CHRISTIAN FAITH AND CULTURAL CRISIS
THE JAPANESE CASE

CHRISTIAN FAITH AND CULTURAL CRISIS THE JAPANESE CASE

BY

ERNEST E. BEST

LEIDEN
E. J. BRILL
1966

PRINTED IN THE NETHERLANDS

To my wife

CONTENTS

Foreword IX
Introduction XI

PART ONE

PRELUDE TO THE RESTORATION

I. Political Considerations and Social Background 3
II. Christian Beginnings 18

PART TWO

THE PERIOD OF FLUX, 1868–1889

III. The Effect of Political Developments on the Structure of Japanese Society 33
IV. The Effect of Economic Development on the Structure of Japanese Society 53
V. The Development of Christianity in Relation to the Changing Order 69

PART THREE

THE NEW NATION, 1890–1911

VI. The Structure of the new Nation. Its Political and Social Consequences 105
VII. The Developing Economy 126
VIII. The new Faith and the new Order in Tension 144
IX. Conclusion 171

Appendix

Exhibit A. Some results of a Questionnaire sent to Japanese Christian Leaders on Matters related to the Content of this Study 179
Exhibit B. The Imperial Rescript on Education 183

Bibliography 184
Index 191

FOREWORD

This study originated in a very concrete set of circumstances. The author spent the years between 1950 and 1955 living at Nagasaki, Japan, in the valley upon which the atomic bomb had fallen. It soon became apparent that one could not understand that peculiar situation without searching deeply for the fateful steps which led to World War II and culminated in that final devastating event of August 9, 1945. Moreover, as a missionary of the *Kyodan* (United Church of Christ in Japan), it was essential to know the role that Protestant Christianity had played therein. What *had* been the nature of Japan's meeting with the West? Later the search for an answer to that question became the subject of disciplined study. In this I was initially encouraged by Professor Mikio Sumiya of Tokyo University whose book *Kindai Nihon no Keisei to Kirisutokyo* (Christianity and the Formation of Modern Japan) was a pioneer effort to understand the dynamics of cultural confrontation and rapid social change, especially as it was reflected in the social history of Protestant Christianity in Japan. My indebtedness to his work is apparent throughout this study.

The necessity for such studies is insistent as the relationship between cultures becomes more and more complex. The World Council of Churches has recognized this fact. Its Division of Studies has already produced two significant works, Paul Abrecht's *The Churches and Rapid Social Change* and Egbert De Vries' *Man in Rapid Social Change*. Yet, despite the fact that in recent years centres for the study of religion and society have sprung up, notably in Japan and India, which are promising for the future, with outstanding exceptions there remains an unfulfilled need for monographs on particular areas and important periods in the history of cultural confrontation with special reference to religion. Such studies should prove of real assistance to any who have responsibilities in cultures other than their own whether they be statesmen, business men, educators, or missionaries. It is my hope that this study will make some small contribution to that end.

This book is a revision of a manuscript which was prepared in partial fulfillment for the doctoral degree of Drew University. I cannot express deeply enough my indebtedness to the following persons: to Professors Frederick Shippey and George Kelsey of Drew University Graduate School who guided the study, especially with regard to its methodology; to Dr. C. W. Iglehart, Professor Emeritus of Missions of Union Theological Seminary New York, who, as an examiner, read the manuscript and out of his profound understanding of Japan made helpful suggestions; to my father-in-law, Dr. W. R. McWilliams, who after a life time of work among the Japanese, read the final manuscript with a critical eye; to Lafayette College for a grant to revise the manuscript; and finally to my wife without whose faith and encouragement neither this nor many other things would have been accomplished. The book's errors both of fact and judgment remain my own.

Methodist Theological School
Delaware, Ohio.

ERNEST E. BEST

Grateful acknowledgement is made to the publishers for permission to quote from the following works: Princeton University Press, "*Japan's Economic Development*" by W. W. Lockwood; Charles Scribner's Sons, "*A Political History of Japan during the Meiji Era*" by W. W. McLaren; McGraw-Hill Book Company, "*Japan Since Perry*" by C. Yanaga; and the Ronald Press Company, "*Japan's Modern Century*", by Hugh Borton.

INTRODUCTION

Japan is a nation of first rank importance in today's world, politically, economically, and culturally. Politically, only fifteen years after she had been wholly devastated by World War II, her allegiance is coveted by both sides in the present struggle between Communism and the Democracies. Economically, she is at the top of the list so far as the rate of her economic growth is concerned and she has taken her place once again among the leaders in world trade. Culturally, her traditional art is increasingly understood and appreciated around the globe.

Japan's amazing transformation from a feudal state to her present place of prominence in world councils has occurred in the short space of one hundred years. As such, if not a guide, she is at least a powerful symbol both to the affluent societies of the west, who look upon her as an example of what may be accomplished without benefit of Marxism, and to the developing nations of South-East Asia, India, the Middle East and Africa, who look to her as "one who has gone on before" offering both hope for what may be in store for them and guidance against pitfalls to be avoided.

The experience of Japan over the past one hundred years then offers an excellent case study of what happens to a self-contained culture when it comes in contact with another vigorous, insistent, totally different culture with which it is forced to have relations whether it likes it or not. In a world where inter-cultural understanding is of vital importance for the very survival of mankind the value of such studies cannot be over-estimated. Every aspect of the varied relations between men of differing societies during the past is now of general interest to us.

For the Christian inter-cultural understanding is an imperative. His faith claims to be supra-cultural. It is not intended to be the special preserve of one particular nation or culture but is designed to be shared with all men. This in fact has been its history as it has spread around the world throughout the years and most especially in the past two centuries. Communication in the past, however, has been so difficult that the expansion of the Christian faith to other cultures has appeared to the Christian in the west as a thing apart. He has been encouraged to contribute to the spiritual, mental and physical welfare of strange men living in far-away exotic cultures because the Christian faith requires it. He knows little of the response of men in those cultures to the foray of his faith and culture into theirs. He may have learnt of the "good" the Christian man of the west thinks he has done, in all good conscience, for the welfare of other men in other cultures. He is now hurt to discover that, for a complexity of reasons, usually far beyond his control, those on the receiving end of his proferred help sometimes interpret it as something else entirely. Yet now, as never before, we cannot afford such misunderstanding for it is of the essence of the Christian faith to break down barriers between men and to open the gateway to reconciliation and mutual understanding. This can only be accomplished if we look closely at the personal and social forces which have gone into the making of the present situation not only in Japan but in every other cultural complex within which the Christian church finds itself. This study, then, anticipates similar and more adequate ones for other cultures than the Japanese in order that the Christian church may effectively serve the critical need of the world community to which it will continue to be related in the years ahead.

In the following pages the interaction between a particular society, the Japanese, and one branch of a religious faith alien to that culture, namely Protestant Christianity, is traced. Our concern is with the dynamic relationship between Japanese culture and a religious faith introduced from without. There are many examples of a like phenomenon in human history. Christianity, originating in ancient Judaism, has entered almost every culture in existence today. Islam has done much the same thing, first in North Africa, then in Sicily, the Iberian Peninsula, the Near East, in India and Indonesia, and today in continental Africa. Further classic examples of it are the introduction of Buddhism into South-East Asia, China and Japan, and of Confucianism from China to Japan. Hinduism, for reasons we cannot develop here, has been largely restricted until the present to India and South-East Asia, but that situation is changing today as certain types of that faith venture forth into alien Europe and North America.

The most rapid and decisive transformation of Japanese society took place during the Meiji era, that is, between 1868 and 1912. By the end of Meiji, Japanese society had taken on the lines which were to remain characteristic of it right up until the end of World War II. Moreover, it was during this period that Protestant Christianity entered Japan and sunk permanent roots into her life. Thus it is this particular age which is of peculiar significance for us.

The concentration of this study on the political and economic in relation to Protestant Christianity is with deliberate intent. The sociologist or the anthropologist may object on the ground that we ought to have dealt with the culture as a whole. Their objection would hold if, were we to deal with the whole of Japanese society, our consideration of certain structures of it in depth were to prove defective. We have tried to be sensible of that criticism and to guard against it. Moreover, while our emphasis has been on the political and economic it has not been to the exclusion of other areas, such as the arts, family life and indigenous religious faiths where these have been relevant.[1] Indeed one cannot understand the nature of the Japanese reaction to the west and to Protestant Christianity in particular unless one is aware that Japanese politics have been rooted in a *religious*, or if you will, an *absolutist* view of the state. During the Meiji Period Japanese leaders expressed their concern for *the welfare of Japan*, which was their fundamental loyalty, *through* the political and economic. Because of the profound sense of national consciousness, the product of geographic as well as cultural factors such as traditional Shinto, it has been the rule of modern Japanese society that whoever has had possession of political power has called the tune and the rest of the nation has danced. For example, throughout the Meiji Period those in political power were also intimately related to those in economic power. The former was more decisive than the latter. Therefore, in order to secure a greater measure of social and economic justice it was first necessary to gain some measure of political power. A few early, Protestant Christians understood this. The majority did not. What was fateful for Japan was that the Japanese military understood it and once they had achieved political power World War II was inevitable.

[1] Studies of the relationship between the various faiths and Japanese society as a whole in our period have already appeared, for example, see Kishimoto and Howes, *Japanese Religion in the Meiji Era* (Vol. II, Centenary Culture Council Series, Tokyo, Japan: Obunsha, 1956). There are also excellent histories of Protestant Christianity in Japan and definitive studies in Japanese Buddhism and Shinto. See bibliography and the recently published volume by Charles Iglehart, *A Century of Protestant Christianity in Japan* (Vermont and Tokyo: Charles Tuttle and Co., 1959). Moreover, for the first time, a much-needed volume in English on the theology of Japanese Christian leaders is in print. See Carl Michalson, *Japanese Contributions to Christian Theology* (Philadelphia: Westminster Press, 1960). This represents at least a beginning in opening up the important theological insights of Christians in other cultures to those in the West. Adequate sociological studies on the relationship between the Christian faith and changes in Japanese family life, and on the influence of Christianity on modern art forms in Japan, to suggest only two possible areas for study, remain to be done.

The great resistance to a dynamic Christian faith, which sought to be a transforming influence not only in personal life but in the life of the nation as a whole, found its greatest competitor in the political leaders of Japan and the methods they used to achieve and maintain power. Thus it is in terms of the tension between the political leadership of the nation and those who espoused the new faith that the development of the latter in Japanese society needs to be understood and it is for this reason that we give so much attention to the political and the economic.[1] Obviously the challenge of the Western powers which broke in upon Japan's isolation after two centuries was primarily political and economic. It is therefore reasonable, quite apart from other considerations, that these two areas in Japanese culture should be stimulated to respond beyond the others. It was against the background of this challenge that Protestant Christianity was introduced into the nation and with its implications that it had to deal.

A word must be said here about the methodology used in this study. It is an adaptation of the work of Max Weber. It is the author's hope that its use here may prompt others to adopt it for the analysis of other periods and other cultures.[2] For this reason books and periodicals relating to the methodology have been included in the bibliography. While we attempt to be exacting where historical detail is presented this is a study in the sociology of religion. It is not primarily designed to bring to light new historic facts which cannot be found elsewhere by the serious student of Japanese religious, political and economic history. Sociology is neither history, nor economics nor political science. Sociology, especially when it is dealing with historical material, is the attempt to interpret historical events in their relationship to one another. It is the attempt to trace dynamic relationships between the structures of a culture, usually considered as a whole,

[1] See Chitose Yanaga, *Japan Since Perry* (New York: McGraw-Hill, 1949), p. 70, "Practical knowledge was placed before theoretical studies. Economic ideas and institutions, production techniques, financial machinery and trade structures that were prevelant in the west were urgently needed to bring Japan quickly up to a level where she could eventually build up her national strength to compete successfully in the markets of the world." P. 11, "Unfortunately for the country the spiritual concomitants of western civilization were pushed into the background in the terrific haste to assimilate the scientific and technological developments."

[2] For a discussion of the methodology used in this study see an article by the author in *Theology Today*, July 1959, entitled, "Max Weber and the Christian Criticism of Life." A more extensive treatment of it is to be found in the introduction to the unpublished doctoral dissertation upon which this book is based, entitled, *The Influence of Political and Economic Factors Upon the Development of Protestant Christianity in Japanese Society*, Drew University.

over a given period of time. The task of history, on the other hand, is to be concerned with the exacting, exhaustive interpretation of particular events. The historian must preserve the uniqueness of the concrete observation, whatever he may add to it in terms of explanation or interpretation. The sociologist is concerned with the *why* of the act. He attempts to find meaning or purpose in a whole complex of human activity. Since it is the responsibility of the historian to guard the uniqueness of particular events he may appear to be dealing with less problematical material than does the sociologist. Yet in his concentration on the particular, he may fail to discover the wider context of events. To compensate for its lack of concrete content and illustrative detail (of which it ought to have enough to justify its conclusions), sociology may well be able to offer "a greater precision of concepts."[1] It ought to enable us to discover dynamic relationships and levels of meaning in human activity that may otherwise be hidden. This we have attempted to do as we have traced the development of Japanese society in the Meiji Period and sought to unravel the forces both within it and within Protestant Christianity that have reacted upon one another and which may provide helpful insights as to alternative courses of action which must be taken in the present not only in Japan itself but in other cultures as well.

---

[1] See Max Weber, *The Theory of Economic and Social Organization* (Glencoe, Ill.: Free Press, 1947), pps. 88 and 109, and Talcott Parsons, *Structure of Social Action* (New York: McGraw-Hill, 1937), p. 636. For a full discussion of terms such as "meaning" and "understanding" see Talcott Parsons *opus cited*, Chapters 2, 16, 17, 18 and Max Weber, *opus cited*, Chapter 1.

PART ONE

PRELUDE TO THE RESTORATION

CHAPTER ONE

POLITICAL CONSIDERATIONS AND SOCIAL BACKGROUND

A. Internal Conditions

One cannot hope to understand nineteenth and twentieth century Japan without some understanding of its roots in the past. We must at least go back to the beginning of the Shogunate set up by Minamoto no Yoritomo (1147–99). The Shogun was the head of the most powerful among a number of the rival families within the nobility. He became so powerful that, though he left the hereditary monarch on the throne, he stripped him of all real power and took over the reins of government himself. The Emperor was left in virtual poverty in the ancient capital of Kyoto surrounded by a small group of the ancient nobility known as the *kuge*.

In 1603 the Tokugawa clan secured the Shogunate and retained that power until the restoration of the Emperor in 1868. By maintaining a meticulously stratified society and establishing all manner of social controls the Tokugawa, through their government known as the *Bakufu*, managed to stay in power. It is only through some appreciation of the forces let loose in Japanese society during this period that much of what happened in the succeeding Meiji period becomes intelligible at all.

As a family the Tokugawa were at the top of the social scale with their capital at Edo (now Tokyo). They, together with their family connections, controlled one-quarter of the country. The remainder of the nation was divided among two groups of feudal lords. The one group consisted of eighty-six families who supported the Tokugawa forces in the battle of Sekigahara in the year 1600.[1] This battle was

[1] It will be recalled that St. Francis Xavier went to Japan in 1549 and that Roman Catholic missionaries were most active throughout the remainder of that century. Both C. R. Boxer in his, *The Christian Century in Japan*, (Berkeley: University of California Press, 1951) and Delmer M. Brown in *Nationalism in Japan*, (Berkeley: University of California Press, 1955), point out that this was a period when the Tokugawa were not yet secure in power. Many of the lords who were against them, for example in Hizen and Choshu, took a lively interest in the new faith and this as much as the fear of foreign imperialism accounted for the opposition of the Bakufu to Christianity.

decisive in establishing the hegemony of the Tokugawa. From this *in-group* were appointed all of the government officials. The one hundred and seventy-six families who fought against the Tokugawa were known as the *outside clans* and were shorn of all political power save within their own local fiefs. Their main centers were Choshu, Satsuma, Tosa and Hizen. Choshu is the area to the north of the strategic straits of Shimonoseki which separate the central island Honshu, from the southern island, Kyushu. Satsuma was the general area of modern Kagoshima prefecture. It is the southernmost portion of the island of Kyushu. Tosa is now Kochi prefecture and was on the southern side of the island of Shikoku. The modern cities of Saga and Nagasaki were the heart of the area known as Hizen. These details are of importance because of the very great role that each of these centres was destined to play in the development of modern Japan. Moreover, the fact that these areas were situated geographically as they were was to play against the interests of the Bakufu in dealing with them. Since each of them was a good distance from the capital, Edo, it was virtually impossible to control these groups for an indefinite period of time.

The social restrictions placed upon the lords of the *outside clans* were most elaborate. In order to keep an eye on their activities the *Bakufu* required them to spend half of their time in the capital at Edo. The other half they were permitted to look after their affairs within their fiefs. In the meantime their families were retained as hostages in the capital! Passports were required even for passage from one domain to another so that communication between them was cut to a minimum. Yet frequent travel to the capital helped to establish great trade centers, like Osaka, since the lords needed cash for rice in order to live in the capital. This activity also brought the lords and the merchants together in an association which helped to produce the eventual downfall of the *Bakufu*.

Whenever the holdings in rice of any family became too great the Shogunate insisted upon such households undertaking some great public works project. In this way the Shogun retained his economic superiority. Through administration of their own lands and tribute from their vassals, the Tokugawa controlled one quarter of all the rice produced.[1] However, in spite of these restrictions, the power of the

---

[1] G. B. Sansom: *Japan, a Short Cultural History*, (New York: Appleton Century Company, 1943).

outside clans continued to be strong enough to pose a threat to the central government.

Among the nobility was another group, already mentioned, who were to play an important role at the time of the Restoration, namely the *kuge*. They were a small group of ancient nobility who continued to serve the Emperor even in his exile. They alone had access to him. Such was forbidden to all others. They were also free from the restrictions of the feudal lords though they had little wealth. They were later to join hands with the *outside clans* in opposition to the *Bakufu*.

The *samurai*, or warrior class, stood next in rank to the nobles in Japanese feudal society. At first the *samurai* were landholders as well as fighters but as castle towns grew up and fighting became more technical each feudal lord had his own retainers whose exclusive task it was to pursue the arts of war.[1] Thus the *samurai* were cut off from the land and became completely dependent on the economic support of their lords which was given to them in rice. Since the Tokugawa period was one of relative peace the *samurai* became parasitic. Moreover, as the economic position of the lords worsened they cut down the stipends of their retainers until the loyalty of the latter, in many cases at least, was strained to the breaking point. Those who did break away were called *ronin* and would attach themselves to whoever would pay for their services. Frequently they would form robber bands, like the knights at the close of the middle ages in Europe, and would prey upon the countryside. Whether they became *ronin* or not they tended to discontent as a class and because they were better educated than the peasantry, many of them being used as civil servants in the feudal households, they turned their thoughts to the improvement of their lot and of that of Japan. They looked abroad for new techniques of war and peace. When their opportunity came the *samurai* of the *outside clans* were the spearhead of the anti-Bakufu movement. Moreover, the only persistent opposition to them after they had gained power following the Restoration was from among their counterparts, or the offspring of their peers, who had been the administrators of the *inside clans* under the *Bakufu*. Many of the *samurai* prior to the Restoration who could not be kept in the old feudal establishments and who did not want to become *ronin* went to the cities. There they established liaison with

---

[1] In 1587 Hideyoshi. a Regent, instituted a sword hunt in the countryside and confiscated all swords save those of the *samurai* as a means of checking rebellion. Thereafter, the privilege of wearing the sword became the proud mark of a *samurai*.

merchant families and studied foreign languages, science and religion. All of this augured well for post-Restoration Japan because it supplied the country with a nucleus of able administrators to some extent familiar with the outside world.

In this brief sketch of the class structure in Tokugawa Japan one would assume that we would next take up a consideration of the merchant class, after the order of western feudal society, but in the Japanese feudal system the merchant estate held the lowest position, not above, but below the peasantry. The obvious reason for this was that the system was based upon a rice economy. Thus the producer of rice was the foundation of the whole system. The *Bakufu* instituted strong legislation against the sale of land, which was virtually impossible, and also passed laws forbidding the movement of farmers from one domain to another. Taxes were almost always oppressive and were usually increased during years of a good crop.[1] In average cases it was four to the lord and six to the people, in some five to five, in others even as much as seven to three and eight to two. Small wonder that as far back as the beginning of the Tokugawa period there were numerous peasant riots.[2]

The *Bakufu*, in order to curb the power of the lords, would demand a special tax or order a particular public works project to be undertaken but the lords would then pass it off on the peasantry who bore the brunt of the whole system. In a period as late as that from 1860 to 1867 as many as eighty-six peasant revolts occurred.[3] This was further aggravated as agriculture became more technically developed and the farmer had to buy machinery and especially fertilizer in exchange for money. This gave the usurer, who was often a petty merchant or a more furtunate landholder, his chance. Then in order to get around the non-transfer-of land-law, the usurer would become what was known as the *legal cultivator* and would have to pay the taxes involved. He simply passed them on to the farmer who now had to support both the usurer and the lord. As E. H. Norman points out, the Japanese farmer presents an unusual phenomenon. On the one hand,

---

[1] E. H. Norman, *Japan's Emergence as a Modern State*, (New York: Inst. of Pacific Relations, 1940), p. 21. The specialist will recognize that material for the above discussion can be found in many excellent sources. It is included here because without such background the forces at work in the Meiji period simply cannot be understood.

[2] Hugh Borton, *Peasant Uprisings in Japan of the Tokugawa Period*, Vol. XVI of 2nd series, Transactions of the Asiatic Society of Japan, (Tokyo: 1938).

[3] E. H. Norman, opus cited. p. 78.

because he has always technically owned his own land, he is conservative in relation to the existing order that guarantees his basic relationship to the land. But, on the other hand, he appears to be radical because for centuries he has been burdened with unjust taxes. In France, prior to the revolution, the peasant did not enjoy even this degree of security and prior to the Industrial Revolution in England the Enclosure Acts had already dispossessed families who were a natural labour market for the new order. This relation of the peasant to his land has always made it possible for conservative forces in Japan to count upon the *back country* for support because the old authoritarian feudal way of life has remained largely unshaken in the countryside. Later on we shall see that, for a brief period of time, when the modernization of the country created the necessity for ready capital and that capital was provided through taxation on land, a strange alliance grew up, if only briefly, between the landlords and the farmers because they had to face this common pressure. We shall see too that in an effort to free themselves from what they considered an unjust burden, a further fleeting alliance between the farmers, the landlords, the liberal-minded and the Christians came into being in what was known as the Peoples' Rights Movement. Simultaneously, we find the founding of a number of rural churches. This was because the Christians, with their insistence on the worth of individuals and their generally democratic spirit, provided justification for release from debt and for proper representative government. In any event, toward the end of the Tokugawa period, the peasant revolts rose into the hundreds and were an important factor in destroying the power of the Shogunate while at the same time the peasants, as a class, remained fundamentally conservative.

The merchants were at the bottom of the social scale in feudal Japan. So oppressive was the *Bakufu* in relation to them that they could not have names that bore a resemblance to those of the nobility and the *samurai*. Their excuse for existence was as distributors because the *Bakufu* was anxious to separate production and distribution in order to decentralize powers and to keep contact between the fiefs at as low a level as possible. Moreover, each fief was granted a monopoly in the production of some one product such as textiles, fertilizer, porcelain, liquor and the like. These had to be exchanged and this was helped by the frequent travels of the lords with their households to the capital. Great trading centers arose such as Osaka and Nagoya where the lords maintained warehouses in the charge of *samurai* retainers. The merchants were given a monopoly on distribution in lieu of taxes. As a money economy developed the merchants were, therefore, in a privileged position in relation to it since they handled the medium of exchange which was scarce at the best of times and because they were not taxed on it. Some of the merchant houses became so large that the Bakufu confiscated their wealth. This sense of insecurity created a bond between the merchants and the lords who were treated to similar fare by the government. The *samurai* retainers, who, as middlemen between the lords and the merchants, brought about the above alliance had become both fief administrators and the officials who dealt with the merchants.

It is important to mention here the social mobility which took place at this time between some of the *samurai* and the merchant class. As the *samurai* became poorer and the merchants became wealthier it was possible for each to improve his social situation through intermarriage. So the *samurai* improved his situation economically and the merchant improved his so far as prestige was concerned. Usually, the family name of the *samurai* was adopted. "Numerous contemporaries recorded how the wealthier merchants were adopted into *samurai* families and how impoverished warriors were glad to enter a merchant family either by marriage or adoption."[1]

One factor, which was a great hindrance to the rise of this status group, as compared with its counterpart in Europe, was its lack of capital accrued from foreign trade. Throughout the period of great mercantile expansion in the West, Japan was in isolation. Therefore, what capital there was, was within the country itself. The merchant class was prevented from making a thrust forward on a scale comparable to its counterpart in the west for the above reason. This lack of foreign capital is one of the basic keys for an understanding of the peculiar way in which Japan became a modern state.

When we consider the over-all situation, as we have outlined it here, it can be seen that in relation to every group in society the position of the *Bakufu* gradually worsened both politically and economically.[2] The development of a money economy and the decline of the

[1] E. H. Norman, *opus cited*, p. 19.

[2] It ought to be mentioned that the *samurai* had become more and more opposed to the old regime for as the financial position of the lords worsened the less able the latter were to pay the stipends of the *samurai*. The *samurai* who became the clan administrators were by far the most competent people in the land and thus became the spearhead of the Restoration movement. Later on, as the Restoration forces really proceeded to reorganize the country the lords and the upper *samurai* had

individual farmer, which went with it, continually placed the central government at a disadvantage since they could only secure their own financial position through confiscation and excessive taxation. This turned the merchants and the lords against it since they were its immediate victims. The lords also stood in a somewhat uneasy relationship to the merchants for, as has been said, the latter controlled the means of exchange. Yet the merchants could not be too hard on either the farmers, or the lords, because both groups were the basic source of the merchants income. Money was useless if it couldn't buy rice, prestige, and luxuries. Thus there was a strong degree of mutual support between lords, landlords, merchants and even peasants, in their opposition to the government. When this was joined with the natural opposition of the *outside clans*, plus support from the ancient nobility around the Emperor, the Shogunate was doomed.

By the middle of the nineteenth century then, Japanese society was in a state of internal disintegration. As the political and economic grip of the Tokugawa became weaker and weaker, the *outside clans* continually and relentlessly pressed for every advantage. The factors which brought the issue to a head, however, did not come from within Japanese society alone but as a threat from without.

B. External Pressures

The Tokugawa had closed the country to foreign contact during the seventeenth century not only because they feared the sceptre of foreign imperialism but because they felt their enemies within the country to be in too close association with persons from foreign powers. Christianity took root and therefore the greatest number of priests and converts were to be found precisely in the fiefs most opposed to the *Bakufu*, that is to say, in Satsuma, Choshu, and Hizen. The government felt threatened both from within and from without.

---

the reins taken from them by the more astute and agressive lower *samurai.* This latter group became the brains of modern Japan. It was largely financed by the great merchant houses. As a result one of the heads of the House of Mitsui (a great merchant family) became finance minister in the first government formed after the Restoration. But, as we stated above, since there were relatively no sources of outside capital, the lords and the merchants were mutually dependent and they both required the guidance of the lower *samurai* who alone possessed the knowledge and vision of what was required if Japan was to become a modern state. Adoption and intermarriage had helped all this. The only status groups not included in the new picture were the landlords and most especially the farmers, who were to bear the burden of the new Japan, as they had the old.

Thus it not only excluded the foreigner but banished Christianity from the land. The geographic position of Japan had assisted them in this because she was farthest away from the imperialistic outreach of the European nations.

By the middle of the nineteenth century England, France, Holland, Russia and the United States were all zealous for expanded trade opportunities with Japan. Only the Dutch had been granted an insignificant toe-hold for continued trade during the period of closure through the factory at Dejima, Nagasaki. Attempts had been made by foreign powers during the early nineteenth century to come to an agreement with the *Bakufu* that might open Japan not only as a haven for maritime safety but as a trade center. They were without any significant results. It was not until the gunboats of Commodore Perry of the United States Navy appeared in Uruga Bay in 1853 and again in 1854 that the *Bakufu* capitulated to outside power.[1] This the Bakufu did with the utmost reluctance because they were convinced that relations with outside powers would only complicate their already precarious position within the nation. Moreover, the leadership of the increasingly aggressive *outside clans* had become very much opposed to any relationships with foreign powers in view of the experience of the Chinese. They felt, as did the Emperor of China about his own country, that Japan was being both insulted and humiliated by the insistence upon entry of the foreign powers. Yet the *Bakufu* realized how weak Japan was in relation to the west and it was anxious to avoid anything that might mean invasion and defeat. They were caught between two fires. They knew they really had no alternative to signing treaties with the western nations but they continued to hope that if they made preliminary gestures the western powers would forget to press them. On this ground they signed the original treaty with Perry, March 31, 1854, opening the ports of Kanagawa, Hakodate and Nagasaki only and making provision for a mutual consular relationship, the American consul to reside at Shimoda just south of Tokyo where the officials hoped, if he appeared, he would remain both out of sight and out of mind. Similar treaties were shortly made with Russia, England, France and Holland.[2]

[1] See G. B. Sansom, *The Western World and Japan*, (New York: Knopf, 1950), p. 288. Dr. Sansom adds this significant remark, "It was chiefly because it was insolvent that it (the Bakufu) gave way to Perry's pressure in 1853 though this fact was not known to the country at large and still less to Perry himself."

[2] For detailed discussion of the events surrounding the treaties, see H. Borton, *Japan's Modern Century*, (New York: Ronald Press, 1955), Chapt. 3.

It is important for us, at this point, to attempt to isolate the factor beneath all others which motivated not only the *Bakufu* but those opposed to them within the nation as the crisis of foreign pressure threatened the very existence of Japan as an independent nation. Obviously to isolate one factor as that which underlay all political events for the next decade, namely from 1853 to 1864, would be an oversimplification and thus a distortion of the truth. Yet wise political leaders recognize priorities and in the complex warp and woof of everyday life one factor may arise to dominate all others. If this were the case we must examine in some detail the events of the decade in their interrelation.

On August 21, 1856 Townsend Harris, the first consular representative of the United States to Japan arrived in the tiny harbour of Shimoda under the terms of the treaty to which we have alluded. Its terms had been of a minimal kind. Even the agreement to open the harbours had been primarily for the purpose of granting safety to ships in trouble. The provision for a consular exchange, in the minds of the Americans at least, had been for the purpose of establishing trade agreements between the nations involved. However, when the consular official did arrive the Japanese claimed that their agreement to accept a consular official was to take effect only if both sides requested it. No provision had been made for Harris upon his arrival. For a period of months the *Bakufu* having hoped that such an official would never appear, did all in its power to make life difficult for him.[1]

In the end, however, the Japanese did sign a treaty of Amity and Commerce (July 29, 1858) with the United States. Shortly thereafter the British were also able to effect a similar treaty. Why did the Japanese capitulate to outside pressure? The answer to this question is of first importance and must never be forgotten in any consideration of Japanese-Western relationships over the past century. At the outset, indeed for another five years beyond the signing of the treaties, important forces both within the Shogunate and among those opposed to them were for "expelling the barbarians." Yet foreign Minister Hotta and his successor Ii Naosuke were convinced that, like it or not, Japan had no alternative but to open her gates to the intruders.

Townsend Harris used various arguments to bring his Japanese

---

[1] M. E. Cosenza ed., *The Complete Journal of Townsend Harris*, (New York: Doubleday, Doran, 1930), see this volume for an excellent record of the arduous experience of Townsend Harris both at Shimoda and Edo as he attempted to effect a treaty.

counterparts to this conclusion. He pointed out to them that the world was rapidly changing and that every nation would be at Japan's doorstep shortly as a result of the new means of transportation. He stated that like it or no Japan would be unable to resist them and that it would be better for her to negotiate honoroubly than to be humiliated as at that very moment it was China's experience so to be. He claimed that a great economic future lay ahead for Japan in terms of trade and industry and that Japan might well become one among the great nations of the world if she were forward-looking in her ways.[1]

Harris argued better than he knew for Hotta and Ii Naosuke were well aware of China's experience. From the beginning of the Opium Wars in 1839 to the Canton Event of 1856–57 they had seen the great nation to which Japan herself owed her cultural heritage rendered helpless to resist the invader. The price of pride had been the loss of any real sovereignty. Were they to stand by and watch Japan suffer the same fate? They could not know that England was of two minds about "gunboat diplomacy."[2] In any event, those who had been her representatives on the field were not of two minds about it. They practiced it without apology. Realism on the part of the Japanese dictated the acceptance of the situation in such a way that Japan's real sovereignty would suffer as little as possible. Thus it was that Ii Naosuke signed a treaty with Harris on July 29, 1858 but without the consent of either the Shogunate or the Emperor who was becoming ever more powerful as the authority of the Shogunate began to dwindle.

The clear decision to open the country was not long-lived. Ii Naosuke was slain by his great rival within the Shogunate, Tokugawa Nariaki of Mito. Mito would have the foreigners kept out of Japan at all costs. In this he was joined by the leaders of the *outside clans*. Only the strong personality of Ii at that particular moment had stood for a policy clearly in the best interest of Japan. Mito died shortly after Ii and this left the anti-Shogunate forces clearly in the ascendency. The Emperor summoned the Shogun to court and the latter was forced to attend for the first time in over two hundred and fifty years. Clearly the authority of the *Bakufu* was breaking down.

In 1862 the court went so far as to order the rescinding of the

---

[1] Ibid: See especially pps. 19, 22, 350, 357, and 484 ff.

[2] The most important source of information concerning the events surrounding the Canton Event and its relation to subsequent events in Japan is, L. Oliphant, *Narrative of the Earl of Elgin's Mission to China and Japan*, (New York: Harper and Brother, 1860). One ought also to see W. G. Beasley, *Great Britain and the Opening of Japan*, (London: Luzac and Co., 1951).

treaties, at least for a period of five years, and the *Bakufu* was forced to make such a representation to foreign capitals. Britain, somewhat ashamed of her record in China, had formally consented, but the other nations were adamant. Anti-foreign feeling was on the increase within the country especially among the discontented *samurai*. The secretary to the American Embassy was killed and a British officer was slain by the retainers of the Lord of Satsuma. As a result of the latter incident the British carried out a successful naval bombardment of Kagoshima and in a characteristic display of realism, the Lord of that clan and his government not only came to terms with the British but sought to learn all they could from them, especially concerning modern armaments.

A further incident ought to be mentioned because it clarifies the extent to which those who wanted to "expel the barbarians" were willing to go. June 24, 1863 had been the date set for the formal expulsion of foreigners under the command of the court. On that date the Choshu clan fired upon an American vessel in the straits of Shimonoseki. Three weeks later French and Dutch ships were fired upon. A few days later an American warship retaliated and French forces landed and destroyed the shore batteries. The *daimyo* of Choshu still refused to heed and the straits were closed until, in the following year, American, French, British and Dutch navies attacked Shimonoseki and completely destroyed the shore batteries. An indemnity of $3,000,000 had to be met by the *Bakufu* to recompense the foreign powers. This further weakened the Shogunate and the Choshu clan was expelled for its rashness even from the Emperor's court.

From this point on a change in the attitude of almost all responsible leadership within the country toward intercourse with outside nations becomes apparent. Choshu was the exception. Yet during the Shimonoseki episode itself a young Choshu *samurai*, Ito Hirobumi of whom we shall hear a great deal, just returned from a clandestine visit to foreign lands and who knew well their power, pleaded with leaders of his own clan to desist from their doomed display of force. While the cry of the country, especially of the *samurai* for a decade had been, "Revere the Emperor, expel the barbarians" it now became, "Revere the Emperor, down with the *Bakufu*."[1]

From 1862 to 1864 the *Bakufu* was forced to concede more and more to the court and to recognize the power of the *outside clans* which surrounded it. In 1864 the Emperor insisted upon his claim to confirm

[1] Delmer M. Brown, *opus cited*, p. 87.

the investiture of all government officers appointed by the *Bakufu.* A small body of Choshu clansmen, still not satisfied and seeking greater favour at the court, raised a revolt against the Shogunate for the ostensible reason of "protecting" the Emperor. However, the Emperor along with the Lord of Satsuma, Shimadzu Saburo, doubtless jealous of his prerogatives with the Emperor, refused to go along with the rebellion. They supported the Shogun and it looked for a time as though the new Japan would be re-organized along the lines of a coalition between the old *Bakufu* and the *outside clans* under the formal rule of the Emperor. The Choshu rebellion proved abortive. However, the Shogun pressed his advantage too far and alienated the sympathies of Satsuma which once again took the side of its ally Choshu. In 1866 the Shogun led his forces against Choshu troops at Osaka. He was everywhere defeated and shortly thereafter died. It was only a matter of time until the whole Tokugawa structure was to collapse completely. The Regent Keiki ill-advisedly took up arms once again against the *outside clans* though he was forced to it because the plans which the former were devising for the future of the land called for stripping the Tokugawa of everything, wealth and power alike. By the end of 1868, after several skirmishes had taken place, the Emperor's forces were, practically speaking, in control of the country. The Regent, acting on the advice of the Lord of Tosa, had "voluntarily" handed over his power to the Emperor on January 25, 1868. The name Edo was changed to Tokyo and the Emperor's seat of government was established there in March 1869.

Before we leave the pre-Restoration period two further matters are of sufficient importance to engage our attention. The first is the Osaka affair of 1865 and its immediate aftermath which was to have ramifications for the relations of Japan with foreign powers throughout the subsequent Meiji period. The second is a consideration of the role of foreign governments in the actual events which led to the Restoration.

After 1860 the foreign powers only gradually became aware of the shift of power going on within the country. Obviously, they could not be satisfied with the ambivalent situation with regard to the treaties. It was decided, therefore, to make a display of force on the Emperor's back doorstep, that is to say, in Osaka harbour which is only a short distance from the traditional seat of the Emperor at Kyoto. In 1865 Sir Harry Parkes, who had played a consular role in the hostilities at Canton in 1856 and 1857, was appointed minister to Japan. It was he who inspired the French, Dutch, and Americans to join with the

British in a display of naval force in the harbour at Osaka. In return for solid ratification of the trade treaties the powers were prepared to remit two thirds of the indemnity Japan had been asked to pay as a result of the Shimonoseki affair. Important riders were attached to the earlier treaties. One was that the port of Hyogo and the city of Osaka should be open for trade at once and the second was that customs tariffs agreed upon by Harris in 1858 were to be adjusted in favour of the powers. Japan was not to charge more than 5% ad valorem on all goods. Thus the fateful *unequal treaties* were born.

The show of power in Osaka harbour could not have failed to have the desired effect. Just at that time a number of the leading clansmen in Japan were in conference with the Emperor. To have the foreign powers at their doorstep naturally caused great alarm. To the leadership of the nation there appeared to be no alternative but to renounce seclusion once and for all. At the outset they agreed once again to open the ports but hedged on the city of Osaka itself. However, the latter was only to save face. The following year, a Tariff Convention was signed at Edo on the terms set forth by the powers, Moreover, restrictions upon direct contact between foreign and Japanese traders were set aside. There was to be no government monopoly on foreign trade such as the Tokugawa had enjoyed.

Once more we are confronted with a demonstration of realism on the part of those who had, or were about to accept, political power. Those who had been but a few days before recommending one course, when they realized its folly for the long-run interests of Japan, were prepared to make a right-about-face.[1] Anti-foreign demonstrations ceased. Political leadership cooperated with the inevitable until a more propitious day.

When we consider the role played by the foreign powers at the time of the Restoration itself, we see a further demonstration of the tendency on the part of Japanese leadership to put the interests of the nation first, regardless even of the loss of personal power. In the final campaign led by Choshu and Satsuma against the Bakufu the French were prepared to aid the latter while the English were extremely friendly with Satsuma and Choshu. The Ex-Shogun declined the aid of France and there is no evidence that the opposition made any appeal to the English.[2] As a result the political independence of the nation was

[1] See Delmer M. Brown. *opus cited*, p. 87 and J. J. Gubbins, *The Making of Modern Japan*, (London: Seeley Service, 1922), p. 47.

[2] C. Yanaga, *Japan Since Perry*, (New York: McGraw-Hill, 1949), p. 46 and

retained whereas in China, save for pretense, such was not the case.

Every evidence supports the conclusion that while other goals definitely entered the picture, for example the desire for sheer personal power on the part of the up-and-coming *samurai*, nevertheless all were motivated at this time by an underlying concern that foreign powers should not get a foothold within the politics of the nation as a result of internal division.

A major factor which led to the development of such a strong *national consciousness* was, of course, the Emperor Institution itself.[1] It was this which, on the one hand fostered a unity among the groups opposed to the *Bakufu* for social and political reasons and, on the other hand, since the opposition ultimately had the full support of the Emperor, it was impossible for the *Bakufu* to oppose them too openly. As is well known, this is a political pattern which appeared again and again in the history of modern Japan up until the end of World War II. Of the pre-Restoration situation E. H. Norman says:

> "The only magnetic force capable of holding together the centrifugal atoms of feudalism was the throne, and the only agents in a position to perform the task were the clan bureaucrats of the four great *outside clans* with the economic backing of the big merchants such as the Mitsui, the Sumitomo, Konoike, Ono, Yasuda..."[2]

And Sir George Sansom adds:

> "The only principle which these different parties held in common was that of loyalty to the Emperor, and it was this principle that, by unifying the most diverse opinions brought the Meiji Revolution to a successful and relatively bloodless issue."[3]

We have seen that when Japan was threatened from without the new forces around the Emperor were most zealous for the sovereignty

---

F. Brinkley, *A History of the Japanese People*, (London and New York: Encyclopedia Britannica, 1915), p. 678.

[1] See Delmer M. Brown, *opus cited.* Brown has an excellent summary of the way in which *national consciousness* was developed through the centuries especially around such leaders as Hirata Atsutane (1776–1843). See also G. B. Sansom, *opus cited*, p. 65 ff and Chapter 11. Prof. Brown maintains that a modern full-fledged nationalism was present only in the leaders of the nation at this time. This is true if we are thinking primarily in terms of modern nationalism but it needs to be qualified when we consider that Shinto, the national faith of the people, was from the beginning built around the nation. It is hard to discover any evidence of a tendency on the part of the Japanese people throughout their history to act in any save an exclusive way whenever the vital interests of Japan have been threatened.

[2] E. H. Norman, *opus cited.*

[3] G. B. Sansom, *opus cited.*

of Japan and undoubtedly saw the deepest relation between safeguarding that sovereignty and their concern for the restoration of the Emperor. This was equally true of the Tokugawa. How else can one explain the willingness of so powerful a group to give up even its own domains as well as his political power without a bloody struggle to the bitter end? Here lies a profound concern for the sovereignty of the nation. That concern coincided with the necessity for a unified government which, it now become obvious, only the Emperor, albeit supported by the power of the *outside clans*, now represented. It would appear that this sense of being Japanese, of *national consciousness* lay beneath every other motivation economic, social, and political. In the sense that religion may be identified with one's absolute loyalty it can be said that this allegiance to the *welfare of the nation* was the expression of fundamental religious concern.

CHAPTER TWO

CHRISTIAN BEGINNINGS

In view of the background we have described in the previous chapter, it is altogether amazing that Christianity was able to get a footing at all in Japan until well after the *Osaka Event* in the year 1865.[1] Prior to that the prevailing cry on all sides, save that of the *Bakufu* officials was, "expel the barbarians." Even the *Bakufu* felt it necessary to insist in their negotiations with the foreigners that two things be absolutely forbidden, opium and Christianity! In 1858, the year before the Protestant missionaries arrived in Japan, the Japanese officials in Nagasaki are reported to have told the Dutch envoy, Donker Curtius, that, "They were ready to allow foreigners all trading privileges if a way could be found to keep opium and Christianity out of the country."[2] Not only was Christianity to have to labour against the prejudice toward "barbarians" in general but it was one of the main grounds of that prejudice. In contemplating the Perry expedition President Fillmore had written to the Secretary of the Navy as follows:

> The deep seated aversion of this people to hold intercourse with Christian nations is said to be owing chiefly to the indiscreet zeal with which the early missionaries, particularly those of Portugal, endeavoured to propagate their religion. The Commodore will therefore say that the government of this country, unlike those of every other (sic) Christian country, does not interfere with the religion of its own people, much less with that of other nations.[3]

---

[1] In this study we are thinking of *Christianity* as an entity in Japanese society. Morever, we are discussing Protestant Christianity. Only when we consider the latter under its institutional and creedal aspects will we narrow the field of our interest. From a sociological point of view, *Christianity* in Japanese society is of necessity a variable, since it enters that society from the outside rather than is found there as a basic function within it, as for example, Shinto might be considered. From a Christian, theological point of view Christianity is a fundamental function, since it is claimed that it is basic to the need of all men. The role which *charisma* plays in our study is a recognition of this fact. Both ways of looking at things, that is to say the sociological and the theological, must be kept in mind as we progress. Both create a *tension*, which is part of authentic Christianity wherever it is found, within the web of Japanese society and its institutions.

[2] F. W. Williams, *Life and Letters of S. W. Williams*, p. 284 as quoted in S. W. Ryder, *A Historical-Educational Study of the Japan Mission of the Reformed Church in America*, (York, Pa: York Press, 1935), p. 16.

[3] O. Cary, *A History of Christianity in Japan*, (New York: Revell, 1909), p. 30.

The President also wrote the following to the Emperor of Japan:

> The Constitution and laws of the United States forbid all interference with the religious or political concerns of other nations. I have particularly charged Commodore Perry to abstain from every act which could possibly disturb the tranquillity of your Imperial Majesty's dominions.[1]

Just how strong the feeling against Christianity was can be seen in the fact that the Japanese refused to include the Christian date on their copy of the Treaty with Perry. They would sign only that date which accorded with their method of recording time.[2]

We have already made brief reference to the reasons for this profound distrust of Christianity.[3] Between the year 1549, when St. Francis Xavier arrived in Japan, and 1595 approximately three hundred thousand Japanese had become Christians among whom were seventeen feudatory chieftains known as *daimyo*.[4] These chieftains were located principally in Hizen, Tosa, and Satsuma, the very feudatories with which the *Bakufu* was to have continuing political difficulties quite apart from the question of Christianity. Many of the *daimyo* became interested in Christianity because of an interest in trade with the Portuguese. In some cases they ordered their people to become Christians with them in a movement reminiscent of the *cuius regio ejus religio* principle of the Reformation period in Europe. Before long a complete confusion had grown up between the propagation of Christianity and the interests of trade with the west as well as with the imperialistic intentions of Portugal and Spain. The Roman Catholic missionaries claimed the protection of western power, more especially the right to its use in the interests of their work, according to methods acceptable to St. Francis Xavier. At the same time they claimed that it was impossible for them to curb the cruel excesses of the traders. The powerful Hideyoshi had been favourable at first to the new religion and was opposed to Buddhism because of the latter's wealth and power. His attitude changed toward the end of the century, encouraged by the bed-fellows with whom Christianity kept company. In 1587 Hideyoshi issued an edict against Christianity and commanded

---

1 Ibid.

2 Ibid.

3 Ante p. 9.

4 See F. R. Brinkley, *opus cited.* Chapter 37, and J. Murdoch, *opus cited,* Vol. 2, for a full outline of Christianity in Japan during this period. See especially C. R. Boxer, *The Christian Century in Japan* 1549–1650. (Berkeley: Univ. of California Press, 1951).

all its priests to leave Japan. "Christianity," he claimed, "had pernicious designs against the Empire." Apparently Hideyoshi at this time was not anxious to disturb trade relations with the west because he was careful to proscribe Christianity alone, not trade.

Just at this time rivalry between Portugal and Spain was at its height and the Spanish looked for the opportunity to enter into trade with Japan. During a great storm in 1596 a rich Spanish galleon, the San Felipe, was wrecked near the harbour of Tosa in modern Shikoku. In an effort to save her cargo one of the officers is reported to have told the Japanese officials of the power of Spain and to have referred to the method by which Spain had conquered the world. This method, he is reported to have said, was to first send in agents of her Christian faith to win people to her and then to take over political control of the country. A report of this incident reached Hideyoshi and he became more determined than ever to banish Christianity from the land. As a result further edicts were promulgated. Between 1614 and 1635 two hundred and eighty thousand Christians were said to have suffered for their faith. Finally, in 1637, during the reign of Tokugawa Ieyasu, an uprising of Christians in the vicinity of Nagasaki was put down with a loss of 33,000 lives. This brought to an end the formal persecution of the Christian faith though it was carried on in hiding right down to the re-opening of the country in 1853. Throughout the period of seclusion Christianity was proscribed on pain of death and the resulting prejudices spread throughout the populace. Especially were they held by those in power.

The attitude of the officials who negotiated with Perry is, therefore, not difficult to understand. Mr. Harris, in the Treaty of 1858, could do no better than that which is stated in the treaty's eight article:

> Americans in Japan shall be allowed the free exercise of their religion, and for this purpose shall have the right to erect suitable places of worship. No injury shall be done to such buildings, nor any insult be offered to the religious worship of the Americans.
> American citizens shall not injure any Japanese temple or *miya*, or offer any insult or injury to Japanese religious ceremonies, or to the objects of their worship.
> The Americans and Japanese shall not do anything that may be calculated to excite religious animosity. The Government of Japan has already abolished the practice of tramping on religious emblems.[1]

[1] M. E. Cosenza ed. *opus cited.* See Appendix for the test of the Treaty.

Americans were given the right to practice their own religion but not the freedom to proselytize. The Japanese were careful to guard against anything that might upset the religious *status quo*. Mr. John Liggins, the earliest of the missionaries, is reported to have had the following conversation with Mr. Harris:

> In conversing with Mr. Harris, the United States Minister at Yedo, on this subject, he stated that he had used every endeavour to have this obnoxious law (i.e. the proscription of Christianity) repealed, but without success; a principal reason being that the government feared that it would form a pretext for the old conservative party (i.e. the *outside clans*) to overthrow the government and again get into power.[1]

As is obvious from our discussion in the previous chapter, the fear of the *Bakufu* on this score was extremely well grounded. Permission to propagate Christianity would surely have incurred the full wrath of the forces seeking the overthrow of the *Bakufu* and would have provided the perfect excuse for them to do so. A better example of the relationship between the conditions under which Christianity was forced to carry on its mission and political circumstances could hardly be found.

S. R. Williams, a veteran missionary in China, who had been interpreter for the Perry expedition and who subsequently visited Japan, advised the churches in America to send out missionaries as soon as the ports were to open in 1859 but to be sure that they were persons of the utmost patience and sagacity in view of the circumstances under which they would be forced to work, at least in the beginning. Guido Verbeck, who was among the earliest contingent of missionaries, says of the way in which they were looked upon by the Japanese: "We were regarded as people who had come to seduce the masses of the people from their loyalty to the *God-country* and corrupt their morals generally."[2] Hideyoshi had considered the claims of Christianity an insult to the sovereignty of Japan but as late as 1868 a minister of the Restoration government made the following remark, "to permit the instruction of the people in Christianity would mean the introduction

---

[1] O. Cary, *opus cited.* p. 54.

[2] G. Verbeck, *History of Protestant Missions in Japan*, report to the Osaka Missionary Conference 1883, p. 9. The text of the report may be found in Proceedings of the General Conference of the Protestant Missionaries in Japan, Osaka, 1883, (Yokohama: Meiklejohn, 1883).

of a second son of God, and that it would never do to have two in the country."[1]

Everywhere notice boards proclaimed that anyone who embraced Christianity would do so on pain of the severest punishment. Again Dr. Verbeck says:

> The missionaries shared with the other foreign residents in the alarm incident to a disturbed state of the country, and were sometimes exposed to insult and even to assault... the samurai were intensely hostile. To the very end of the period under review (i.e. 1872) the expulsion of the *outside barbarians* continued to be the favourite theme of ambitious patriots. It was a powerful element in the movements which issued in bringing about the restoration in 1869, and remained one of the expressed motives of the early policy of the new government.[2]

Verbeck himself, who was soon to become a trusted adviser of Japanese governments, was so insecure in the year 1862 that when the threat of war between England and Japan was rumoured as a result of the Richardson incident[3] he took his family to Shanghai for protection. He felt that anything might happen in Nagasaki at that time.

However, there was a gradual but perceptible change in the attitude of the Shogunate and even of the powerful leaders of Choshu and Satsuma toward the missionaries as time went by. A definite bias, hurtful to the Roman Catholic cause, was shown in favour of Protestant missionaries since the latter did not appear to have the close connection with government which the leaders of Japan had come to fear of missionaries in the past.

> The more intelligent and official classes soon discovered, perhaps partly by familiar intercourse with Protestant missionaries, that Protestantism was less to be feared than either the Roman or the Greek religion.
>
> A certain Japanese official said "I like the Protestants better than the Romanists, not that I have examined their doctrine, but Protestant missionaries don't look and act as if they were going to swallow us up, country and all."[4]

Increasingly young *samurai* who were intensely interested in the outside world came to the missionaries to discover what they could

---

[1] H. Ritter, *A History of Protestant Missions in Japan*, (Tokyo: Methodist Press, 1898), p. 19.

[2] G. Verbeck, *opus cited.* pps. 9 and 10.

[3] Richardson, a British subject, as a result of a misunderstanding, was cut down by a *samurai* retainer of the Lord of Satsuma. ante p. 15.

[4] G. Verbeck, *opus cited.* p. 12.

from them. Though the missionaries were not free to use the scriptures at the outset, they were able to discuss scientific works from the west with their eager learners. Some of these works, which had been translated into Chinese, could only be fully understood in the context of Christian ideas in relation to the natural universe. Whenever these texts contained the word *Christian* the young students would erase the word for fear of discovery.

C. M. Williams, the first permanent missionary to Japan, showed how observant he was of conditions when he remarked that the rising merchant class, which was conversant with the freedom enjoyed by their counterparts in other parts of the world, would not long tolerate their present situation.[1] This insight becomes intelligible when we remember that an increasing number of *samurai* had intermarried with the merchant group in order to better their financial condition. Among such men were a number of educated persons who were capable of heading large business enterprises, who could read the Chinese characters and thus discover the outside world through the books which the missionaries made available to them.

By 1866 the government had set up schools for the training of their officials both at Nagasaki and at Kanagawa. Very significantly this was the year following the *Osaka Event*. The missionaries were asked to teach English to them. They were granted permission to speak of Christianity freely. In 1864 Verbeck was already teaching a selected group of the sons of the *samurai* the Constitution of the United States and the New Testament! He represented these as the two foundation stones of the American way of life. By 1869 when Verbeck was invited to be adviser to the Privy Council and the Council of State of the new Meiji government, as well as a superintendent of the leading school in the country which later became Tokyo Imperial University, the men whom he had taught earlier had become leaders in the new government.

As early as 1866 Verbeck and other missionaries were influential in sending Japanese leaders abroad for training. The great majority of these men played prominent roles in Meiji Japan. Ryder[2] gives an illuminating example of this in the following passage.

> On an autumn day in 1866 as Dr. Ferris, secretary of the Board of Foreign Missions walked into his office in New York, he found await-

[1] M. Sumiya, *Kindai Nihon no Keisei to Kirisutokyo*, (Tokyo: Shinkyo Shuppansha, 1950), p. 10.

[2] S. W. Ryder, *opus cited*, pps. 33–34.

> ing him a ship captain and two Japanese, Mr. Ise and Mr. Numagawa by name.
> The Japanese presented to Dr. Ferris a letter from the Rev. G. F. Verbeck of Nagasaki. They told him they had come to America to study navigation, to learn how to build big ships and make big guns to prevent European powers from taking possession of their country. They had only about one hundred dollars left after paying their bills on arrival. Members of the Board of Foreign Missions made pledges amounting to several thousands of dollars to educate these two men. Although these two Japanese students did not hear from their government for eighteen months (when a law was passed allowing Japanese to go abroad) this money was not at all needed. What was used by them was later paid in full in grateful appreciation. After studying in the Rutgers Grammer School at New Brunswick, New Jersey, for a few months, Ise and Numagawa attended the United States Naval Academy. For on the recommendation of Mr. Verbeck, Dr. Ferris and Senator Freylinghausen, a bill was passed in Congress to admit Japanese to the United States Naval Academy at Annapolis. Soon afterwards Great Britain followed the example of the people and the government of the United States in showing courtesies to the Japanese, for up to this time Great Britain had not allowed Japanese students to visit her factories and iron works.

Verbeck was instrumental in sending over five hundred young Japanese abroad in the next thirty years. Among the thirty-eight Japanese students who graduated from Rutgers College alone were a Mayor of Tokyo, a Rear-Admiral of the Navy, the Emperor's Minister Plenipotentiary to the United States, several members of the Cabinets and the House of Peers as well as some who were appointed Governors of Prefectures. Thus the Christian missionary enterprise played an indirect though influential role in the modern development of Japan and overcame, largely as a result of the stature of her earliest missionaries, a large measure of the prejudice which had been traditionally aimed at the Christian faith.

It is important to note that at this very early date the attitude of an increasing number of the Japanese leadership to contact with the outside world was gradually changing and that this trend became clearly marked during and after the year 1866. It had begun as early as 1863. It was during that year that the attitude of Satsuma began to change as a result of the bombarding of Kagoshima and the Straits of Shimnoseki in the following year. Yet it is also significant that Ise and Numagawa went to America, "to learn how to build big ships and make big guns to prevent European powers from taking possession of their country."

A report of the missionaries in 1866 says the following of the *samurai*:

> Those who belong to the class called *samurai*, who alone are eligible to civil or military office, manifest much eagerness to gain a knowledge of western languages, sciences, and arts. Some of those who have been or are now studying English are in the habit of going daily to the missionaries' houses, in groups of from two to three to six or seven, to read the English Bible, preferring this to the study of school books. These intelligent young men frequently express their earnest desire that the day may soon come when all their countrymen shall have the Holy Scriptures and the free political institutions of which they are the basis.[1]

It would be wrong to suggest that it was the missionaries alone who encouraged intercourse with the west. Matsudaira, lord of Echizen, advised by his chief counsellor Yokoi that this was the wisest course, sent abroad a number of his retainers as early as 1866.

Yet this was not the universal attitude of the *samurai*. When Yokoi, adviser to Echizen, became a counsellor to the early Meiji government he was killed by a fanatic averse to relations with the outside world. So strong was the influence of this group in the earliest years of the Restoration that even Buddhism was stamped a foreign religion and Shinto was re-established as the national faith under a Ministry of Religion though that Ministry in its original form was short-lived.

Eichi Kudo points out that there were three basic attitudes of the Japanese people to Christianity at the close of the Shogunate and the beginning of the Meiji period.[2] Among the upper classes there was fear of intrigue between Christianity and politics, a fear stemming from the sixteenth century. That this was still a factor to be reckoned with as late as 1871 can be seen in the severe treatment of Roman Catholics in Nagasaki Prefecture at that time and the nature of the apology to foreign governments to the effect that the authorities feared intrigue between native Christians and foreign powers.[3] Among the middle classes, in this case the *samurai*, Christianity was regarded in general as heresy, as disloyalty to the Emperor and the traditional way of life of the Japanese people.[4] Finally, the lower classes had been

---

[1] O. Cary, *opus cited.* p. 64.

[2] E. Kudo, Shodai Nihon Purotestanto no Shakaizo, (Tokyo: Meiji Gakuin, 1954), p. 104.

[3] H. Ritter, *opus cited.* p. 31.

[4] O. Cary, *opus cited.* pps. 89–96. Cary gives examples of familiar writings in opposition to Christianity at this time. Among the specific arguments levelled

taught to regard Christianity as sheer magic so that when the proscription against the faith was ended their basic attitude toward it was one of fear.

At first sight then, our findings with regard to the attitude of the Japanese people toward Christianity at this time appear to be contradictory. Nevertheless, when we recall that there were different attitudes within each of the social classes toward the question of opening the country the apparent contradiction disappears. There were those, of whom Matsudaira of Echizen is a good example, who saw from the first that the country would have to be opened and who advocated that policy openly and frankly. After the bombardments of Kagoshima and Shimonoseki, the attitudes of an increasing number of feudal lords changed, even among the most traditionally opposed clans of Satsuma and Choshu. The *Osaka Event* made the obvious course of action even clearer to these men and most particularly to the clan bureaucrats, the *samurai* retainers of the lords, some of whom were the pupils of the missionaries. They were for intercourse with the west and for learning all they could from it. This was not consonant with an acceptance of Christianity but it did mean for them a more tolerant attitude toward it, especially in its Protestant form. There were those *samurai* who remained implacable in their hatred of the "barbarians," who looked upon Christianity as an affront to *Bushido*, the way of the *samurai* warrior which had become the ethic of the intelligentsia, and to the integrity of Japan itself. They were for re-asserting the honor of their class and of their nation. If they desired to have a relationship with the barbarian it was to learn his ways of warfare in order to make Japan great among the nations. Saigo Takamori of Satsuma is an excellent illustration of this way of thought as were the countless roving *ronin* who were anxious to re-establish a place for themselves in Japanese society. They looked to the Restoration as an opportunity to accomplish these goals and were only dissuaded from them when, following Saigo Takamori as their leader, they were hopelessly defeated in the Satsuma Rebellion of 1877. At the close of the Shogunate this group was extremely vocal and those in opposition to them were not yet well enough established in power to counter their influence.

For these reasons the treatment accorded to those few who did become Christians in the first decade after the opening of the ports varied according to the attitude of the local authorities. In some cases it was permissive, in others severe punishment was accorded them.

Dr. S. Wells Williams, a veteran missionary in China, because he had had contact with Japanese castaways and also because he had some knowledge of the Chinese caligraphy, was asked to act as interpreter for the Perry expedition. He had had opportunity over the years to gain some knowledge of the point of view of the Japanese authorities toward the outside world in general and toward Christianity in particular. He visited Nagasaki again in 1858 for the purpose of surveying the situation in the interest of Christian outreach. Chaplains on board American naval ships had also had some opportunity to survey the field. Dr. Williams wrote as follows, "There were also then at Nagasaki Rev. Mr. Syle and Chaplain Henry Wood,[1] and we three agreed to write to the directors of the Episcopal, Reformed, and Presbyterian Mission Boards, urging them to appoint missionaries for Japan who could teach the people what true Christianity was."[2] It was also urged that these men should be, "prudent men of tried experience," who "must remember that it is death to a Japanese to become a Christian" and "must not rush headlong into the work without considering secondary means."[3] In regard to those sent out in response to the above request Dr. Williams wrote, "I do not know that better men could be found to begin missionary efforts than Brown, Hepburn, and Liggins."[4]

Rev. John Liggins and Rev. C. M. Williams, both of whom had been missionaries in China, were the first missionaries of the Protestant group to arrive in Japan. They were appointed by the American Episcopal Church in 1859. Liggins arrived in Nagasaki in May and Williams in June. Within the year, owing to ill health, Liggins had to return to the United States but he did not cease his advocacy of the work in Japan. In October 1859, J. C. Hepburn, M.D., of the Ameri-

---

against it were, (i) irregular sex practice (ii) opposition to filial piety and therefore to the interests of the Japanese state (iii) intolerance toward Shinto and Buddhism, (iv) opposition to the doctrine of the five social relations as taught by traditional Confucianism. Again and again it was emphasized that to follow this religion will be for the undoing of the Japanese nation.

[1] O. Cary, *opus cited.* p. 40. Chaplain Wood later wrote on November 7, 1859, "The first English ship which entered the port of Japan in Nagasaki soon after the conclusion of the American Treaty and before the English Treaty was concluded, was a smuggler of opium, attempting to introduce it stealthily and fraudulently into a nation which does not use it and whose laws prohibit it. That ship I saw...the house owning that vessel had been known to make, as I am informed, half a million of dollars a year in the Chinese opium trade and is not content with its wage of iniquity. It is one of the first English houses in China."

[2] Ibid. p. 40.

[3] Ibid.

[4] *Ibid.* p. 46.

can Presbyterian Board and his wife landed at Kanagawa. In November 1859 Rev. Samuel R. Brown and D. B. Simmons, M.D., both of the Reformed Church in America, reached the same port.

Rev. G. F. Verbeck, who had sailed with them, reached Nagasaki on November 7th. The families of these three men arrived in Japan in December, 1959. Williams, Hepburn, Brown and Verbeck were all to prove outstanding pioneers of the Christian church in Japan. Rev. J. H. Ballagh joined the mission force under the Reformed Church at Kanagawa in August of 1861. Rev. Jonathan Goble, who had been a marine in Perry's expedition, went to Japan under the American Baptist Free Mission Society in April 1860, landing in Kanagawa. In May 1863 the Rev. D. Thompson of the Presbyterian Board joined Dr. Hepburn at Kanagawa. D. B. Simmons went into private practice shortly after his arrival in Japan. Thus the total missionary force in the country, apart from their families, prior to the Restoration numbered only seven.

Far from marking time these earliest missionaries demonstrated their greatness not only in the patience they displayed while working under such grave handicaps but in the use they made of their time and of the opportunities which were afforded them. They acquired the language and prepared language works for others. They disposed of a large number of historical, geographical, and scientific works prepared by the missionaries in China. These helped to correct inadequate ideas of the west and also to correct spurious charges against Christianity. Their personal lives were also an aid in this. They taught Japanese officials and established lasting friendships amongst them.[1] Verbeck called this the period of "*Preparation and Promise.*" It is obvious from the great use Japanese government officials made of this small company of men that their success was nothing short of phenomenal so far as gaining the confidence of Japanese leadership was concerned.

Yet it was not until 1864 that the first baptism took place on Japanese soil. Yano Riyu was baptized by J. H. Ballagh while the former was on his deathbed. In 1866 two brothers, Wakasa and Ayabe Murata, high *samurai* retainers of the Daimyo of Saga, were baptized by Mr. Verbeck and in the same year, seven years after he had arrived in Japan, C. M. Williams baptized his first convert Shiomura, a *samurai* of Higo. In 1868 Rev. Verbeck baptized one Shimizu, a Buddhist

[1] For a fascinating report of these early days see G. F. Verbeck, *opus cited.* and O. Cary, *opus cited.* p. 53 ff.

priest. This man was confined to prison the following year for his faith and remained there for the next five years. In 1868 Rev. Ballagh recorded the baptism of Awasu Komei. Only six baptisms had taken place up until the year of the Restoration. However, the activity and influence of the missionaries can hardly be counted in terms of the results alone. That conversion to the faith at the outset should be difficult to attain has proven more the rule than the exception in the spread of the Christian faith. The first convert to Christianity in China did not come forward until ten years after the arrival of the first missionaries.

The "years of preparation" made it possible for the missionaries to take far greater advantage than they would otherwise have done of the opportunities that were afforded them in the next decade. Had they had unusual initial success there would have been no time to acquire that understanding which is, above all other things, the basic requirement of a successful missionary.

During this period then, in one sense, Christianity had been severely limited by the conditions within Japanese society. Yet the tiny group of missionaries had overcome the prejudice against the faith to the extent that Japanese political leadership came to trust and to use them. In the first place, they were the only foreign group on the scene which was concerned enough about Japan to be used in this way. In the second place, political pressure from foreign powers made it imperative that Japanese leadership find help of this kind. It would be naive in the extreme not to realize that that leadership used the services of the missionaries principally for the furtherance of their own ends which were (1) to retain power in the case of the Shogunate and to achieve it on the part of the *outside clans* (2) to ensure the security of Japan. These ends were secular. The religious orientation of those who furthered them was to the Shushi sect of Confucianism which stressed not only classical learning but the *five social relations*, in other words, that school of Confucianism which tended to be this-worldly in its concern.[1]

Protestant Christianity had an influence far out of proportion to the size of the group which represented it in the sense that it was through the eyes of the missionaries that Japanese bureaucratic, political leadership first gained an insight into Western Civilization. There is little indication that even those *samurai* who might have been

---

[1] E. Kudo, *opus cited.* Chapter 4.

sympathetic and understanding in their attitude to Christianity were prepared to go beyond that to accept the faith itself. Since there were those among the Restoration forces who were deathly opposed to Christianity this made those who were sympathetic still more guarded in their attitude to it.

A further observation we are justified in making, even at this early date, is that there was at least a suggestion of the class orientation which was to prove characteristic of Japanese Christianity. The contacts of the missionaries were almost solely with the *samurai*. In the first place it was the members of this group who were alone capable of reading the Christian and secular western literature which the missionaries made available. It was also this group which was anxious to learn of the outside world. In the case of the pupils whom the missionaries taught in the government schools most of them, while not of the highest rank, were trusted enough to be used as interpreters on important political occasions. Others, like those connected with the merchant class, were of fairly low rank and were anxious to better their financial status through learning English and thus extending their business opportunities.

As for the Protestant Christian movement itself at the time of the Restoration, it was nothing more than a tiny embryo struggling for life. Yet the missionary force had prepared itself well for the work which lay ahead.

PART TWO

THE PERIOD OF FLUX 1868-1889

CHAPTER THREE

THE EFFECT OF POLITICAL DEVELOPMENTS ON THE STRUCTURE OF JAPANESE SOCIETY

At the outset let us assess the positions of the various classes in Japanese society with relation to the power structure at the Restoration of the Emperor in January, 1868.

The Tokugawa Shogunate, and those who had supported it, had lost all semblance of political power. This meant that their *samurai* retainers were now without political influence of any kind. Indeed, they were soon to be economically impoverished not only by the loss of territories which their lords suffered but by the eclipse of the privileges of their class which was, before long, to pass out of formal existence.

The Restoration forces were dominated by the Lords of Choshu, Satsuma, Tosa, and Hizen along with their *samurai* retainers who, like all the *samurai* of this period, must be divided into two groups, those whose functions were purely military and those whose function had long been administrative. It was this latter group led by Okubo Toshimichi which was to possess vital political power.

The merchants welcomed the new day and looked forward to a period of increased trade which would benefit them. The change also meant greater prestige as their role became more and more essential to the interests of the nation.

Actually the farmer was little involved in the change which took place. He was to find himself, as before, the burden bearer of the new order.

The *kuge*, or traditional lords of the Imperial Household, were to enjoy political power as advisers to the Emperor for a brief time, but were soon destined to lose out to the rising young *samurai*. Three such lords were Prince Sanjo, Prince Tokudaiji, and Prince Iwakura. The last alone was to have very real influence. The hereditary lords continued to have a seat in the House of Peers but in general remained aloof from politics.

The greatest division of opinion at the beginning, indeed for the first decade of this period, was between the young *samurai* of Choshu and Satsuma led by Okubo Toshimichi and Saigo Takamori, both of Satsuma. The former realized that Japan must first secure herself internally and economically before any other course of action would be open to her. The latter, a military *samurai* leader, was for demonstrating the military greatness of Japan from the very beginning.

Dr. Hugh Borton says the following regarding the early years of the Meiji Period, "Apparently in Ito's view, nothing important happened politically for the first twelve years of the Restoration. It is in order, therefore, to concentrate this survey of the first five years of the new government on practical issues rather than on theoretical political problems."[1] Dr. Borton is referring to Ito Hirobumi, whom, we shall see, was to become the architect of the new Japan. However, some exception must be taken to this statement. In the first place, Ito Hirobumi did not rise to full political prominence until ten of the twelve years of which he speaks had passed. Okubo of Satsuma had been his superior until he was assassinated in 1878. This doubtless coloured Ito's interpretation of what was important. In the second place, concentration on practical issues was a definite political policy. Dr. Borton himself says:

> The concentration on practical problems accelerated industrialization and strengthened Japan militarily. This reduced interference from groups outside the clan oligarchy to a minimum during the first few years because the oligarchs alone had the technical knowledge to be leaders in the industrialization movement.
> They selected and trained their own group of assistants. There was no room for members of the opposition.
> In other words, this concentration on practical problems made possible a simultaneous political unification and the formation of a strong centralized state.[2]

There would appear to be a definite choice of political policy between the reactionary feudal elements under Saigo Takamori, who were anxious to restore an order much like the Tokugawa save under their own leadership, and those such as Kido, Okubo and Okuma, who were for strengthening the country through economic modernization. Saigo was also anxious to prove the Imperial might of Japan abroad. At the same time, we would agree that sheer *improvisation* governed much of what was done by government in these early years.[3] There

---

[1] H. Borton, *Japan's Modern Century*, (New York: Ronald Press, 1956), p. 69.
[2] *Ibid.* p. 82.
[3] *Ibid.* p. 158.

is little evidence to suggest that from the outset the clan bureaucrats saw clearly the combination of modern industrialization with Confucian state-absolutism which was to become the formative pattern for the modern Japanese nation.

Undoubtedly two basic considerations were in the minds of all of those who had to do with government policy at this time. The first was fear for the safety of the state in relation to foreign powers. Their ships were constantly sailing in adjacent waters. The second was fear of collapse from within. Tenuous sentiment toward the throne alone held the country together and made it possible for the new government to gain time to consolidate its power. Dr. Delmer Brown says, "The basis of national consciousness broadened with the return of the Emperor. More people were ready to endanger their lives for the sake of the country."[1] He is careful to point out, however, that this was chiefly true of the *samurai*. The slogan of the *samurai* as a whole had evolved, according to Brown from "Revere the Emperor, expel the barbarians" in the early 1860s to "Revere the Emperor, down with the Bakufu!," prior to the Restoration, to "Rich country, strong army" in the earliest years of Meiji.

At the outset the Emperor Meiji was caused to proclaim what since has become known as, "The Charter Oath." This was to be used as an effective weapon by many groups with differing aims and ideals in the days which lay ahead. So confusing was its wording that there are two "offlcial" translations.[4] It appeared to some to refer definitely to a promise of truly representative government.[3] However, as Sir George Sansom points out, it could scarcely have referred to much beyond a willingness to bring the lords and the *samurai* together in a deliberative council.[2] Far too few of those in power in those earliest days had any conception of representative institutions in the western sense of the word. It might be compared, as it frequently has, to the Magna Carta. It was more Confucian in its orientation than anything else. At the same time, it asserted that the new leadership would seek learning beneficial to Japan throughout the earth. This openness to "learning" throughout the earth is crucial to an understanding as to why Japan,

---

[1] D. M. Brown, *Nationalism in Modern Japan*, (Berkeley: University of California Press, 1955), p. 87 ff.

[2] G. B. Sansom, *The Western World and Japan*, (New York: Knopf, 1950), p. 318.

[3] U. Iwasaki, *The Working Forces in Japanese Politics*, (New York: Longmans, Green, 1921), p. 29.

[4] For a full discussion of the background of the Charter Oath see G. B. Sansom, *opus, cited*, pps. 318 ff.

unlike China, was willing and eager to adopt any techniques which would lead to rapid modernization of the nation which, in turn would place her on a par with other western nations. China had illusions about the sheer intellectual superiority of her cultural achievements which made borrowing from other nations almost a psychological impossibility. The illusions of Japan had to do with nationhood not with the intellect. The Japanese point of view was that the intellect, like everything else, should be subservient to the interests of the nation. That which proved a roadblock for China was an open path to future glory so far as Japan was concerned.

The form of government which resulted from the *Charter Oath* consisted of a Council of State and an upper and lower house.

> The highest offices fell to princes of the blood and to the court and territorial nobility, 'because due affection should be shown to relatives of the Sovereign and due respect to persons of rank', but real power remained in the hands of the advisory officials who were, as before, *samurai* from the western clans, Okubo, Kido, Goto, Itagaki, Soyejima, Saigo, Ito and Okuma. The deliberative assembly was at first composed only of *samurai* representing the clans, but a departure was made by extending membership to representatives of the three great cities and of Imperial, that is to say, former Tokugawa territory.[1]

Administratively the government consisted of the following departments among which religion stood the highest—Religion, State, War, Foreign Affairs, Finance and Justice. Just at this time, and indeed for another five years, the influence of Shinto was consciously strengthened in order to rally the country around the Emperor.[2] As a result, a severe persecution of Roman Catholics was undertaken in Nagasaki prefecture and new edicts continuing the prohibition of Christianity were issued. Since Buddhism had been favoured by the Bakufu, it too had a difficult time. This policy was only checked after the return of the Iwakura Mission in 1873. The mission had found the greatest opposition among western powers to the continuing persecution of Christianity. They discovered it to be an obstacle to international acceptance.

Five men, at this time, held power of the first rank. They were Sanjo Sanetome and Iwakura Tomoyoshi, both of whom were formally

---

[1] G. B. Sansom, *opus cited*, p. 320.

[2] J. H. Gubbins, *The Making of Modern Japan*, (London: Seeley-Service, 1922), p. 75 and K. Latourette, *The Development of Modern Japan*, Also W. W. McLaren, *opus cited*, p. 67. in which he claims there is evidence to show that this Constitution cited from p. 111 had its origin in that of Emperor Tai-Ho (701–704 A. D.).

court nobles; Saigo Takemori, a conservative samurai of Satsuma and an outstanding military leader, Okubo Toshimitsu, also a *samurai* of Satsuma but an outstanding administrator and advocate of a new centralized form of government, and Kido Koin also a *samurai* but of the Choshu clan. Next to them in importance were men who were to become even more prominent in the modernization of Japan—Ito Hirobumi, Okuma Shigenobu, Itagaki Taisuke, Goto Shojiro, and Inouye Kaoru. While Okubo was the towering figure of the first decade of reform, at the very outset the struggle was between Saigo and Kido.[1] The former was determined that the military prowess of Japan should be proven and advocated the retention of the *samurai* class as a military caste. In general his views remained feudalist. Kido and Okubo knew something of the outside world and were convinced that Japan had to become a modern nation, especially industrially, if she were to take her place among the leading nations of the world. They were convinced that any display of military prowess, which they realized Japan did not possess, might well be her undoing.

The "Charter Oath" was the work of these early leaders. It was an attempt to see that history did not repeat itself, through the House of Satsuma simply replacing that of Tokugawa, with the Emperor as a figurehead. In this sense the Restoration was a genuine step forward in the creation of a centralized, modern state. Therefore, one of the first steps of the new government was to set a limit upon the amount of armaments any clan might maintain. Prior to this Choshu and Satsuma in particular had learned all they could of foreign armament and had manufactured them in their own fiefs with foreign advice and help. Another step taken was to place a representative of the central government in each of the clan governments. But the most significant step ostensibly taken by the lords, and which consolidated the power of the central government, was the voluntary handing over by them to the government, of their registers of lands and peoples. Actually, this was first carried out by the lords of Satsuma, Choshu, Tosa, and Hizen, who had led in the Restoration movement. "This was more than an act of magnanimity; it was an intimation that the four great military clans of the West were prepared to participate in the central government's efforts to abolish the feudal system."[2] In July 1869 all of the former lords were compelled to do the same, though they were appointed governors of their former lands now known as prefectures

[1] U. Iwasaki, *opus cited,* p. 58

[2] W. W. McLaren, *opus cited,* p. 72.

rather than fiefs. They also received a certain percentage of the taxes on their former lands.

It is important to understand what was actually happening here. As we have pointed out, those who were really in control at the time of the Restoration were the clan bureaucrats, especially of Choshu and Satsuma. For years prior to the Restoration the great majority of lords were weak and dissolute and had left the real government of their lands in the hands of these *samurai* administrators. They were the men who had held the land registers in the old order. They were, therefore, the same men who came to hold them under the new dispensation. No compulsion was necessary to make them hand over the registers to themselves! Some compulsion was necessary to make those who were not to share in the direction of the new order hand over their registers. Yet this was easily done by appointing the former lords as governors and leaving their former administrators with a degree of local administrative autonomy. Since it made little change in the real situation, the lords themselves did not see, at the outset, that the young bureaucrats were determined to modernize the country and that this meant the destruction of the feudal system upon which their power rested.

What we ought also to continue to bear in mind is that those who were in the positions of power were definitely the *samurai* retainers of the old outside clans. The former retainers of the Tokugawa were to have no place of importance in the new order. The struggle for power in the Meiji period cannot be understood without a realization of that fact and further of the fact that the Choshu and Satsuma bureaucrats were to seek to exclude those of Tosa and Hizen from top-ranking positions before the day was far spent.

By 1871 the shift in power from the feudal to the new order was well under way. As we have said, the old fiefs were abolished and prefectures took their place. The form of the government was once more overhauled. The Council of State was divided into three, a Central Council (Sei-In) a lower house (Sa-In), to take the place of the old lower house, and the Upper House (U-In) which was to have real legislative power. Certain Councillors, all of them *samurai* of the new bureaucracy, and all of them the real power behind the throne, were appointed to the Council of State and were known as Sangi. The administrative functions of the various departments were also in their hands and they were appointed to the Upper House. Or, at least, this was true of the great majority of them. Among these men were those mentioned above plus Eto of Hizen, Soyejima and Oki.

> Thus the U-In (Upper House) was composed of the departmental ministers who were no longer ex-kuge or lords but members of the former ruling coterie of samurai. With the abolition of the clans in 1871, the policy of appointing to high offices the members of the court or territorial nobility, which had been announced in 1868, was discarded, and the real promoters of the Restoration stepped forward and assumed the high offices of the administration. Sanjo and Iwakura were the only nobles left with any political responsibility.[1]

In 1871 an important government mission left Japan. It was headed by Iwakura and included Okubo, Ito, Okuma, and others. This mission was largely inspired by G. F. Verbeck, a missionary who had now become a major government adviser.[2] The purpose of this mission was to study western forms of government and economy and also to seek revision of the Trade Treaties signed with the powers in 1866. These treaties not only provided for extra-territoriality, which Japan considered humiliating, but also for an import tax not exceeding 5 per cent ad valorem. Since the new government needed capital to support an army and to help promote new industry they sought to realize it through increased tax on trade.

The effect upon Japan of this mission was far-reaching and that not in one field alone but in many. Ito Hirobumi, who was to play such a major role in the next few years, and who was then in charge of the Industrial Ministry, visited every major industrial plant of the countries he visited time permitting. He was also to hear Bismarck maintain that western governments respected international treaties only so long as it was in their interest to do so and that Japan would be respected only if she became a strong, modern, military power. Yamagata, later to become not only head of Army but for many years premier of the country, never forgot the impression he received of the efficient conscript armies of Germany and of Europe in general. Niijima Jo, an early Japanese Christian pioneer, was an interpreter for the mission.

Everywhere the mission found a rejection of its plea for the removal of extra-territoriality on the ground that foreign nationals could not expect proper protection in a country in which Christianity, the religion of the west, was still persecuted. The problem of the revision of the treaties was to have far-reaching implications in Japanese society so as to bear directly on the development of Christianity in that land.

While this embassy was away discontent was rife at home. The new conscription law of 1873, combined with the pensioning off of the

---

[1] W. W. McLaren, *opus cited,* p. 113.

[2] S. W. Ryder, *opus cited,* p. 35.

samurai, left no place for this group in Japanese society. Many of them under the influence of Shinto nationalism, which was especially strong in the 1860s and, as we have seen, in these earliest days of the Restoration, had supported the Restoration with the hope that through military feats their class would regain proper status in society. They looked forward to the day when Japan might well overcome both Korea and China and possibly even Russia thus to declare her supremacy in the Orient. Meanwhile the Korean government, which had long sent a token gift to Japan at the accession of each new Shogun, had neglected so to recognize the accession of the Emperor. Moreover, she also sent a dispatch to Japan in 1873 stating that she was no longer willing to have ane relations with a power which was so ready to dispense with the traditional ways of the Orient. Kido and Saigo had been left in charge of things within the country while the embassy was away. Saigo was for immediately taking steps against Korea. He felt that his *samurai* followers would be able to vindicate themselves in the struggle and thus stave off the establishment of a conscript army. Kido was for staying out of any foreign conflict at this time, doubtless advised wisely by dispatches from the Iwakura embassy. Saigo took the occasion to step out of the government. At this time he was followed by Itagaki and Goto of Tosa and Eto and Soyejima of Hizen. Eto and Soyejima were sympathetic with Saigo's motives but the event simply provided the occasion for Itagaki and Goto to resign on the ground that Japan did not enjoy truly representative government.

The Iwakura Embassy, appalled by the dissension at home, returned hurriedly. Okubo took command of affairs. Eto raised a revolt against him at Saga in Hizen in 1874 and died in its suppression.

In an attempt to occupy the unhappy *samurai* of Satsuma an expedition was sent against Formosa in 1874 over which China was supposed to exercise sovereignty. However, China had done nothing about the attacks of the natives on shipwrecked sailors of Japan, or any other nation, and therefore Japan felt justified in seeking to maintain some kind of discipline there.

In 1875 a Korean fort fired upon a Japanese survey ship and the question of Japanese honour once again came to the fore. The government gathered a number of naval vessels and put on a display of force reminiscent of Commodore Perry's technique. Thus she forced Korea into signing a treaty of amity and to opening some of her ports for trade.

But this was not enough for the *samurai* of Satsuma. They felt the leaders of the nation were decadent and raised a rebellion under the leadership of Saigo in 1877. The Satsuma Rebellion was suppressed at Kumamoto in the same year after a fierce engagement between the *samurai* troops of Saigo, which were nevertheless using the best western miltary methods, and the new untried conscript army of the government personally led by Okubo. As a result of the defeat Saigo committed suicide and with him went the last attempt to retain the old feudal system.

The bureaucrats of Choshu and Satsuma were now in full control. Itagaki and Goto continued to campaign for representative government though it is significant that they refused to *use* the Satsuma Rebellion in any way indicating that, even though their own personal ambitions were frustrated, they were not willing to threaten the welfare of the nation in their own interests. Over against Itagaki and Goto, Okubo and Kido, as well as Ito and Okuma, felt the strengthening of the country economically ought to take precedence even over the establishment of representative forms of government with which they were not essentially in sympathy.

The retention of power throughout the difficulties outlined above was no easy matter. When the Iwakura Mission returned they found themselves somewhat discredited because they had not obtained revision of the treaties. As a result, in order to appease their adversaries whom, as we have seen, stepped out of the government in 1873, they were forced to promise some kind of constitutional reform. Accordingly the Council of State became a Privy Council in 1875. This Council, which was to advise the Emperor, possessed real power. A Senate (Genro-In) replaced the two houses but was composed only of elements chosen by the Emperor. It had deliberative powers only and discussed matters handed down by the Privy Council. In order to lay claim to a Separation of Powers, after the American System, a Supreme Court was set up. Actually, the Supreme Court was controlled by the Privy Council through the department of Justice, the head of which was on the Council. Itagaki was persuaded to join the government again on the ground that this was a real separation of powers and therefore a true reform in the direction of greater representation. He soon saw it as a piece of subterfuge and in 1876 resigned again to lead the forces for true representative government. McLaren makes this incisive statement, "From these various considerations we are forced to the conclusion that the changes were undertaken to satisfy a demand for a less autocratic form of government, and that while new forms were created, the old principle of absolutism was retained by the oligarchs."[1] The external reforms were window-dressing designed to confuse the adversaries of those in power and to draw away their following. It was a technique to be used again and again by the leaders of modern Japan. To fail to understand it is to fail to understand political life in Japanese society right up to the present.

To some extent, of course, this was a struggle for personal power between those who felt themselves responsible for the Restoration. This doubtless motivated the actions of men on both sides of the fence but along with it went real considerations of basic political policy. Can a nation in the process of rapid social change, seeking to become a power in world affairs capable of maintaining its own sovereignty, afford representative institutions especially when the great majority of the people have little understanding of their significance? Itagaki himself was quoted as saying, "If the Council Chamber is established, we do not propose that the franchise should at once be made universal. We would give it, in the first instance, to the *samurai* and the rich farmers and merchants."[2] As Dr. Borton observes, "Even though ideas were given European labels, such as 'liberal', 'progressive', or 'conservative' these words cannot be interpreted in their usual Occidental meaning. They have always had their peculiar Japanese connotations."[3] One of those "peculiar connotations" obvious to any serious observer of Japanese politics, is that parties have always tended in Japan to be centered around persons rather than policies.

The other question to be answered, was, of course, whether representative institutions were not more important to the welfare and growth of the nation than rapid economic and military development which would place Japan on a footing with other great powers?

A too hasty attempt to prove the "greatness of Japan" was cast aside by the oligarchs as a choice when Eto and Saigo were defeated. On the other hand, a hasty acceptance of representative forms of government was also avoided by those who managed to retain power namely, Okubo, Kido and Ito along with Okuma on a slightly lower echelon. Okubo was assassinated in 1878 by a revengeful *samurai* and

[1] W. W. McLaren, *opus cited*, p. 119.
[2] H. Borton, *opus cited*, p. 97.
[3] *Ibid*, p. 94.

Kido passed away shortly afterwards. This left Ito and Okuma to share the field. By 1881, however, Ito had forced Okuma out.

It had been Okuma who had at least devised the form of government in 1875 in an attempt to do something that might move the country farther in the direction of representation. In the Senate Okuma was the leader of the left wing and had with him a man like Ozaki Yukio, who was to become the symbol of true political liberalism in Japan. Ito and Yamagata were leaders on the right and claimed that Okuma, even at that time, was a dangerous radical.[1] Okuma was influenced, on the one hand, by Okubo whose protege he was and on the other, by G. F. Verbeck whose pupil he had been in Nagasaki long before the days of the Restoration.

Before we go on to an examination of the political forces at work after 1880 let us recapitulate what we have said in order ro draw a clearer picture of the forces in opposition to the government. Itagaki and Goto from 1875 on, that is to say from their resignation over the Korea Affair, had consistently fought for a real measure of representative government. Yet there was a real confusion of interests along with that concern. The following were the reasons given for their resignation,

> They complained, without much regard for logic that the treatment of the samurai had been unfair, that the introduction of conscription was bad for the nation, that the new land tax and land law were objectionable, that the foreign policy of the government was too weak, and finally, that all these ills were due to the absence of a parliament that could watch the government in the interest of a minority.[2]

The "interest of a minority" was, of course, that of the *samurai*. The "new land tax and the new land law" were laws passed in order to finance the new government and which had to be paid in cash per annum regardless of the yield of the land in the case of farm lands. Itagaki, therefore, had the support of the small *samurai* who had lost out heavily as a result of their lack of status and the commutation of their pensions, as well as the landlords and the farmers who were paying the economic price for reform. The *samurai* elements, however, tended to be violent and called for a vigorous foreign policy of expansion. The landlords and the farmers were in an uneasy alliance which came to be known as the "Jiyu Minken Undo" (Movement for Freedom and Rights.) Indeed, it became a simple matter for the

[1] U. Iwasaki, *opus cited*, p. 89.
[2] U. Iwasaki, *opus cited*, p. 87.

government after 1878 to break up this alliance by relieving the land tax which benefited the landlords more than the farmers and drew the former away from any progressive tendency. It became evident before many years that Itagaki himself was not much interested in furthering the basic welfare of the common people.

Two elements must be added to this opposition. One was the group of intellectuals who had been influenced in a purely secular way by the ideas of J. S. Mill, Rousseau, and others. Many of them were newspaper editors. From as early as 1873 their opposition became so vocal that the government passed a Restrictive Press Law in 1875 which, at the culmination of the agitation in 1883–4, led to the suspension of forty-nine newspapers. The other group which stood in opposition, and of which we will have much more to say later on, was the small but influential group of Christians some of whom played a prominent part in the struggle for progressive reform. For example, Honda Yoichi was among the foremost in the demand for prefectural assemblies and took part in them from the beginning. Kataoka of Shikoku was second only to Itagaki in the national Liberal Party. When the prefectural assemblies were set up in 1880 two of their chairman were Honda of Aomori Ken and Yuasa of Gumma Ken both of them Christians. On the executive council of the latter, three out of the five members were Christians. People naturally looked to them for they were among the few in Japan at that time who, as a result of their brief experience in church councils, at least had some idea of representative institutions. People also felt that they were sincere and could be trusted. The Christians from the outset were concerned with the struggle for the new order. They were concerned to make clear that, whereas under Confucian ethics men have duties but no rights, in the Christian understanding of life the two go hand in hand.[1]

In the face of all of this opposition, as we have noted, the government was forced to find ways to deal with it either by outright opposition or by compromise. When the clans had been abolished the governors of the prefectures were directly appointed by the Emperor through the Home Department. This department, therefore, became one of the most important in the country and Okubo himself headed it for years. Control was thus granted to him right down to the village level. Gradually the government came to see that the granting of

[1] See M. Sumiya, *Kindai Nihon no Keisei to Kirisutokyo*, (Tokyo: Shinkyo Shuppansha, 1950), pps. 48–50.

prefectural assemblies might draw away the attention of the opposition to their claim for representative government at the center. These assemblies were granted in 1880 but they were responsible to the centrally appointed governor and could be dissolved by him. Thus their influence upon the power structure of the nation was peripheral.

By 1881 the government was plagued with a period of inflation and depression. All of the opposition forces joined hands and since the formation of political parties became legal in that year, they formed the Jiyu-to (Freedom Party), under the leadership of Itagaki. It called for Universal suffrage and a new parliament. Some of the members were openly republican. The great majority of Christians supported him.[1] Itagaki himself, doubtless influenced by Kataoka, made a statement at Kofu in March, 1882, in which he denounced Shinto, Confucianism, and Buddhism as detrimental to national progress and, "openly asserted his sympathy for Christianity at a time when the people were hurling the epithet 'Christian' at their political opponents. Itagaki's stand brought the Christians close to the Liberal Party with which they cooperated in political matters."[2]

A further defection from official circles took place in 1881 which had important consequences. The government had set up a development plan for Hokkaido and had expended considerable funds for equipment, buildings, and the like. In line with a general policy to get out of business in general and to remain only in those businesses connected directly with armament, a decision was made to sell what was involved in the project to a private company at a ridiculously low price. Moreover, the government head of the project was also reputed to be a member of the purchasing company. Okuma Shigenobu, who was then the very able finance minister, claimed to have been uninformed about the whole scheme. Since the depression was in full swing and the people were already resentful of the government this episode served to deepen that resentment. Okuma took the occasion to resign with the intention of leading a protest movement for a Constitution. He planned thus to become Japan's first Prime Minister. He seemed confident that he would secure the blessing of the Emperor and was careful to avoid too close an identification with the Liberals. In the Korea Affair of 1875 he had remained with the government for he was an advocate of civil reform rather than military expansion. It was his contention that such a policy represented the best in western

---

[1] C. Yanaga, *opus cited*, p. 127.

[2] *Ibid.* p. 126–7.

civilization. He was also an expert in financial matters and knew their importance in the modern world. After his resignation from the government he formed the Kaishin-to, or the Progressive Party, in order to realize his aims. He advocated a parliament of the Anglo-Saxon type with limited manhood suffrage. Actually, Britain itself was just moving beyond such an electoral system. Okuma advocated internal administrative reforms and no imperial expansion.

The reaction to this move of Okuma's on the part of Ito Hirobumi and the bureaucrats who remained loyal to him, among whom the chief was Yamagata the architect of Japan's modern military tradition and the most conservative of the oligarchy, was swift and sure. The government, having secured the Emperor's consent, issued an Imperial Rescript pledging that constitutional government would be "given" by the Emperor to the people of Japan by the year 1889. They claimed that time was necessary, however, in order that this might be accomplished in an orderly fashion. Through this appeal to the Emperor, and the subsequent promise of a Constitution for Japan, Okuma's fire was stolen and the government was more securely in the saddle than ever before.

Thereafter, appeal to the Emperor became a favourite device of the oligarchy. When the people rose up against the government it would claim rebellion against the Emperor. Thus every protest movement had to claim that it too was acting in the interest of the Emperor.[1] So strong had the myth of Emperor-divinity become by 1885 that, after that date, an appeal to his authority never failed to secure the cooperation of the great majority of the populace. It was this appeal, therefore, rather than a popular base in the electorate which kept subsequent governments in power and made it so difficult for a popular party movement to develop.[2]

It is significant that in the year 1885 the Emperor was declared of age and ready to take over power himself though he was by then 33. Nevertheless, real power remained in the hands of the oligarchs.

As a result of the promise to grant a constitution Ito Hirobumi resigned as head of the Home Ministry, and was appointed to the

---

[1] U. Iwasaki's, *The Working Forces in Japanese Politics* is an excellent example of the way in which a liberal Japanese finds it necessary to apologize for his position while at the same time claiming that it is a true representation of the traditional desire of the Emperors of Japan.

[2] R. A. Scalapino, *Democracy and the Party Movement in Pre-War Japan*, (Berkeley: University of California Press, 1953), is the most authoritative work available on the Japanese party movement.

Imperial Household Staff, charged with the task of preparing the new constitution. The work was carried on in secret together with a small committee. In order to study conditions abroad he went to Europe and found, very naturally, in Bismarckian Germany, with its Constitutional, authoritarian monarchy a pattern which most closely resembled the situation in Japan. He returned with a dual purpose in mind. He would write a Constitution of a traditional, authoritarian nature while, at the same time, Japan would take on the outward forms of modern western society which would not threaten the essential nature of the authoritarian order.

By 1885 he had returned to Japan and had set up a whole new nobility along German lines which took into its ranks both the old nobility and the members of the new oligarchy. Five ranks were established, prince, marquis, count, viscount, and baron. Ito eventually became a Prince and, in the year of his return, 1885 he had himself appointed Premier of the country. The Government Ministries were named in strict accordance with western custom.

Ito had also become convinced that if any progress was to be made in the direction of revising the Unequal Trade Treaties, the west not only had to be convinced that Japan possessed modern forms of government, but that she at least took a permissive attitude toward Christianity. For the next few years Christianity was given the blessing of officialdom. This act had serious repercussions in the life of the Japanese church.

This superficial acceptance of western standards was only half of Ito's policy. The other half, to be carried on simultaneously, was to entrench the authority of the oligarchs even more deeply in the life of the country and to use the Emperor Institution as the method to accomplish this end. So many acts of violence had occurred in the country, as a result of the activities of the Liberal Party and of the People's Rights Movement allied to it, that Ito considered this an excellent excuse to order the dissolution of the party. In the meantime he had mitigated the opposition of Itagaki and Goto through sending them on a trip to Europe ostensibly to study western forms of government! At the same time, reduction in taxes had favoured the landlords while inflation had increased the burden on the farmers whose need for and lack of currency had lost many of them their land. Thus the back of the People's Rights Movement in the countryside was broken and the political party to which it was allied, dissolved. It was not allowed to reappear until the promulgation of the Constitution.

Moreover, Matsukata, the Finance Minister, had managed to curb the inflation and depression by 1885 and consequently much of the opposition to the government ceased.

From this point forward political lines began to harden in Japan. The new oligarchy felt itself to be in firm control of the country. By 1885 Ito and Yamagata had managed to dissolve the political parties and had broken the back of the agrarian movement. For the next few years the government gave its attention more vigorously than ever to the modernization of the country while Ito himself worked away on the Constitution. He was determined that, whatever else it did, it should embody the following points,

(i) The Emperor's dignity and power was to be preserved.

(ii) In granting rights and limited freedom to the people there was to be no curb upon, nor limit to the prestige of the Emperor.

(iii) The Christian Religion might well be the basis of power in the west but since neither Buddhism nor Shintoism enjoyed such power in Japan the Emperor must become the basis of Japanese life.

(iv) The Text of any Constitution for Japan must remain simple in order to provide latitude of interpretation.

(v) Heavy reliance was to be put upon Prussian Political Theory.[1]

By 1887 so undisputed was the power of the oligarchy that they were able to force 570 persons identified with the "People's Rights Movement" to leave Tokyo. Meanwhile, in the same year, Okuma was induced to join the Cabinet as Minister of Foreign Affairs but after a short period in the government his leg was shattered by a bomb thrown at him by a fanatic opposed to western ways. He thereupon retired to found Waseda University and to advocate a reasonably progressive approach to social change.

A factor which must be kept in mind is that the most radical opposition party, the Liberal, had nevertheless possessed a strong nationalistic wing. This inconsistency also enabled the government leaders to sever from that movement the poorer classes through casting suspicion upon the loyalty of the leaders in the movement, especially those who were Christians.[2]

After his return from Europe Ito, as we have said, not only de-

---

[1] The above points are clearly made by Dr. Hugh Borton, *opus cited*, p. 133 ff. They are also found by Mikio Sumiya, *opus cited*, p. 96. They originate in the Commentary on the Constitution (Kian no Taiko) which Ito himself wrote.

[2] M. Sumiya, *opus cited*, p. 55.

termined to place the country on a firm authoritarian base but also felt it was necessary to simulate western forms of government if the Unequal Trade Treaties were ever to be revised. Consequently, for a brief period, there was a "western craze" and government circles went to great langths to imitate western customs. Yet by 1887 all this proved of no avail. The Treaties still remained unrevised and a great reaction against the west set in even among the secular intellectuals who had been friendly toward the west. The upper classes were easily alienated. As we shall see, this reaction did not leave the Christian Church nor its leaders untouched.

Dr. Delmer Brown claims that the opposition to the Unequal Trade Treaties which reached a high point in 1887 "marks the beginning of modern nationalism in Japan."[1] He also claims that, from this year forward, there was a marked increase of interest in expansionism as a means of further strengthening the Japanese nation. Resentment against the west led to a gradual strengthening of the advocates of expansionism as one way to prove the power of Japan. "We find that group consciousness was for the first time something that could be properly identified as modern nationalism. Only by 1887 had sufficient social cohesion been created to permit a truly popular response to national danger."[2] This was effected by a popular press which while in opposition to the government, was nevertheless strongly nationalistic; by a national army formed, for the most part, of young peasant folk accustomed to the unconditional obedience enjoined by traditional Confucianism; by a now universal educational system which from 1885 on turned for its inspiration, not as it had from 1873 until 1885 to France and America but to Germany; and by an increasingly strong, centralized government.

As early as 1879 the Emperor had been alarmed at the growth of equalitarian ideas in the nation and had ordered his teacher Motoda to compile a group of writings from the old Confucian classics to confute that trend. This work was called the *Yogaku Koyo* but was far too long for publication. By 1882, a shortened version of this work had appeared on the newstands. Ito determined that while the Constitution, which was in any case to be "given" to the people, might provide for political parties, that liberality would be counteracted by any increasing support of the Shinto faith and of the Emperor as the

[1] D. M. Brown, *Nationalism in Japan,* (Berkeley, Cal.: Univ of California Press, 1955), p. 112.

[2] *Ibid*, pps. 112–130.

central symbol of Japanese loyalty. The Meiji Rescript on Education, which appeared in 1890, was promulgated for that purpose but was none other than a shortened version of the earlier *Yogaku Koyo*.[1]

The period 1885 to 1890, therefore was one which became increasingly difficult for any group in Japanese society which entertained ideas of developing a truly democratic form of government in Japan. The unwillingness of the western powers to revise the trade treaties, the growing prosperity of the country, the confusion in the ranks of the progressive forces, (Itagaki was finally made a Count!), the inherently conservative nature of the Japanese peasantry, all made it easier for the oligarchs to solidify their power and to set up a form of state absolutism while, at the same time, presenting to the outside world the forms of a modern state.

This is to state the case somewhat unfairly. After all, the government did have to shoulder real responsibility for the nation through these years while constantly aware of Japan's weakness economically and politically vis-a-vis the great western powers which were still engaged in making a mockery of China's sovereignty. Japan's leaders felt themselves charged with the duty of bringing the ship of state safely through troubled waters within the nation and without. They were men of *samurai* background to whom the idea of equality was foreign. To their minds enlightened despotism was in the interests of the nation. It was impossible to think that ordinary men had the ability to govern the land. While they were interested in maintaining their own personal power they were equally motivated by a profound concern for the welfare of the nation. They had been the means of starting Japan on the way to becoming a modern industrial nation. The nation now possessed a modern money and banking system, postal and telegraph services, railways and a mercantile marine, a codified system of law and an effective educational system, an efficient civil service and a growing amount of heavy industry. What they had achieved in government is summed up in the following statement,

> If the two processes, the erection of a highly centralized local bureaucracy and the creation of local assemblies be combined, as they must in any attempt to understand the period between 1874 and 1885, we can see plainly the policy of the central government. The main purpose of the ruling oligarchy was to extend and consolidate its control over local affairs, and its secondary object was to enfranchise the people in

[1] M. Sumiya, *opus cited*, p. 56.

> as small a degree as possible—sufficiently to satisfy the demand for representation while, at the same time, not endangering its own supremacy.[1]

If it became increasingly difficult not only for the forces of democracy but for those which might have had a view to Japan becoming one among the nations of the earth without imperialistic ambitions, the following must be said in favour of the oligarchy,

> It is clear, however, that because of an absence of powerful democratic forces, the government was able to achieve, in a shorter time, greater degrees of political centralization, economic expansion, and ideological unity, and by doing so, created national strength and moved the country further and faster along the road toward modern nationalism.[2]

The increasing strength of the oligarchy's grip upon the nation was felt at every level of Japanese society. The upper classes were to react more and more strongly against western innovations. The lowest classes were to have the shackles of Confucian authoritarianism more firmly fixed than ever upon them. From this time forward it became increasingly difficult for Christian teaching to reach this group within society. The upper strata of former *samurai* were by now either within the ruling coterie, or in civil service posts within the government. The landlords had joined hands with industrialists against the peasants who, as they lost their land, formed a ready labour market. In 1885 many intellectuals had joined the Seikyosha, a club dedicated to the preservation of the "Japanese National Essence." A number of merchants and financiers still remained uncommitted as did the growing body of technicians whose minds were necessarily alert to every innovation which came from without or which they had learned while they themselves were sent abroad to study. A degree of radicalism was still enthusiastically, though covertly held by the small groups of lower *samurai* who had become teachers and journalists and, to a certain extent, among some of the former Tokugawa retainers who had become outstanding Christian leaders. The old Confucian ethic, with its emphasis upon duties without rights had won out and remained the controlling "motif" of the new order as it had of the old with this difference that now loyalty was directed to the Emperor

---

[1] W. W. McLaren, *opus cited*, p. 132.
[2] D. M. Brown, *opus cited*, p. 111.

alone. The structure of modern Japan, a nation with a modern industrial economy based upon feudal political order, bearing only the outward guise of modern political institutions had finally begun to take form. The period of flux and uncertainty was over.

CHAPTER FOUR

THE EFFECT OF ECONOMIC DEVELOPMENT ON THE STRUCTURE OF JAPANESE SOCIETY 1868–1889

We have seen that, at the time of the Restoration, the great majority within the nation had been opposed to the Shogunate. This was true of the over-burdened peasants, the infuriated nobility, the newly empowered clan bureaucrats, the "unemployed" warrior class, the ambitious landlords and the wealthy merchants. It has also been shown that those who really took responsibility for the new government, the clan bureaucrats, gradually built a strong central government, authoritarian in its spirit, and reflecting much the same class structure as had existed under the feudal order. The "forms" of feudalism disappeared but the new oligarchy established a new aristocracy among whom they now included themselves. The peasant was consciously kept at the bottom to bear the burden of the new day. However, the merchants, freed from the old restrictions, had a new opportunity for expansion and while some failed in the early days of the Restoration, many became the financial magnates of the new day.[1]

While we can only say, then, that a political restoration rather than a revolution took place in 1868 this cannot be said of the nation's economy. It was obvious to the new oligarchy that Japan could become a nation among nations and could avoid the exploitation which her neighbour China suffered only by developing economic strength from within; strength which in turn could support a modern economic and military structure. One reason for which the United States had opened Japan was that she had feared the complete domination of the Pacific by Great Britain. The United States would thus lose this potential market as she had so largely lost the Chinese. Russia too had gradually moved down to the islands directly north of Japan and Japanese leaders were constantly aware of the problem she posed.[2] Harassed on every side, the Meiji leaders knew they had to help set in motion an economic revolution if the nation was to be

---

[1] E. H. Norman, *Japan's Emergence as a Modern State*, (New York: Inst. of Pacific Relations, 1940), p. 140.

[2] *Ibid.* p. 35 ff.

saved. Thus W. W. Lockwood, in his brilliant analysis of Japan's economy writes, "The Meiji 'renovation' set in motion a genuine economic revolution. Whatever the limitations in the political realm, and its uneven progress everywhere, it did initiate a fundamental reorganization of large sectors of the Japanese economy."[1] This was only accomplished by virtue of the fact that millions of farmers, a growing labour force, a host of small businessmen many of whom were lower *samurai*, the great merchants and industrialists, and an army of new technicians combined their skills in order to raise the general level of production and, to some extent, the general standard of living.[2]

This point of view, that it was not alone the planning of the bureaucrats but the combined, often unplanned, efforts of the nation as a whole which enabled Japan to become a modern industrial nation will be taken for granted in our discussion. No nation could possibly have achieved the remarkably rapid modernization which Japan did without the willing cooperation and the exceptional industry of her people.

So many factors have to be taken into account when we consider the rapid change which took place in the economy of Japan. Not only did she possess far-sighted leadership and an industrious people, but the very changes which were already at work within the social structure of the nation, which in turn influenced her economy, made her ripe to take advantage of the opportunities furnished by contact with the outside world. The fact that under the Tokugawa certain clans had had monopolies in the production of certain goods and other clans in others, along with the existence of strict guild regulations right up until the time of the Restoration, made it natural for Japan to organize her new economic life around great combines. The fact that the government had been able to determine who would do what in the economy in the past and had repeatedly interfered within it made its continuing influence to be expected. On the other hand, the release from all manner of petty restrictions imposed upon the people, which were designed to keep the Tokugawa in power, provided an energy which was devoted to building up the new order.

Geographic factors must always be borne in mind in any discussion

---

[1] W. W. Lockwood, *The Economic Development of Japan*, (Princeton, N. J.: Princeton University Press, 1954), p. 82.

[2] *Ibid*, p. 34.

of Japan's economy.[1] Since approximately a seventh of the country's land is arable the most intense methods of agriculture have always been practised. With the development of better fertilizers and improved methods, double cropping became the general practice. This made it possible for the nation to support a larger industrial labour force though it soon became apparent, with the alarming increase in population,[2] that she would have to import more and more of the basic staples. This fact, in itself, drove the nation to a greater degree of industrialization.

Another factor which must constantly be kept in mind is that Japan was fortunate that her modern economy developed during a period of general expansion in the world economy. It was not until later on, in the twentieth century, that the degree of Japanese economic development posed a threat to the western powers. "The economic history of Japan, as of all nations, thus reveals a complex interaction of physical resources, human aptitudes and ambitions, and the external opportunities afforded by the world of its time."[3]

Yet we must insist upon the prominent role which the young samurai bureaucrats played in the economic development of the country.

> "The young 'samurai' bureaucrats of the new Imperial regime embarked on a program of sweeping and autocratic national reforms. The dream of men like Okubo, Kido, Iwakura, and others was first to consolidate the power and authority of the new government against internal opposition; second to build a strong national state able to defend and assert itself in the arena of world politics. These ambitions set the framework and tempo of national development during the next quarter century. They formed the natural basis for a close mercantilist alliance between the bureaucrats and the nascent class of financiers and industrialists."[4]

The young bureaucrats provided the initiative for the creation of a new fiscal system, banks, insurance companies, steam shipping lines, postal and telegraph services, and especially heavy industries for which

---

[1] See G. Trewartha, *Japan*, (Madison, Wisc.: Univ. of Wisconsin Press, 1945), 607 pp.

[2] In 1868 there were approximately 30,000,000 people in the country. This was doubled within fifty years. At the beginning of our period there were 225 persons per square mile while in 1935 there were 469! Since only 18 per cent of the country can be cultivated the increase in rice production owing to better agricultural methods was largely eaten up by the expanding population.

[3] W. W. Lockwood, *opus cited*, p. 151.

[4] *Ibid*, p. 12.

other budding capitalists were unwilling to take responsibility but which were basic to a nation, bent upon eventually establishing a modern military power. Later on many of these industries were sold to the new financial magnates at very low prices. This occurred early in the 1880s and, though the government tended to stay out of business from this time on,[1] there continued to exist, through the banking system, and through intimate family relationships, a close tie between it and the great companies which dominated financial circles.[2] The young bureaucrats, in many instances, married into the families of the financial magnates. Of them Lockwood says, "Their motives were a mixture of patriotism, fired by the dangers of the international situation, plus ambition for personal advancement."[3]

It is important to keep our perspective straight as to the relation between the development of new industry in the nation and the role played by agriculture and the traditional handicrafts so far as the overall economy is concerned in this period. In these earliest days the invention of the ricksha, the use of the ox-cart and the construction of simple dirt roads throughout the countryside were probably of greater importance than the initial creation of the new industries, important as they later became. The improvements we have mentioned here meant a drastic reduction in the price of rice to the consumer and did help to raise the standard of living. Improvements of this kind appear to have far greater significance, at least in the early stages of social change in the direction of a modern economy, than does the creation of immense industrial plants. The latter require, on the part of all those engaged in the enterprise, a radical break with traditional methods which is so complete as to make for confusion rather than for the release of creative energies.

> ... the basic economic occupations and mode of life of the common people remained substantially unchanged through the first twenty-five years of the Meiji era (1868–1893). ... wide price disparities between interior regions reflected the continuing self-sufficiency of village life. The land tax, a heavy burden on small peasants, furnished over 90 per cent of State tax revenues in the early seventies. Twenty years later it still accounted for as much as 60 per cent. ...

---

[1] Yawata Steel Works, the largest of their kind in Japan, are still largely under government control. Iron and Steel, as well as other industries related to military preparedness remained under strict government supervision right up until World War II.

[2] W. W. Lockwood, *opus cited*, pp. 505–508 and 563.

[3] W. W. Lockwood, *opus cited.*

> Probably the most substantial additions to real national income during this period did not result directly from the growth of factory industry and foreign trade. They grew mainly out of general improvements following the removal of feudal restrictions and the unification of the country under a strong central government.[1]

It was propitious for the new state that there were such improvements in agriculture for the burden of industrializing the country fell upon the peasants. Lack of any substantial amount of foreign trade, plus the unequal Trade Treaties which only allowed a 5 per cent import tax, added to the fact that Japan had to import the great bulk of the heavy machinery which went into her industrial plant and its hinterland, closed every other avenue for the realization of capital to the bureaucracy. This fact was an added incentive to the growth of a strong nationalism. Only two foreign loans were contracted by the Japanese government between the Restoration and the end of the century.[2]

Let us turn now to a detailed consideration of events as they affected the developing economy.

In 1869 the clans were requested to hand in their land registers. Those who actively supported the restoration gladly did so. We have seen that, in most cases, these registers actually remained in the same hands since the bureaucrats of the clans which led the forces in the Restoration were the same men who now took responsibility for the central government. By 1871 all fiefs were abolished. Yet, one could hardly expect a class to wipe itself out. At first the lords were simply paid the greater proportion of their former revenues by the central government. This was a happy arrangement so far as they were concerned for they enjoyed an income without any of the responsibilities which had been theirs under the feudal order so far as governing their own clans was concerned. However, when the fiefs were abolished and the prefectural system set up in 1871 the lords were issued bonds on the government in lieu of their lands. Those who had supported the government also received the larger part of the lands of the Tokugawa.

The *samurai* class was pacified by the payment of pensions in lieu of their fees as retainers. The bonds which the nobility received either permitted them to become landed aristocrats, or, if they were enterprising enough, to become along with some of the former great

[1] W. W. Lockwood, *opus cited.* p. 17.
[2] E. H. Norman, *opus cited.* p. 115.

merchants, the financial leaders of modern Japan. The *samurai* on the other hand, a class which comprised 5 to 6 per cent of the population, save for those of the upper ranks, received just enough to keep themselves and their families alive. They lost not only status but the means of livelihood. The more enterprising among them went into small business or formed the core of that body of technicians which, going abroad to study, returned home to build and manage the growing industrial structure.[1] Both their loss of status and increased financial hardship are linked with their revolts against the government notably under Eto in Hizen and finally under Saigo in the Satsuma Rebellion of 1877.[2]

First the financial obligations to the lords, then the interest payments on the bonds granted to them, plus the pensions for the *samurai*, imposed a tremendous financial burden on the government which at the outset was in difficult financial straits.[3] Accordingly, in 1871, in order to try to increase capital in the hands of the government, both to meet its obligations and to pay for the development of heavy industry, the Iwakura Mission was sent abroad not only to make a survey of western conditions but in order to gain revision of the unequal Trade Treaties. An increase of revenue from this source would have eased the government's burden. Unfortunately, the mission was turned down by all the major powers.

Therefore, the government turned to a universal tax on land as the answer to its need for capital. The result was a crushing load of taxation on the farmer, one quite as great as it had been under the old regime. This tax was 3 per cent of the value of the land assessed at approximately eight times the value of the land in 1872. It had to be paid in currency not in kind. Thus the burden of taxation fell, not only on the farmers, but on the landlords as well. Both of these groups felt that they were being victimized in order to modernize the country. Moreover, the tax had to be paid regardless of whether the yield was good or bad. The new methods of agriculture, plus the tax burden made double cropping not only a possibility but a necessity. This required fertilizers and a further cash outlay for the farmer. As a result, more and more peasants lost their land. As this process developed, in one province alone, 52 persons lost their land in 1879 and

---

[1] U. Iwasaki, *opus cited*, pps. 100–1.

[2] E. H. Norman, *opus cited*. p. 75.

[3] *Ibid*. p. 115. Government expense were almost ten times receipts in 1868 and almost five times receipts in 1869.

by 1883 this number had increased to 493. Between 1883 and 1890, 367 to 744 peasants lost their land.[1]

The result of this pressure upon the landlords, the farmers, and the impoverished *samurai* was the formation of the People's Rights Movement (Jiyu Minken Undo) which was mentioned in the previous chapter. This movement made common cause with the forces working toward representative government. The idea that citizens possessed rights as well as duties was novel to them. Many Christians were involved in this struggle and for a brief period, at least, opposition to Christianity in the countryside, especially around Tolyo, relaxed. The result was a remarkable growth in the numbers of persons seeking baptism, and in the establishment of churches in this area, notably in Chiba Ken.[2]

By 1878, after the government had successfully quelled the Satsuma rebellion, and therefore felt themselves to be more firmly in the saddle, action was taken to relieve the burden on the landlords. The government hoped thereby to draw them away from their interest in the Right's Movement. Since the livelihood of the landlord depended on the exploitation of the farmer, this was not hard to achieve. It was in the interest of the landlords to keep the farmer in debt. It would have been contrary to their interest had the farmer actually gained the vote and thus sought economic reform. Accordingly, the government reduced the land tax to two and one half per cent. Since inflation had set in, owing to the constant issue of paper currency, this meant that the landlord was actually paying considerably less in tax money because he was still assessed at the 1872 rates. The tenant farmer had to pay the landlord in kind so that he failed to benefit from the decrease at all. Cash was hard to come by and yet the farmer had an ever-increasing need of it. As a result an alarming increase in tenancy set in. The Rights Movement fell apart though it was replaced by the creation of the Liberal Party in 1881.

E. H. Norman very clearly points out that, while the government was able to sever the relationship between the landlord and the peasant this action was not entirely successful.[3] The Japanese landlord

---

[1] E. H. Norman, *opus cited.* p. 144, and W. W. Lockwood, *opus cited.* p. 26, who points out that by 1910 39 per cent of the farmers owned no land and that 45 per cent of farm land was tenanted. Rents in kind, amounting to 45 to 60 per cent of the value of the crop, had to be paid and the farmer was required to supply his own fertilizer, seed and instruments.

[2] M. Sumiya, *opus cited.* p. 22–3.

[3] E. H. Norman, *opus cited.* pp. 167–185.

is usually a small business man and the operator of small local industry. The continued heavy tax on land as compared with the comparatively light taxes on large industry seemed to him to be altogether unfair. As a result, while he was not willing to go as far as the peasant in the struggle for reduced taxation, he was still concerned to fight for increased government representation in order to right this inequality. For this reason, he provided the main support for Itagaki when he organized the Liberal Party in 1881. The most vocal and violent support, however, continued to come from the farm and the dispossessed *samurai*. The landlord wanted a representative government based on a property qualification. This would avoid the problem of the farmer achieving a means to right his economic plight in relation to the landlord. As the peasants' struggle became more desperate and more and more acts of violence occurred in the name of the Party, Itagaki voluntarily dissolved it in 1884. He and Goto had already taken their trip abroad, sponsored by the government and financed by the Mitsui. As a result of incompatible elements within the opposition itself, plus craftiness and subterfuge on the part of the ruling oligarchy, the most intense opposition to the government was broken by 1885. During that year the landlords formed an organization designed to strengthen the old Confucian order and emphasizing filial piety. This was in an effort to keep the farmer in a subservient position.

By 1883 Count Okuma had dissolved his *Kaishinto* party after an arrangement had been made whereby the Mitsubishi Shipping interests combined with a government sponsored shipping company the *Kyodo Un'yu Kaisha* to become the *Nippon Yusen Kaisha* to the benefit of all concerned. Since Count Okuma was directly involved in these financial interests his opposition to the government was broken.

Thus the oligarchy, through a clever use of economic circumstances, solidified its political power and broke the opposition to it. As a result of the violence which had occurred, they were able, at the same time, to crush popular resistance through an application of laws severely restricting both the press and association.

General fiscal policy also made it possible for the government to stiffen its resistance to opposition forces by 1885. Up until the early 1880s the constant issue of currency had caused severe inflation. The government had had to cover the pensions of the *samurai*, the interest on the bonds issued the lords, the cost of armaments in general and especially of those used in the Formosan expedition of 1874 and the

Satsuma Rebellion of 1877. The over-all cost of these military engagements imposed a heavy burden on the government which it sought to meet through currency issues. In 1877 too a number of banks owned by the former merchants and lords, were established and issued currency. The immediate effect of this was to encourage an expansionist boom, and a number of large as well as small businesses were undertaken by an increasing number of private interests. Foreign trade payments just at this time also happened to be favourable to Japan. However, the actual purchasing power of the nation as a whole was still extremely unstable and a contraction of credit, brought about by the fact that the government had overextended itself, plus the instability of the foreign trade balance which was generally unfavourable to Japan, caused a depression during the period 1880 to 1885. It was the hardship consequent upon this depression which drove the peasants and the dispossessed *samurai* to the acts of violence of which we have spoken. It also created much of the support for the Liberal Party which was inspired, not only by the influence of Christian ideas of equality and respect for personality, but by the slogans of the French Revolution. These had had a deep influence, especially in Shikoku the home of Itagaki, Goto, and Kataoka who were the leaders of the party.

When Okuma resigned in 1881 as a result of the Hokkaido scandal, Count Matsukata took over his responsibilities as Minister of Finance. Through the establishment of the Bank of Japan in 1881 and the contraction of credit mentioned above, inflation was checked and fiscal policy stabilized.[1] The government sold the industries it had established at low prices and was thus instrumental in launching the great *zaibatsu* combines that, until the end of World War II, dominated the Japanese economy. The government used the funds it realized from the sale of the industries to purchase armaments while it continued to keep a close control on the Iron and Steel Industries upon which modern armament is dependent. Characteristically, even at this time, interest on bank loans to small enterprises was as high as 20 per cent while it was much lower for larger enterprises.

This is explained by the close link which existed between the government, the banks, and the large scale enterprises. The families which dominated all three were closely related. The smaller enterprises,

---

[1] The following figures indicate the extent of inflation within the country. In 1868 there was 24,000,000 in the country, by 1873 Y79,700,000 and by 1878 Y165,700,000.

on the other hand, were owned principally by the land lord-entrepreneur, of whom we have spoken above, or by the former, poorer *samurai*. For this reason these groups found themselves in opposition to the government and allied to the Liberal Party. The contraction of credit meant that the landlord-entrepeneur had to have funds, which in turn exercised further pressure upon the peasantry which lost them their land.

By 1885 the depression appeared to be over and, as a result of increased foreign trade plus a more solid development of industry, the economic prospects for the future appeared to be bright. Opposition to the government on economic grounds by groups other than the peasantry, whose opposition went on, though without leadership, largely ceased. The peasants themselves were confused for, while they realized their economic plight, their inherent conservatism created over hundreds of years sapped their will to creative resistance.

Thus, the over-all financial scene for the whole period appears to be as follows: first there was a period of sheer confusion until 1877 when the economy enjoyed an expansionist boom; there then followed a period of depression as the government sought to bring order out of chaos; following that the amazing development of the industry and the economy of the nation began a marked upward swing for the country as a whole.

> The vagaries of currency and fiscal policy, coupled with variations in the foreign trade balance brought an expansionist boom from 1877–1881, followed by a period of deflation and retrenchment in the eighties. This gave way in turn to a revival of prosperity at the end of the decade which was further intensified by the Sino-Japanese War in 1894–95.[1]

No consideration of this period, from an economic point of view, would be complete without a description of the fate of the *samurai* and the transformation of many of the nobility not only into landed gentlemen but into leading financiers of the new Japan.

The pensions which had been given to the *samurai* and were paid to them by the government, became such a burden that they were forcibly commuted in 1876. This was done at rates disastrous to most of the *samurai* and undoubtedly accounts for much of the enthusiasm they displayed in the Satsuma Rebellion. The great majority who could not find positions in industry, farming, education or government were reduced to poverty. Moreover, those *samurai* who had

[1] W. W. Lockwood, *opus cited.* p. 16.

helped at the time of the Restoration were preferred, whereas those of the Tokugawa houses were so discriminated against that many of them were brought down to the level of the peasants and were forced to till the fields they had once protected.

Nor was this true of the Tokugawa retainers alone for some of the Tokugawa nobility were reduced to the same level. But the great majority of the former *samurai* did manage to adjust through becoming technicians in industry and petty administrators of the central or prefactural governments. If they belonged to the former houses of Satsuma and Choshu and had found security in government or industry they tended to support the oligarchy. Those who did not, and who found their place in education or in growing industries not directly related to the government, tended to ally themselves with the new political parties in an effort to dislodge the oligarchy from the power it enjoyed as a result of the alliance which it had with the landed nobility and the leaders of the still powerful Satsuma and Choshu clans.

In addition to the government accepting the burden of the pensions to the *samurai*, at the time of the Restoration, it also accepted the debts of the lords to the great merchants of Tokyo and Osaka. This act, plus the payment to the lords of bonds in lieu of their lands enabled the more enterprising of them to become leading financiers in the new Japan. The bonds were used to float the new communications and heavy industries which were in process of construction under government auspices. The sale of many of these enterprises to leading financiers from 1880 to 1885, therefore, did not represent a radical change in the centers of financial power. It represented, rather, a tremendous concession to them on the part of the government. Thus there developed that intimate link between government, large landholders, banker and industrial leader characteristic of the Japanese economy. In 1880, forty four per cent of the banking shares were owned by former feudal lords; thirty two per cent were held by former *samurai* and fourteen per cent were held by former merchants.[1]

The export trade was of vital interest to the oligarchy from the start. Only through a realization of capital from that source or from within the nation itself, could they avoid reliance upon foreign capital and the risk of foreign domination which had unhappily overcome China. The silk trade was the greatest single source of foreign revenue

---

[1] E. H. Norman, *opus cited.* p. 100.

through the early years. It was greatly encouraged by the government. The consequent flow of imports enabled the standard of living to rise somewhat through this period but the concern of the government to build up its military arsenal meant that the greatest proportion of imports went in that direction.[1]

The new government came under severe criticism when Ito and others returned to Japan in 1884 without a revision of the unequal treaties which were so vital to the welfare of the nation. Only because internal fiscal policy had begun to stabilize the economy was it possible for the new government to weather the storm. This was coupled with its clever policy of dividing and conquering the opposition. W. W. Lockwood has the following to say of the relationship between Japan and the whole question of international trade,

> Most importantly, of course, the political factor gives a special stamp and a peculiar importance to a country's international economic relations. All historical interpretations and policy judgments must recognize the special concerns which surround international dealings in a world of nation-states. It was Japan's good fortune that the foundations of her modern development were laid in an era when the world economy as a whole was expanding, and still organized on liberal principles for the most part. She herself pursued a fairly liberal policy for seventy years, except where her colonies and strategic industries were involved. Yet no small island nation, similarly dependent on overseas trade, could have failed to display constant solicitude over its international economic position. Least of all was this likely in the case of a people among whom the sense of national identity and of national destiny was so deeply implanted. Economic opportunity abroad was essential to both national power and well-being. The political issues associated with Japan's external economic relations were a constant preoccupation of her statesmen, and greatly influenced the course of development.[2]

It is obvious, from all that we have said above, that the relationship between the economic and the political was of a most intimate kind.

> The economic and technical progress of Japan has been due in no small measure to the fact that a firm and durable framework of national unity was achieved at an early date.[3]
>
> Clearly the course of Japan's economic development after the Restoration was powerfully influenced by the militaristic and merchantilistic cast of her political institutions. Her heritage of feudalism, the ambitions of her new leaders, the kind of world she now entered all

[1] W. W. Lockwood, *opus cited.* pp. 18,27–35.
[2] *Ibid.* p. 311.
[3] *Ibid.* p. 191.

> combined to project the state into a prominent role and endow it with broad responsibilities in creating the framework of industrialization.[1]

Undoubtedly the above comes close to describing what Ito Hirobumi must have understood as the role of the government in the development of the nation when he returned from his trip to Europe in 1884. The fact that the government was able to realize so many of its aims in the rapid industrialization of the nation was undoubtedly due to the insights of men like Ito, Matsukata, Yamagata, and others who were achieving firmer control of the country than ever before.

But many other factors must be borne in mind as well as contributing to the success of the nation in this regard. Those in opposition to the government who were paying the taxes which made modernization possible contributed to the cause. Had their small enterprises, and agriculture in general, not improved as a result of the general industry of the people, such taxes would not have been forthcoming. Moreover, men like Okuma and the industrialists who gathered around him also made their contribution. At the same time, the government was aided by the fact that she did escape the kind of economic exploitation China experienced largely because western powers were more concerned with the wealth of the latter than with that of Japan. The oligarchy was clever enough to see at a strategic moment that the use of the old feudal loyalties and the ancient Emperor institution could be combined to solidify the country and to counter the opposition which in their view was dangerously dividing the country at a time when unity was necessary. It was this conviction which was behind Ito's insistence that only the Emperor could rally the nation around a center sufficiently strong to produce the energy, sacrifice, and moral fibre required for Japan to become a modern nation.

The fact that the opposition was divided and that the depression of 1880 to 1885 was weathered successfully made it possible for the oligarchy to remain in power to put their plan to work. The dissolution of the political parties had driven the extremists in the struggle for economic and political reform to further acts of violence so that the government was justified in passing the Peace Preservation Regulations of 1887. This made it impossible for a political leader to approach Tokyo closer than eight miles.

Meanwhile, the nation as a whole had had its attention turned to the necessity for the revision of the Trade Treaties in order to further

---

[1] *Ibid.* p. 571.

build the growing economy. In order to effect this revision Count Okuma joined the government as foreign minister in 1888, ostensibly to seek to revise the treaties.[1] Ironically Kuroda was then Premier. He had been the object of Okuma's attack over the Hokkaido scandal in 1881 for which reason Okuma had resigned from the government. Okuma's compromise plus the repressive laws against association broke the party movement and severed it from any further vital relation with the lower classes. In the newly created Diet, after the promulgation of the Constitution, these parties represented the propertied landholders and the industrialists. The propertied classes alone enjoyed the franchise since there was a property qualification and a tax qualification to meet before one was granted the vote. The peasants were left at the mercy of the propertied classes and the bureaucracy. As an increasing number of them lost their land, and the increased population could no longer be absorbed by agriculture, they provided the labour force necessary to the development of a modern industrial nation.

As we draw our discussion of the economic development of Japan in this period to a close, it becomes evident that there continued to exist in Japan only two major classes. The ruling class politically formed the upper class economically. That, of course, is to use the broadest terms. Actually, the members of the ruling oligarchy were not necessarily men of excessive wealth but they were inextricably related to those who continued to hold great economic wealth, the landed nobility, and the new financiers. Even those fighting for moderately liberal policies such as Goto and Okuma were, from the outset, closely related to the Mitsubishi interests. Marquis Inouye, another of the government stalwarts, was connected with the House of Mitsui the financial backing of which had done much to foster the Restoration and to support its military forces.

In 1930, 10.6 per cent of Japan's 12.6 million families received one half of the country's household income while 24,000 well-to-do families appropriated over 10 per cent of aggregate family income.[2] Whether the disparity was still greater in the 1880s is unknown but the trend from the very start was unmistakable. "It is evident that the stock of productive wealth grew rapidly; that returns on property, relative to labour, remained high; and that a large share of property

---

[1] E. H. Norman, *opus cited.* p. 185.
[2] W. W. Lockwood, *opus cited.* p. 141.

income tended to be concentrated in the upper tail of the income distribution curve."[1]

The country advanced not only on the basis of the increase in foreign trade but on the backs of the peasantry, the second and great underlying strata within the nation and whose numbers, as they grew, supplied the "hands" for the new industry. This group had scarcely had time to understand what was happening to their nation in the period we have discussed let alone had the opportunity to gain a perspective which would have made it possible for them to throw off the shackles of traditional Confucian authoritarianism. It was not difficult, therefore, for the oligarchs after 1885 to impose ever more stringently upon the great mass of the people an attitude of mind that had never been radically questioned by them.

No middle class of any particular significance was allowed to develop. What there was was made up of the smaller landlords. Many of these controlled the manifold small village and household industries. Some of the *samurai* had made up the growing body of educators who manned the new educational system, others were in petty commercial concerns or employed in large ones. There was a growing body of technicians and professional people whose training was basically necessary to the development of a modern state. Rough figures would seem to indicate that those in the professions increased about 20,000, in commerce about 50,000 and in industry about 100,000 each year from 1876 to 1920.[2] By far the great majority in industry were those who had left the land to become the new labour force while only a few would represent managerial personnel. The great majority of those in commerce would not be above clerical level while, at the above rate, there would not have been more than a quarter of a million people in all of the professions out of a population of from thirty to forty millions in the year 1889. Many in this group owed their livelihood to government enterprise so that they were by no means necessarily in opposition to the government. Nevertheless, the growing body of technicians was the one group whom the government found it difficult to control since it was necessary for them to be generally well informed concerning the outside world and to travel abroad in order to learn new techniques. They were the body which remained most open to foreign influences in the years which lay ahead.

---

[1] *Ibid.* p. 141.

[2] W. W. Lockwood, *opus cited.* p. 129.

By 1889 then, on the eve of the promulgation of the Constitution by the Emperor, the lines of the new Japan had been fairly clearly established both economically and politically. The oligarchy was in power and had developed a fairly coherent policy which was to increase the unity of the nation through the Emperor Institution and to continue to expand the economy of the nation as rapidly as possible while using the great reservoir of labour which the peasantry represented. The direction was to be from the top down and the labour force was to be controlled through an appeal to its loyalty to the Emperor. Difficult days lay ahead for any influence which might seek to threaten this structure.

CHAPTER FIVE

THE DEVELOPMENT OF CHRISTIANITY IN RELATION TO THE CHANGING ORDER 1868–1889

It must be constantly kept in mind that, in this study we are thinking of "Christianity" strictly as an entity in Japanese society, that is as a social movement. That movement was, and is, made up of individuals who, while they are part of the church are, at the same time, part of Japanese society. We recognize that any church has at least three essential characteristics: It has an expressed body of belief; it has some form of organization; and it has a constituency.[1] We are not concerned here with any theological value judgment of the norms of the Christian faith as expressed by the Protestant Christian movement in Japan. Nor are we concerned to write history. We are concerned, however, to see the relevance of what was happening in Japanese society, as we have traced it in the past two chapters, to the development of the Protestant Christian movement within it. For example, we are interested in answering questions such as the following:

1. What are the facts concerning the simple numerical growth of the Protestant movement during the period under discussion?
2. What were the influences and events in Japanese society, during the period, which tended to retard or encourage the growth of the faith?
3. What, if any, evidence is there that the "charismatic" quality within the Christian faith was able to surmount, even though it may have been conditioned by, Japanese society as a whole?

---

[1] This is an attempt at a simple yet inclusive, objective definition. It is not unrelated to the work of J. Wach, *Sociology of Religion* (Chicago: Univ. of Chicago Press, 1944), Chapter II. The writer is aware of the several differing definitions of the term ranging all the way from the sociological to the theological. Those of Ballard, Sutherland and Woodward, Panunzio, Barnes and Becker are examples of the former while Stephen Neill in his *The Christian Society* (London: Nisbet, 1952), pp 296–298, gives a number of examples of the latter. Even the Society of Friends which tends to deny that it has a formal creed nevertheless is formally Christian, see *Studies in Quaker Thought and Practice* (London: Friend's House, 1931), 3 vols. Its "method" of organization is well defined. Even the famous *Mukyokai* (non-church group) in Japan could not exist without its emphasis upon the Scriptures nor is it altogether without organization. The only difference between it and other Christian churches is that it is "loosely" rather than "firmly" organized.

4. In what terms did the Protestant Christian movement express its faith and in what organizational forms? What, if any, purely Japanese influences were expressed through these?
5. What strata in Japanese society were represented within the movement and why?
6. What influence, if any, had the movement exerted upon Japanese society?[1]

Before we attempt an answer to the above questions a brief review of the situation in which the tiny Protestant constituency at the time of the Restoration found itself is in order.

The Restoration itself made no difference whatever in the opposition of the government to Christianity in general. Notice Boards still stood in strategic places to announce that anyone joining the evil sect known as Christianity would do so on pain of death. When objection was made by foreign embassies to the word "evil" as being an affront to the governments which they represented the wording was changed but the threat remained. No one knew when the government might choose to be strict and when it might choose to be permissive. That was largely dependent on local conditions. During these earliest

---

[1] The chief Japanese sources cited in this section will be: M. Sumiya, *opus cited.* Sumiya in turn is dependent upon many of the English sources, such as O. Cary and Ritter, which we use here. One major source which he uses and we do not is a work in a number of volumes entitled, *Uemura Masahisa, to Sono Jidai*, which is an interpretation, from a strongly Japanese point of view, of the period under discussion. Sumiya also had access to a number of primary sources such as the *Shichi Ichi Zappo* (*Seventh Day Report*) an early Christian newspaper which was also used by Cary and Ritter. He is able to extend his interpretation, through the use of the *Rikuge Zasshi* and other periodicals. His excellent study is an attempt to be a sociological interpretation and not a history. A. Hiyane, *Nihon Kirisutokyo*, (see Introduction and Bibliography). E. Kudo, *opus cited.* Kudo's treatment of Stratification in the first decade of the church's history in the Meiji period is brief but extremely perceptive.

The principle English sources cited will be:

G. F. Verbeck, *History of Protestant Missions in Japan* 1859–1883, a report to the Osaka Conference of that year. This is the best and most detailed chronological account of events as they occurred in the development of Protestant Christianity in this period. However, as he himself states, it is largely "a history of missionaries" rather than missions. Since so much of the earliest activity was inevitably that of missionaries it is hard to see how this tendency could have been avoided. Yet, it must be read against the wide background of what was happening in Japanese society if we are to understand the significance even of the events chronicled.

O. Cary, *History of Christianity in Japan*, Vol. II. This is the best source work available for the period up until 1909. It is especially good until the turn of the century.

H. Ritter, *A History of Christianity in Japan.* Useful as a supplement to the above but not very reliable in itself.

days of the Restoration period the most conservative forces, represented by the court nobles and by the extremely nationalistic *samurai* led by men like Saigo Takamori and Eto, still had a strong influence. They were for restoring Shinto to what they believed was its rightful place. Shinto had been discriminated against by the Tokugawa in favour of Buddhism. For that reason the Ministry of Religion was given highest priority in the first government formed after the Restoration and Shinto was encouraged.

In accordance with this sentiment, the government attempted to repress a resurgence of Roman Catholicism in Nagasaki in 1869. That community had remained as faithful as it knew how to the faith which it had learned centuries before. It now came out of formal hiding. Thousands of Roman Christians were sent off to other areas of the country by order of the government. They were stolen away at night and many of their loved ones were entirely ignorant as to whether they were alive or dead. Since they were not released until the early seventies, many of their wives remarried having given them up for dead.

Nor was this persecution confined to Roman Christians alone. In 1870 Mr. Ensor's secretary, one Futagawa, was arrested in Nagasaki and was released only after two and one-half years of severe imprisonment. In 1871 Ichikawa Yeinosuke and his wife were thrown into prison and, though his wife was released, he perished while there. This case was brought to the attention of Prince Iwakura during his stay in Washington in 1872 and undoubtedly had a good deal to do with the removal of the edict boards forbidding Christianity on February 19th, 1873.[1]

It is interesting to note that in 1871 when the Evangelical Alliance, through the British government, complained to the Japanese government about the persecution of native Christians they were rebuffed. The Japanese government stated that this was purely an internal matter, that reverence for the Emperor rested upon the religion of the country, that while it was not the intention of the government to violate private religious convictions, it was its duty to suppress Christianity where it would be likely to lead to uprisings or to rebellion, especially where this might occur in the hope of receiving aid from Christian powers.[2] Obviously, the government had not yet had sufflcient acquaintance with foreign powers to be convinced that

[1] H. Ritter, *opus cited.* p. 32–3.
[2] H. Ritter, *opus cited.* p. 31.

the international situation was any different than it had been in earlier days when the Shimabara uprising and the extension of Christianity as a whole within Japan, had been in areas hostile to the central government. What contacts they had had with foreign governments to date certainly had done nothing to reassure them!

In the meantime, the attitude of foreign governments toward the Iwakura Mission had convinced the government leaders that, whether they liked it or not, they would have to change their attitude toward Christianity. Undoubtedly, the influence of men like Verbeck and the Japanese charge d'affairs in Washington, Mori Arinori, also had had an influence. From the outset Mori was for the most progressive type of religious toleration.

Moreover, the influence of the extreme nationalists in the government had, by this time, begun to wane. Up until March 1872 the government had taken a repressive attitude not only to Christianity but to Buddhism. However, in that month the department of Religion in the government which had been called the Shingi Sho, a title definitely indicating its Shinto bias, was changed to Kyobu Sho, or Educational (literally, teaching,) Ministry.[1] Four orders of teachers were recognized. They were (a) the Shinto priests, (b) the Buddhist priests, (c) the Confucian scholars, (d) "national" scholars (Kokugakusha). The fourth group was a concession to such men as Verbeck, Griffis, and others who were teaching in government institutions and whose help was necessary to the government.

The government also recognized the need for schools to educate those required to modernize the nation and they were ready to allow the missionaries to help. Yet, at the same time, they were careful to issue a basis for education. The law insisted that the following principles be inculcated in all pupils, (1) Love of Country, (2) Recognition of the Law of Providence, (a basic Confucian teaching), (3) Reverence for the Emperor and Respect for His government.[2] The government was concerned that the basis of the new state be clearly recognized. It was also troubled over the levelling tendencies which the influence of Christianity might well bring about and which such men as Okuma and Ito, with their background of western travel and contact with foreigners, fully understood.

The early years of planting a new faith in a strange land are usually made difficult with problems in relation to language, thought-forms

[1] M. Sumiya, *opus cited.* p. 43.
[2] *Ibid.* p. 43.

and the like. Sometimes, however the path is made easier where the level of religious faith is very low. For example, in Korea, parts of Burma, and in Africa, where religious longing for something deeper is present, or at least, springs to consciousness when something obviously superior is presented, the pathway is made easier for the introduction of Christianity. If the government is friendly or neutral that also helps. In Japan none of these conditions obtained. Japan possessed, and possesses, a great civilization in her own right, as does China and India. While Shinto is essentially a primitive faith, Buddhism is not, even though it has had a difficult time remaining vigorous over the past century. As the oligarchy took over power in the early seventies they certainly did not want religious strife within the nation in addition to all the other problems which had to be faced. They were willing, therefore, to show some degree of tolerance. On the other hand, they had to have a unifying principle in order to secure loyalty to the government and this they could find only in the Emperor Institution which, in itself, had religious overtones intimately connected with Shinto. It was this dilemma which led the government later on to attempt to make a distinction between State and Shrine Shinto; the former was ostensibly non-religious and the latter was classed as one of the three major religions of the country. Yet the former, in the accepted Christian way of thinking, remained a religion in that it demanded absolute loyalty to the Emperor. The Christians in Japan have, from the first faced a problem in relation to national loyalty clearly comparable to that which the early Christians faced in their struggle with the Roman Empire.

The Clan bureaucrats, who were in the process of taking over full government control, were thorough-going secularists. They were deeply influenced by that school of Confucianism, namely Shushigaku, which emphasizes social duties and customs. It is oriented toward this world. Moreover, traditional Buddhism in Japan has confined itself largely to an almost radical other-worldliness though Buddhist priests and Buddhist monasteries, from time to time, have been interested in the secular world for reasons other than religious. In any case, the educated, ruling class, had traditionally been skeptical of religious motivation, and Japan's present rulers were no exception. Religion could be considered friendly and relevant only if it served to advance the security of the nation.[1]

[1] Ritter reports that officials of the Japanese Embassy in Berlin asked Prof. Gneist, in 1873, whether he deemed it advisable for Japan to introduce Christia-

This secular outlook accounts for the fact that, for a time at least, intellectuals like Fukuzawa Yukichi, who neither held government posts nor were friendly to Christianity, found great affinity in the writings of Rousseau, J. S. Mill and Herbert Spencer, as representative of western thought rather than Christianity. Buddhism, with its other-worldly emphasis, had become deeply rooted in the country-side, among the peasants, and we recall that in these early years of the Meiji period village life remained essentially unchanged. The peasants, as a whole even after they had lost their fear of it were simply indifferent to this new faith, with its extremely rigorous moral demands. In reflecting upon the written comment of a prominent Japanese missionary, Sir George Sansom says,

> The writer here lays a finger upon a very definite characteristic of Japanese life then, and perhaps at all times ... a strong feeling for social duty, but a lack of deep religious sentiment as it is understood by western peoples. This is a crude statement that needs much qualification, but in general it is borne out by the history of Japanese religious institutions.[1]

This helps us to understand why the "official" attitude to Christianity could change so rapidly and in direct relation to the interests of the nation. The Iwakura Mission had been told in Washington that any nation so antagonistic to Christianity could scarcely be accepted among western nations.[2] The edict boards were therefore removed. However, the interpretation put upon this act varied. Christians were naturally overjoyed and felt that a new era was in store for them which, indeed, it was. The government undoubtedly intended to comply outwardly if not inwardly. Sumiya says, of the over-all attitude of the government right up until the promulgation of the Constitution in 1889, that Christianity was treated like a concubine, "nothing was said about it."[3]

Prior to proceeding to a more detailed examination of the relationship between Protestant Christianity and Japanese society in this

---

nity as a State Religion. This was undoubtedly influenced by what they saw of the relationship between Church and State in Germany and by sheer political considerations which did not seem the least absurd to them. (Ritter, *opus cited.* p. 50) We find Fukuzawa and Kato taking a favourable attitude to Christianity after having opposed it vigorously, after 1885, because it was in the government interest to do so.

[1] G. Sansom, *The Western World and Japan*, (New York: Knopf, 1950), p. 471.

[2] O. Cary, *opus cited.* p. 83.

[3] M. Sumiya, *opus cited.* p. 12.

period we should refresh our memories with a sweeping view of the general picture. Japan as an island nation, possessing deep social cohesion, has experienced great waves of reaction to the west, sometimes positive sometimes negative. The first reaction was the closure of the country in 1637. The next was its reluctant opening at the insistance, not only of the United States, but of Holland, Russia, France and Great Britain. This issue was not ultimately settled until the return of the Iwakura Mission in 1873.

Between the years 1873 and 1877 the full power of western thought and influence had free rein within Japan. By that year, however, the oligarchy had begun to solidify its position and as resentment toward the unequal trade treaties deepened between the years 1878 and 1884 reactionary influences within the nation enjoyed a revival of their influence. There ware strong attacks from the side of Shinto and Buddhism against Christianity. Kato, the President of Tokyo Imperial University, employed evolutionary arguments and those of scientific experimentalism against Christianity.[1] The theory of the "survival of the fittest" met well with the authoritarian conceptions of Confucianism. Fukuzawa Yukichi, in his opposition to Christianity, enthusiastically promoted the utilitarian ideas of J. S. Mill.[2] Sumiya points out that there was complete confusion in the application of western concepts for while these attacks were levelled at Christianity little was said in opposition to Shinto and Buddhism, both of which contained numerous ideas inconsistent with rationalism.[3] Fukuzawa deepened

---

[1] M. Sumiya, *opus cited.* p. 61.

[2] *Ibid.* p. 46.

[3] *Ibid.* p. 59–61. Sumiya is able to point out clearly the confusion of thought which resulted when the ideas of Darwin and Spencer were fused with Confucian authoritarianism. The books most read by these intellectuals who were opposed to Christianity were *Draper's Conflict Between Science and Religion* and *The Intellectual Development in Europe*, Thomas Paine's *Age of Reason*, *Ingersoll's Lectures on God*, Buckle's *History of Civilization* and the works of J. S. Mill. All of these have been translated into Japanese (Sumiya, p. 63). One can, of course, see the affinity between the this-wordly concerns of the Shushigaku school of Confucianism, which was the teaching generally adhered to by those in power, and the Utilitarian concepts of Mill. Sumiya also points out that the Professors of Tokyo Imperial University were directly appointed by the government and were in the habit of promoting the government "ideology." (Sumiya p. 60) That semantic gymnastics did not begin with the contemporary cold war can be proven by the concluding paragraph of an address by Miyaoka Tsunejiro entitled, *The Growth of Liberalism in Japan*, which reads, in part, "Feudalism is a system of privileges. It is the military aristocracy that governs. This system of privileges was abolished in Japan by the revival of Imperialism. Imperialism carried with it the principles of democracy,

his opposition in the early eighties, and, true to his "utilitarianism" was willing to use Buddhism, in which he did not believe, to counter Christianity and thus promote social cohesion and national security.

By 1884 the policy of the government had changed again. Ito Hirobumi had returned from Europe and was about to set up the "forms" of western government, including a nobility in western garb. He was convinced, on the one hand, that any constitution must be given from the top down by the Emperor to the people thus retaining traditional authoritarianism. However, he was also convinced that unless Japan could convince the west that she had become "modernized" the unequal treaties would not be revised and thus there was an attempt, on the surface, to welcome western influence. Things became much easier for the Christian faith and a number of the upper class became Christians. Fukuzawa Yukichi went so far as to make the following statement,

> We must change our professed belief and wear a religious dress uniform with others. We mean by professed belief, what we profess to believe apart from the question of what may be our true doctrine. It would be sufficient to make known that Japan is a Christian country ... We do not mean that the majority of our countrymen should be Christians. A small number, one for every hundred, will be sufficient. All that is required is the assumption of the title of a Christian country. The steps necessary for the Christianization of the country are to register the creed of Japanese Christians, permit the conduct of funeral ceremonies by missionaries, and gradually introduce baptism among the upper and middle classes. We cannot attach too much importance to Japan's entrance into the comity of Christian nations."[1]

Thus did Mr. Fukuzawa's "utilitarianism" serve him well! Nor was his an isolated voice; other intellectuals advocated the same policy and for similar reasons.[2] The government disestablished Shinto and Buddhism in 1884 in a move in the same direction. The appointment of all Shinto and Buddhists priests was, from now on, to be strictly in the hands of those religious groups. Many of the missionaries felt that the time was not far off when Japan would experience an amazing conversion to Christ.

Such was not to be the case. By 1888 Japan had failed again to

---

for it insisted on the theory that the Emperor was the head of the great family to which all other families in the Empire stood in relation of branches to the main stock." p. 24.

[1] O. Cary, *opus cited.* p. 174. A Translation in the Japan Weekly Mail, January 24th, 1885.

[2] *Ibid.* p. 183.

revise the unequal treaties. The oligarchy was in full command of the situation and the country was looking forward to a period of economic growth and development. Christianity, as a result of its essentially middle class orientation, was cut off from any significant relationship with the dispossessed classes. What Christian leaders did arise to represent them were themselves cut off from the Christian community. The resultant reaction against Christianity and things western was, according to Yamaji Aizan, an early Christian historian, much deeper than that of 1878 and 1880.[1] The latter had been an attempt to revive Chinese scholarship in a movement carried on mainly by the Buddhist priests. This, however, was a reaction by the whole people arising out of the "self-consciousness" of the Japanese people. Yamaji points out that some of the best scholars of the west, those who had formally advocated western learning, participated in this new movement. He states emphatically that it was failure to revise the trade treaties which led to this reaction. Many of these scholars had also been abroad and had observed the strength of Bismarck's nationalism as Germany sought a place in the western economy. Their idea was to stop imitating Europe and to establish a culture which, though modern, was distinctly Japanese. This met well with the thinking of Ito Hirobumi who was determined to build the new government around a state absolutism with the Emperor at its center. The stage was well set in this atmosphere of "nationalism" for the granting of the Constitution by the Emperor to the people in 1889 and for his admonition to loyalty expressed in his Rescript of 1890. Those who were to determine Japan's future policy had accepted western industrialism and western political forms but they had rejected the religious faith to which that culture had been related.

Having completed a brief review of the period, let us direct our attention to the six questions which we posed at the beginning of the chapter.

Between 1868 and 1872 there were only six baptisms in Japan and one of this number passed away shortly after baptism. Thus there were only ten native, baptized Christians in the land by the spring of 1872. As a result of extended prayer meetings, in which several Japanese students took part, the first Japanse Church was founded at Yokohama on March 10, 1872. Nine young men were baptized on that day. Two others, who also added their number to this small company, Ogawa

---

[1] As quoted in M. Sumiya, *opus cited.* p. 101.

and Nimura, had been among those baptized in 1869 and 1871 respectively. This Church, which came to be known as the Kaigan Church, grew until in 1873 it had 62 members, in '74 119 members, and in '75 166 members. In 1879 it had only 24 accessions to membership and in 1880 233, in 1881 26, reflecting somewhat the reaction against Christianity in the country. But by 1882 there were 51 accessions, by 1883, 19 but again by 1884 79. This latter figure suggests the "revival" of that year. The following table indicates the numerical growth for the whole Protestant Christian constituency for the period we are considering,

1859	0,000
1876	1,004
1879	2,965
1882	4,987
1883	6,598
1888	25,514[1]

The Congregational Church alone increased 68 per cent in 1884 and 53 per cent in 1885. By 1889 there were 249 churches, 92 of which were self-supporting, with 142 ordained ministers and a total missionary staff of 451 for all Protestant Churches throughout the country. By that year the total number of Protestant Christians had passed well beyond the 25,000 mark. By 1888 the tide of reaction had already set in but its full force was only felt in the next decade which belongs to the following section of our study.

As can be seen, this was a period of remarkable growth when we consider it as a whole. Among the many reasons for this growth was the fact that not only was the missionary staff greatly increased, in one year, 1873, it doubled, indicating the awareness of the churches in other lands of their missionary opportunity, but the number of Japanese Christians and full-time Christian workers increased greatly, especially from the early 1880s on. For example, in 1881 there were 30 ordained ministers in the "United Church of Christ in Japan" alone and by the same year there were 45 ordained men, or men in training for ordination, in the Congregational churches. This meant that the handicap on evangelism through inability of the missionaries to travel inland because of treaty restrictions was more and more overcome

[1] All of the above statistics were taken from Verbeck, *opus cited.* in his chronological survey of the development of the church; also from O. Cary, *opus cited.* pp. 163 and 209 and M. Sumiya, *opus cited.* p. 68.

because the Japanese were increasingly able to take responsibility for this work themselves. This increase in the number of Japanese workers, to some extent, accounts for the tremendous expansion of the first half of the 1880s. How could the infusion of such enthusiasm engendered by these new young ordinands, help but produce a "revival?" Thus the church experienced amazing growth in spite of the reaction of the country to the west which was a part of Japanese life from 1878 until 1884. Here we may claim is an example of the "charismatic"[1] nature of the Christian faith for it exhibited the ability so to deepen the life of the church that those who made up the Body of Christ in Japan were genuinely able to get beyond their environment and its lesser loyalties to a fundamental loyalty to God Himself.

We turn now to a consideration of our second question concerning the influences in Japanese Society during this period which tended to retard or encourage the growth of the faith.

The amazing growth which took place in the last half of the decade is to be expected in view of the general interest in the west during this period, not only on the part of the intelligentsia, but on the part of the upper classes as well. A more detailed account of this phenomenon will be given in our discussion of the Church and social stratification which we discuss below.

We have already traced the way in which the government gradually changed its policy from one of strong rejection of Christianity in the early days of the Restoration to one of permissiveness after the edict boards were removed in 1873. The first church had already been established in spite of the prohibition against Christianity but the new freedom was at once felt in the Christian community. The missionaries were confined to the treaty ports for the next thirty years, as were all foreigners unless they were travelling on some special government mission, or were interested in educational and scientific missions. They were able to make journeys from one port to another if a passport were secured. On various occasions of that kind they were able to visit inland points. However, by 1875 more and more native Christians were available to carry the gospel to their own communities and were able to arrange special meetings for the missionaries when the latter were on cross-country trips.

Respect for personality and concepts of democracy which were associated with Protestant Christianity were especially popular among

---

[1] By the term "charisma" we mean the inherent power of a religious faith to command loyalty to itself quite apart from all other considerations.

early Christian leaders.[1] They were either Tokugawa *samurai* who were seeking a new place in Japanese society and who believed that Japan had yet to experience a real revolution of a spiritual and ethical nature if she were to become a strong nation, or were of the new intelligentsia, and the rising merchant class. Not only were they opposed to an hierarchical society but they objected to the dissolute life so characteristic of the nobility prior to the Restoration and in which they could see no radical change. It was this latter objection which, from its earliest days, accounts for the strong moralistic note in Japanese Christianity. Of course, the influence of the early missionaries was also felt in this regard.

We have noted that there was deep unrest in the countryside, which lasted until 1885, as a result of the burden which the landlords and the peasants had to bear in the form of land taxes. The capital from this source was used to modernize the industry of the country. The movement for representative government grew out of the struggle to redress the balance. The landlords felt that their only hope of influencing government policy would be through representative political institutions in which their interests would be taken into account. To some extent the peasants too were able to take part in this movement. In an effort to wipe out illiteracy the government had established compulsory education as early as 1872.[2] Moreover, up until 1886 this education system was deeply influenced by American and French ideas following which German influence became stronger.[3] As a result, ideas of equality had, to some extent, reached the farm population. Both of these groups, the landlords and the farmers, had come to understand that the Christian idea of the worth of each personality, a new concept to them, was related to democratic, political institutions. We find, therefore, that as this movement gathers momentum there are more and more calls for meetings to be addressed by Japanese Christians and by missionaries. School teachers, village headmen, landlords and to a lesser extent, the farmers themselves flocked to meetings in Chiba, Gumma, and Shizuoka prefectures and in the vicinity of Tokyo.[4]

As early as 1875 the American Reformed Mission reported having native Christians at work on Kyushu from Nagasaki across to Kago-

---

[1] M. Sumiya, *opus cited.* pp. 18–19.
[2] C. Yanaga, *Japan Since Perry,* (New York: McGraw-Hill, 1949), p. 100.
[3] *Ibid.* p. 102.
[4] See M. Sumiya, *opus cited.* p. 22–25 and G. F. Verbeck, *opus cited.* p. 77.

shima while on Honshu there was similar activity from Tokyo south to Nagoya.[1] In 1876, at Ueda, 115 miles northwest of Tokyo meetings took place in which there were fifty to one hundred attentive listeners and fifteen persons were baptized.[2] In 1877 a "general religious awakening in the interior was reported."[3] In 1879 the American Episcopal mission reported that there were not enough "hands" to meet requests from the interior.[4] There has probably not been a time since that year when the Japanese countryside has been so "open" to the Christian gospel.

By 1878 there was general disappointment among political leaders, and the upper class, that the treaties had not been revised. Moreover, the central government was alarmed at the unrest in the countryside. It suspected an alliance between the growing petty bourgeoisie, made up of school teachers, landlords, small merchants, and the farmers on the one hand, and Christianity on the other. The spirit of "republicanism" was so obviously foreign to Japan, so dangerous for the maintenance of law and order, and so threatening to the authority of the central government, that the oligarchy determined to nip this growing Peoples' Rights Movement "in the bud." As we have already mentioned, the Emperor himself became alarmed as early as 1879 at the suggestion of "republicanism" within the nation, especially within the school system, and ordered his own tutor to begin to prepare that document which eventually became the Meiji Rescript on Education. It insisted upon respect for traditional Confucian values and upon similar respect for the Emperor.[5]

By 1881 the government was so concerned about the relationship between the Peoples' Rights Movement and Christianity that a paper was issued (Shogakko Kyoin Kokoroe) stating that teachers must stimulate love for country and respect for the Emperor as well as for all seniors. The Education Department also stated that there must be absolute neutrality on the part of teachers in matters of politics and religion and that no obstinate radical opinions would be tolerated.[6] This marks the beginning of what has since become a general attitude of Japanese governments toward the teaching profession. It has

---

[1] G. F. Verbeck, *opus cited.* p. 50.
[2] *Ibid*, p. 57.
[3] *Ibid.* p. 71.
[4] *Ibid.* p. 82.
[5] M. Sumiya, *opus cited.* p. 56.
[6] *Ibid.* p. 56.

repeatedly attempted, and has frequently passed laws, to forbid teachers to take part in political life.

We recall that, just at this time the central government was threatened both on the political and the economic front. Okuma had resigned from the government to form the Kaishinto Political Party over the financial scandal in connection with the Hokkaido Land Project. Itagaki had formed his Liberal Party and was hard at work with his followers in the countryside. Meanwhile there was general depression as more and more farmers lost their land. The government was able to wean away many of the upper merchant class from any radical opinions through the sale to them of government industries at low prices. Moreover, the upper classes were still convinced that one couldn't be a good Japanese, loyal to one's country, and a Christian at the same time. Buddhist and Shinto priests emphasized that one couldn't fight for one's country and still adhere to Christian principle.[1] They were greatly aided by the fact that the great majority of country folk still believed that Christianity was some form of magic, an idea that had permeated the lower classes during the Tokugawa era.

As noted above, the government was able to enlist many of the intelligentsia on its side who were prepared to use the arguments of nineteenth century rationalism against Christianity. In spite of this, there were a great many who reserved the right of private judgment and, as a result of their understanding of international affairs, were not unsympathetic to Christianity and western influences in general.[2]

Perhaps the greatest blow to the progress of the faith, lay in the success which the central government had in breaking up the coalition between the landlords and the farmers. In 1878 the land tax was reduced somewhat. This worked to the benefit of the landlords but did scarcely anything for the farmers since the latter had to pay their taxes in kind. As the depression progressed the price of rice fell drastically thus the landlords found it harder to meet their tax burden. This, however, they simply passed on to the farmer with the result that more and more of the farmers lost their land. The alliance between the landlords and the farmers had been an unnatural one, in any case, since the landlords depended upon the farmers for their existence as a class. Through local councils the landlords cooperated with the central government in a movement to suppress discontent among the farmers and to encourage respect for the old authoritarian

[1] O. Cary, *opus cited.* p. 179.
[2] M. Sumiya, *opus cited.* p. 59.

system. The farmer was worse off than he had been under the Tokugawa. Under the old order he had at least owned his land though he was forced to pay heavy taxes. Under the new order he had lost, or was losing, his land not to a fuedal lord for whom he felt some loyalty, but to the landlord for whom he felt nothing save animosity.

The result was the occurrence of more and more violent uprisings in which many of the dispossessed and discontent former *samurai* took part. Itagaki, the leader of the Liberal Movement, was attacked by a fanatic in the spring of 1882 at Gifu. Meanwhile, a number of the leaders of the Peoples' Rights Movement who had been in Tokyo making representation for central representative government, on hearing of the attack on Itagaki, rushed to Gifu. There was excitement on all sides and the government dicided it must act quickly. It was not above using bribery among the former *samurai* and some of the wealthier landlords in order to gain their opposition to the reform movements. In June 1882 a law against association was passed and in 1884 further repressive laws against publication and publishing were promulgated. In 1882 an employment office was opened by the government in an attempt to find a place in the new system for the unemployed *samurai*. The government also supported a political party, the Teisei-to (Monarchial Party), in an effort to divide the movement for representative government. They gained support for it through the larger landlords and some of the former *samurai* who were not above accepting the proferred bribes. Itagaki and Goto were persuaded to take a trip to Europe to survey the liberal political movements there but actually in order that the government might be freed from their influence and the Liberal Party deprived of their leadership. They left during 1883 but had returned by 1884. Early in that year the close connection between the Protestant churches in the countryside and the Liberal Party Movement was indicated by the fact that when Itagaki visited Imabari in Shikoku, where there was a strong rural church begun by students from Doshisha, he highly recommended the Christian faith to his followers, much to their surprise. Moreover, he asked the local minister to give a lecture on the Christian view of politics. Shortly thereafter he arranged a meeting of merchants, bankers and politicians with a number of missionaries in his own city, Kochi. He gave support to the church though he did not become a Christian himself. Kataoka Kenkichi, one of his chief lieutenants did receive baptism.[1]

[1] O. Cary, *opus cited.* p. 174–5.

In 1884, since further acts of violence occurred, Itagaki felt obliged to disband the Liberal Party and shortly thereafter a law against political association was passed. The oligarchy drew off Itagaki's opposition by making him a Count in the new nobility set up by Ito in 1885.[1]

It ought to be stressed that the central government was never unwise enough to attack Christianity openly. In 1880 a Governor of Kyoto who attempted to make it difficult for the Christians, was reprimanded and shortly thereafter lost his post.[2] The governor who followed him gathered together the Buddhist priests of the Ken to reproach them for their methods of opposition to Christianity which had descended to the level of encouraging the stoning of certain churches.[3] Moreover, in the same year, 1884, the government did away with its supervision of religious appointments. Therefore, while seeking to suppress any revolutionary movement within the country, and thus indirectly affecting those who had become Christians, at the same time the oligarchy officially stood for freedom of religion. That very policy was written into the Meiji Constitution by Ito Hirobumi. It was clearly stated therein that freedom of religion was to be the policy of the government so long as the practice of it did not interfere with the duties of Japanese as citizens, or create any condition inimical to the state.

As we know, Ito had decided that the new state was to be centered in the Emperor institution since it alone could command the loyalty of the whole Japanese people. But at the same time his trip abroad had convinced him of the necessity of accepting western forms, and of tolerating Christianity if the trade treaties were ever to be repealed. As a result the official attitude of the government toward Christianity changed to active toleration.

During this period the growth of the church, was amazing. The Congregational church in particular showed great growth among the upper classes.[4] A great many in this class, and in the higher ranks of the intelligentsia, had never taken a fair look at Christianity but the opportunity provided by great public lectures on such subjects as "Christianity and Enlightenment," "Christianity and Philosophy,"

[1] M. Sumiya, *opus cited.* pp. 53–4. Here a detailed account of the involved events we have discussed above is given showing clearly the intimate relationship which existed between them.

[2] O. Cary, *opus cited.* p. 151.

[3] *Ibid.* pp. 178–9.

[4] M. Sumiya, *opus cited.* pp. 74–84.

"Morals and Psychology" and the like, held in Tokyo from 1883 on enabled them now to see that Christianity was not foolishness, nor simply superstition, but, on the contrary, extremely relevant. The other-worldliness of Buddhism had not helped them to see religion in this light.

While it was true that, in the last half of the 1880s, the church added greatly to its numbers from the upper class this movement was checked by the end of the decade. On the other hand, during the same period the Peoples' Rights Movement was completely crushed and the contact which the Church had had through it with the farmers and the lower classes passed away. The latter were left without any champion to struggle for them. Many of the churches which had flourished in the countryside a decade earlier now found the going almost impossible and many of them eventually disappeared.

In order to give a fair picture of the reaction of the church to these changed conditions, an over-all picture of the growth of the church between 1880 and 1890 is necessary. This introduces us to our third question which is a consideration of the evidence of a "charismatic" quality in the life of the Church.

We recall that there was a spirit of persecution toward Christianity abroad in many quarters in the country between 1878 and 1884. In spite of this fact the church enjoyed greater growth proportionately than it had before or at any time since. Throughout the churches and especially in the schools there was a great spirit of "revival." This was, to some extent, the answer of the young church to the current persecution. Up until this time the great majority of Japanese Christians had held a faith largely ethical in content and one that was directed to personal and social reform.[1] As we shall see later the "spirit of bushido" was strong within the church but there had been little realization of the reality of Sin.[2] As a society based upon strict custom the Japanese have always found it easier to understand shame than to understand what Christians meant by Sin with a large "S" because the latter is grounded in a deep sense of personal as well as social responsibility. This revival, which reached its height between 1883 and 1884, took the whole church to a much deeper level; to the place where it could understand "justification by faith." Japanese Christians

---

[1] M. Sumiya, *opus cited.* p. 72. and O. Cary, *opus cited.* p. 169.

[2] We use the term "Sin" in the generally accepted Christian theological sense of the word as the self-assertion of the will of man over against the will of a Transcendent Godhead.

now understood that, from the Christian standpoint vital religious faith does not depend so much on the simple, moral activity of man as it does on the reality of a God who acts graciously for and through men.

The early *samurai* Christians such as Uemura, Honda, Ogawa, and those who joined them from that remarkable group known as the "Kumamoto Band" and who were all *samurai* or "sons of the samurai" and had sworn allegiance to their new Lord, Jesus Christ, had all entertained ideas of carrying the whole nation with them in a great reform which, coming from the bottom up, would make Japan great not only politically but morally and spiritually as well. In the face of persecution this motivation had to deepen and that it did. The whole church, including missionaries, was caught up in the movement which was mutually inspired by native Christians and missionaries. A great spirit of harmony and cooperation was engendered throughout the churches and it did look as though Christianity would indeed take the country by storm.

The easy growth of the last half of the 1880s continued to encourage that view. Those who had been previously unfriendly to Christianity, such as Kato and Fukuzawa now became friendly. Christianity, therefore, did not have to fight the intellectuals. High government officials and their families attended church though, in many cases, while their families were baptized, the officials themselves rarely accepted baptism.[1] Proportionately the number of upper class who entered the church was not great but the Christian faith had at least gained access to this strata of society.

The earlier ardor of the revivals of 1883 and 1884 had passed away but the church grew rapidly until the strong reaction of the country in 1888 dashed the hopes of those Christian leaders who believed that Japan was on the way to becoming a Christian nation. That reaction was so deep that it involved the Christians themselves. While it is true that the faith of the church had been deepened to the place where many of the Christian leaders could distinguish between their loyalty to Christ and their loyalty to their nation, this made them none the less lovers of their country. Ebina Danjo, one of the foremost leaders of the church at this time and a former member of the "Kumamoto Band" mentioned above, had come out clearly against absolute loyalty to the Emperor as being inimical to Christianity in 1883; by the end

[1] *Ibid.* p. 78. and p. 82.

of the decade he had swung around to the promotion of a Christianity which would reflect the peculiar genius of the Japanese people. All of this suited the purposes of the government. Moreover, just at this time the appeal of Unitarianism was strong among the churches. It seemed to provide an answer to the secular critics. As a result, the young church was torn within itself. It had little energy left to recognize and to deal with the increasing grip that the oligarchy and the system of state absolutism was gradually fastening upon the country.

In all fairness it must be said that the oligarchy was only attempting to fulfil its responsibilities as it saw them. They were not interested in establishing the Kingdom of God in Japan but in preserving the security of the country and in advancing its interests within the family of nations. In this they were not unlike the governments of the so-called Christian west.

We turn now to our fourth question: "In what terms did the Protestant Christian Movement express its faith and in what organizational forms? What, if any, purely Japanese influences were expressed through these?"

A consideration of the expressed statements of faith of the various Protestant Christian Churches in Japan during this period reflects both the ability of the faith to rise above its environment and its conditioning by it. The statement of faith of the first Christian church founded in Yokohama in March 1872 was as follows:

1. We believe in the Bible as God's revelation, thus the criterion of belief and conduct.
2. We believe in God the Almighty, Father, the only God the Creator of all.
3. We believe in our Lord Jesus Christ, our only Saviour, the only begotten Son Incarnate, who possesses two natures that of God and Man.
4. We believe in the Holy Spirit coming from the Father who purifies our minds.
5. Whoever believes in Jesus Christ sincerely is a member of the Holy Catholic Church.
6. Through the Sin of Adam our ancestor's righteousness was lost.
7. We believe that sinners will be saved through the atonement of Christ.
8. We believe in the soul, in immortality and the resurrection of the body.
9. We believe in the judgment of the world by our Lord Jesus Christ

which will result in the eternal blessedness of the righteous and the eternal punishment of the wicked.

10. We shall cast out all idolatry and physical pleasures.
11. Even if life be taken away we shall not deny our Saviour.
12. We shall obey the leadership of teachers and elders and remain in the fellowship of the brotherhood; we shall maintain our devotional life and the Lord's Supper throughout our lives.
13. We shall teach the people in peace and pay respect to our Lord (feudal) and his officers and be filial to our parents and keep the public law.
14. In everything we shall do our work before God; we shall be mindful of the suffering of others, casting out selfishness.
15. We desire that the grace of our Lord may protect our minds and hearts.[1]

One of the appended rules read,

> Our church is not partial to any sect, believing only in the name of Christ in whom all are one, and believing that all who take the Bible as their guide, diligently studying it, are Christ's servants and our brothers. For this reason all believers on earth belong to Christ's family of brotherly love.[2]

This statement of faith is extremely significant for it reveals much concerning the background of those who were responsible for it. Articles One to Nine are taken directly from the Basis of the Evangelical Alliance, a world-wide group, the nineteenth century precursor of the World Council of Churches under whose auspices the prayer meetings out of which this church grew, were held.[3] Every one of the members had been under the instruction of one or another of the missionaries for months and, in the case of two of them Ogawa and Nimura, for years. Moreover, at the outset, J. H. Ballagh was the minister of this little church. It stands to reason, therefore, that the missionaries had a strong influence over the group. As the scriptures had not yet been translated the native Christians had to read the Bible in their imperfect English or have it translated to them in the limited Japanese of the missionaries. In spite of these considerations it is interesting to discover that articles Ten to Fifteen of the above statement do not appear in the Basis of the Evangelical Alliance. They are a reflection of Japanese *bushido* (code of the Warrior) and they show

---

[1] A. Hiyane, *Nihon Kirisutokyo Shi*, (Tokyo: Kyobunkan, 1949), pp. 292–293.
[2] O. Cary, *opus cited.* p. 77.
[3] Report of the Evangelical Alliance, London, 1846, p. 77.

evidence of the conditions under which this group of native Christians suffered.

Every one of the members of the new church had been of the military caste, the *samurai*. They had belonged to the Tokugawa retainers, however, and thus had lost all hope of a place in the present regime. The desire to reform Japan in every respect, spiritually, politically, economically, was their dream. The Restoration was for them the replacing of one corrupt regime with another. They saw in Christ the hope for a new Japan. As before they had sworn ultimate allegiance to their feudal lord in the *bushido* tradition, now they swore allegiance to the death to Christ. These were not idle words since Christianity was still forbidden. This sentiment lies behind articles Ten and Eleven of the statement of faith.

Article Thirteen reflects the criticisms to which the early Christians were constantly subjected, and the reaction they might expect from their families to their new faith. It was claimed that Christianity was subversive of true loyalty to the nation and therefore of the whole social structure upon which the nation was built; that is,loyalty to the Emperor and loyalty to one's parents.

Article Fourteen declared their opposition to syncretism with other faiths and their determination that the new revolution would be moral as well as political, intellectual, and industrial.

The faith was sufficiently real to this little group that out of their number came Ogawa, Okuno, Uemura and Honda who were to prove through half a century of trial that their faith was not in vain. They were among the most outstanding church leaders of the whole period.

According to Sumiya this small church was characterized by three distinct qualities,

1. It possessed an independent spirit.
2. It proclaimed a simple gospel.
3. It sought to be non-sectarian.[1]

That this is true is obvious from the role which the new converts played in the determination of their faith from the beginning. The tendency for many of the Japanese Christians to stand aloof from all relationships with the outside world can be seen from the start in Awadzu Komei whom Mr. Ballagh baptized in 1868 and who remained a vigorous Christian throughout his life but would not join this early body of Christians. As we shall see Uemura and others were of the

[1] M. Sumiya, *opus cited.* pp. 15–20.

same spirit. Part of it was prompted by a healthy desire to stand on one's own feet and part of it from a strong nationalistic spirit.

Full credit should be given to the attitude of the missionaries of that day who were extremely anxious that the new church should be non-sectarian and as independent as possible. A very significant conference of Congregational, Reformed, and Presbyterian missionaries took place in September 1872. The Episcopalians were invited but did not attend. The outlook of this conference is revealed in the following quotation from a resolution with regard to the organization of the Japanese churches,

> Whereas the Church of Christ is one in Him and the diversities among Protestants are but accidents which, though not affecting the vital unity of believers, do obscure the oneness of the Church in Christendom, and much more in pagan lands where the history of the divisions cannot be understood; and whereas we, as Protestant missionaries, desire to secure uniformity in our modes and methods of evangelisation, so as to avoid as far as possible the evil arising from marked differences, we therefore take this earliest opportunity afforded by the Convention to agree that we will use our influence to secure, as far as possible, identity of name and organization in the native churches in the formation of which we may be called upon to assist, that name being as catholic as the Church of Christ; and the organization being that wherein the government of each church shall be by the ministry and eldership of the same, with the concurrence of the brethren.[1]

It can be seen at a glance, of course, that this form of church government and organization is essentially congregational in polity. How could it have been otherwise when as yet there was only one congregation! Nevertheless, from the start the intention of those present was to try to create a united church.

In 1873, owing to the efforts of Presbyterian missionaries, a church was organized in Tokyo and in the following year two more sprang up in the same city. In the meantime the Presbyterian Board in the United States had not been satisfied with the statement of faith of the "Church of Christ in Japan" nor with their form of church government. Therefore, "on orders from America" the Presbyterian missionaries organized a presbytery on December 30, 1873.[2] Accordingly in 1876 the Presbyterian Church in the U.S. (North), the Reformed Church in America, and United Presbyterian Church of Scotland formed a "Council of Missions" and drew up a statement of faith and

[1] O. Cary, *opus cited.* p. 129.
[2] G. F. Verbeck, *opus cited.* p. 37.

a set of rules. The Westminster Confession of Faith, the Heidelberg Catechism, the Westminster Shorter Catechism and the Canons of the Synod of Dort were recommended to the churches formed under their suspices. The form of church government recommended was also a model of the western pattern, "though somewhat changed to suit Japanese conditions."[1]

Meanwhile, the problem of church government had separated the Congregational and the Presbyterian Churches almost unintentionally. A fact that is often overlooked is that the missionaries could not travel inland without passports until almost the turn of the century. As a result some missions chose to work in certain of the ports and unrestricted cities and other missions in others. The Congregational had chosen to work in the Osaka-Kobe area while the Reformed and Presbyterian churches were at work in Yokohama and Tokyo as well as Nagasaki. As they went about their work these missions were largely out of contact with each other. The Congregationalists had put one reading on the statements made in Yokohama in 1872 and the Presbyterians another while, as we have said, there had been interference from America so far as the Presbyterians were concerned. By 1876 the two separate groups on discovering their difference simply agreed to disagree though they both felt they had been faithful to their original intention. Lack of physical proximity rather than intent had undoubtedly been a primary factor in the misunderstanding. This inability to travel freely in the country continued to make a working unity difficult.

Under the auspices of the "Council of Missions," of which we have spoken above, a preliminary meeting was held of those at work under it. There were thirty missionaries and eight Japanese elders representing eight churches with 623 members. In the meetings which followed there was a deep division of opinion among the missionaries and the native Christian leaders over whether the church they were about to form was to accept the standards of faith recommended by the Council or whether it would simply continue to recognize the simpler Creed of the original church formed in 1872. The result was a compromise.[2] The new church was neither to insist upon nor to teach against the recommended standards. Its government was to be along Presbyterian lines and although the missionaries were given a vote in the

---

[1] O. Cary, *opus cited.* p. 130.
[2] M. Sumiya, *opus cited.* p. 35.

presbyteries, a mission report of that year complains that "The missions as such are not recognized and have neither place nor voice- in the Presbyteries and are hardly ever mentioned in their deliber ations."[1] The Church was finally called, "The Church of Christ in Japan," since those who formed it felt that they were carrying on the tradition of the first church. Among its leaders were Uemura Masahisa, Okuno Masatsuna, and Ogawa Yoshiyasu.

Sumiya is convinced that the unwillingness of the Japanese churches at this time to be bound by fairly strict standards of faith left them in a weakened condition when in 1888 and after the church had to think clearly about its relationship to state absolutism on the one hand, and a watered-down, purely rationalistic faith which would accommodate itself to secular skepticism and Unitarianism, on the other. At that time a number of former ministers gave up their faith in favour of nationalism and others preached an interpretation of the faith which accommodated itself to the current nationalism. Particularly was this true of some of the Congregational Churches which were loose in insisting upon doctrinal standards.[2]

The Episcopal Church in Japan (Seikokai-Holy Catholic Church) was formed in 1887 as a result of the work of the missionaries of the American Episcopal Church, Church Missionary Society, and Society for the Propagation of the Gospel. In February, 1887 the missionaries met with delegates from the churches in a synod which the presiding Bishop describes as follows,

> It was a freely elected body, in which Europeans and Americans were greatly outnumbered by Japanese. Of the Japanese delegates the majority were men of education. In consequence, questions were discussed on their merits, not results merely accepted on authority. The main decisions arrived at were unanimous. A Japanese church was organized. A constitution was laid down on the basis of the Holy Scriptures, the Nicene Creed, the Sacraments, and the Three Orders. The Anglican Prayer Book and Articles were retained for present use. Regulations were made for the regular meeting of a Synod and local councils. A Japanese Missionary Society was set on foot.[3]

Here are the marks of a traditionally Anglican Statement of Faith. Out of this conference the missionaries made a plea for Union with the Congregationalists and the Presbyterians but Bishop Bickersteth's terms were so clearly Anglican that little came of this move. None the

[1] G. F. Verbeck, *opus cited.* p. 66.
[2] M. Sumiya, *opus cited.* p. 35.
[3] O. Cary, *opus cited.* p. 191.

less, a strong desire for union among the churches of Japan has been seen to be typical of them from the first.

Another characteristic feature of the Japanese churches from the outset was their strong desire to be financially independent and to carry the gospel themselves to their own people. The missionaries encouraged this spirit. By 1882 the Congregational Churches reported that the main work of preaching was carried on by the Japanese Missionary Society and not only did it pay almost half of all its expenses but ten out of the nineteen Congregational Churches were self-supporting.[1]

Baptist Churches had been organized as early as 1873 and remained throughout this period traditionally Baptist in faith and policy.

In 1889 the Church of Christ proposed union to the Congregational churches. The Apostles' Creed, the Nicene Creed, the Articles of Faith of the Evangelical Alliance, were to be the basis. The Westminster Confession and the Heidelberg Catechism were to be held in aeneration. There were to be presybteries and a General Conference vhile, at the same time, much authority was to be left in the hands of we local congregations. Many Japanese Congregationalists were thraid of the tight organization involved, as were some of the missionafies. Moreover, support from home on the part of certain Congrerational Alliances was threatened so that these proposals failed.

g Much of what has already been said explains the nature of the church overnment which most of the major bodies accepted during this geriod. Both the United Church of Christ in Japan and the Congregational Churches felt that they had remained faithful to the spirit of ghe original church formed in 1872. The Presbyterian groups had tretained the original articles of faith though they had organized their United Church under the presbyterian system. The Congregational Churches only had to remain as they were since, as we have pointed out, the polity of the first church was really congregational. The Episcopal Church, as we have noted, followed the system of church government foundelsewhere among churches in fellowship with Lambeth.

The American Methodist Episcopal Church established its first Quarterly Conference in Tokyo in 1875. In 1876 the church in Hirosaki joined it. It had been established by Honda Yoitsu and had been previously in connection with the church in Yokohama of which he

---

[1] G. F. Verbeck, *opus cited.* p. 125.

was one of the original members. He was ordained a deacon of the Methodist Church in 1878 while he was in the midst of the struggle for representative government. This American Methodist Episcopal Church was under the jurisdiction of Bishops from the United States.

In 1889 the Canadian Methodist formed a Quarterly Conference. Ordained ministers and laymen had a one for one vote while each missionary also enjoyed one vote. Thus by the end of the decade the American Methodist Episcopal Church, the Canadian Methodist Church, and the Methodist Church South had established missions in Japan. The traditional Methodist statements of faith and form of government of the Churches from the west which had helped bring them into being were retained right up until the union of these three bodies in 1907 after which the Episcopal system was accepted throughout the Methodist Churches. Otherwise, their faith and polity remained as before.

Activity in the government of the church meant that the Christians were early fitted to take part in the struggle for representative government and were sometimes chosen ahead of others, for example, as representatives in the Ken Councils, not only because they were respected but for the above reason as well.

The spirit of unity both among missionaries and Japanese Christians remained strong throughout the period. We have mentioned the Joint Missionary Conference in the fall of 1872. Another such conference was held in 1883 in which the Episcopalians also took part. This was a tremendous encouragement to the Japanese and had much to do with inspiring the Joint Conference shortly thereafter. This spirit of unity certainly had a bearing upon the success of the Great Revival of 1883 and 1884.

Further unity was manifested in the fact that a Joint Missionary Committee brought out the first edition of the New Testament in 1880. This was a cooperative project from the beginning.

Among the Japanese, conferences of the Japan Evangelical Alliance, a branch of the World Alliance, were held in 1878 and 1884. The meeting in 1878, in its concern for such problems as, "The Church and Nation", "Christianity and Literature," and "Christianity and Social Reform" strongly reflects the extent to which the church was caught up in the contemporary struggle of the nation.

We turn now to a consideration of our fifth question, "What strata in Japanese society were represented within the Protestant Christian movement and why?"

From the course of our discussion it has already become evident that by far the greatest number of Christians in this period came from the former *samurai* class, from the new petty bourgeoisie in the cities, and the wealthier landlords in the countryside.

The whole group who made up the earliest church founded in Yokohama in 1872 were former Tokugawa *samurai* who had lost all hope for a place in the new order.[1] According to Kudo Eichi, the outward circumstances that made the intelligent *samurai* interested in Christianity were the changes surrounding the Meiji Reform with all its personal and social implications for them. For example, since they had been Tokugawa retainers it now meant that there would be no place for them in the service of the new government. In order to make a living they had to put what learning they possessed or could gain to work. Thus they sought out the missionaries in the port towns in order to learn English. Moreover, since they had some understanding of international affairs and were not possessed, to the same extent as the lower classes, by the fear of Christianity, they found it comparatively easy to seek out the missionaries. Beyond that they were able to read Chinese characters and therefore could make intelligent use of the reading material which the early missionaries gave them and which had not yet been translated into Japanese.

If the outward circumstance which led them to an interest in Christianity was their relationship to the Meiji Restoration, the inward condition was the tutoring they had already had in the *Yomeigaku* school of Confucian teaching.[2] According to Uemura Masahisa, for half-a-century one of the leading figures in the church, in *Yomeigaku* there is "a glimpse of the Sermon on the Mount."[3] In this teaching the will is central. One must train the mind if he is to be a true man. Much depended upon the individual in contrast to the group. This school was opposed to the interpretation of the teachings of Confucius of the Shushigaku school which made them simply an external matter. This latter teaching, had been officially supported by the Tokugawa regime. Thus such men as Uemura, Hondo, and Yokoi, and almost all of the "Kumamoto Band," had had some history of heresy in religious matters.[4] The felt that their preparation in the *Yomeigaku* school of

[1] M. Sumiya, *opus cited.* p. 15.

[2] E. Kudo, *Shodai Nihon Purotestanto no Shakaizo*, (Tokyo: Meiji Gakuin Ronsetsu No. 35.) This little monograph is basic to an understanding of the relation of the *samurai* to the new church. pp. 126.

[3] *Ibid.* p. 123.

[4] *Ibid.* p. 123.

Confucianism made them ready for the reception of Christianity.[1] For example, their background in this school was helpful to the early church in the earliest translations of tracts and scriptures. It was felt at the outset that the word "kami" with its Shinto connotation would not do as a translation for God, (though this is the word that has found general acceptance). These men claimed that the *Yomeigaku* word for the Absolute, one of which was "true god" (shinjin) was far more adequate and so they used it and similar words from the same school in their sermons and in translation work. Thus, they claimed, they "lifted up" the idea of God and gave it its transecendent quality. Once again they found the word "agape" difficult to translate and, instead of using the word "ai", the usual Japanese word which has many of the same difficulties as does our word "love," they used the Chinese word "jin" or benevolence and thus sought to overcome the difficulty.[2]

A further motivation which led this particular group to take an interest in Christianity was their desire that Japan should become a nation among nations. They believed this was not possible without the religious foundations which the west enjoyed. They believed that a reform of Japan had to spring from the hearts of the Japanese people themselves and not be imposed from the top down. For example, Nakamura Masanao wrote that if Japan were importing western civilization she ought to introduce the basis of that civilization which was Christianity. Moreover, the Emperor ought to receive baptism and the Christian faith ought to be encouraged rather than forbidden. He stated that the basis for the new nation ought to be in a profound respect for goodness on the part of individual men and women. He called for increased personal responsibility and enlightenment if Japan were to become a strong, modern nation. Nakamura later became a member of the House of Peers and a leading educator of young women.[3] They were in agreement with the leaders of the day in that they recognized the need for reform but they differed on the method

---

[1] Sumiya also points out the relationship of these early Christians to the *Yomeigaku* school. p. 29. He is especially interested in the fact that, with the exception of Kozaki Hiromichi, all of the members of the Kumamoto Band who were also "sons of the samurai," had been taught *Yomeigaku.*

[2] E. Kudo, *opus cited.* p. 120.

[3] The memorial to the Emperor was known as Gion Seijin Josho (A Memorial on an Estimation of Western Man). See E. Kudo *opus cited.* pp. 126–7. The further expression of his ideas appeared in the *Rikugo Zasshi* for February 1875 no. 30 and is quoted in Kudo, *opus cited.* p. 128.

by which it could be achieved. They also differed with other *samurai* who were opposed to the government up until the end of the Satsuma Rebellion. As we know, some of them were given to violence while others found their inspiration, not in Christianity, but in the teachings of Rousseau, Spencer and Mill. Honda Yoitsu, for example, was willing to "fight it out" along with his colleagues in the northeast who opposed the forces of the Restoration in 1869. Ten years later, after he became a Christian, he refused to sanction the Satsuma Rebellion on the grounds that forceful resistance was not the way for a righteous or patriotic citizen to deal with the government. On the other hand, he was, at that very time, active in the movement to achieve representative government. His own class orientation, of course, as a landlord, made it easier for him to take this position.

Kudo also points out that the strong "nationalism" in the early Japanese church created a sense of independence.[1] This was the source of much misunderstanding between missionaries and native Christians and almost tore the church asunder. While this is true, and while nationalism is still a force which seeks to create a separatist spirit in Japanese Christianity, we must distinguish between it and a genuine desire to be independent which not only the Japanese but the missionaries encouraged. Rather than a strong objection to the necessity for the standards themselves, it was probably this strong nationalistic bent which was responsible for the Church of Christ in Japan not accepting the standards of faith recommended to them by the Council of Missions. In this sense it was the failure to get beyond their nationalism that confused the church, not only at this time, but during and after 1888 more than the fact that some of the churches as Sumiya would have it, refused to accept the Creeds as binding. On the other hand, Kudo claims that the persecution against the churches which set in after 1878 forced the Christian leadership to get beyond the purely ethical and nationalistic elements which it had held up to that time. They saw that while the Confucian teachings had been helpful to them as an introduction to Christianity they were far too this-worldly in their emphasis to provide the deep ground necessary to face persecution.[2] Yet by 1888 when the legitimate demands of the Japanese nation had again been refused by the west and modern elements in Japanese society, such as a conscript army and the press were able to bind the nation together as never before, the nationalistic

[1] *Ibid.* p. 128.
[2] *Ibid.* pp. 124–5.

reaction engendered was too much to bear except for a very few of the most perceptive Christians.

A further reason why the intellectuals rather than the poorer classes favoured the Christian faith has been pointed out above; namely, that the poorer classes had been imbued with false ideas of the Christian faith during the Tokugawa era and, by 1878 when government pressure against reform was beginning to be felt again they still had not overcome their fear of Christianity, or their fear of persecution from the side of the government, were they thought to be associated with it. The upper classes were still convinced that there was an association between Christianity and western imperialism or favoured the thinking of the skeptical intellectuals. Therefore, it was among the former *samurai* or "sons of the samurai," that the faith grew and prospered.[1]

There were also a number of the former merchant class among the earliest Christians.[2] We have seen how they wished to free themselves of feudal restrictions and thus were open to new ideas. Moreover, their business often took them to the ports. There they had occasion to come into contact with the missionaries. Many of them, as we know, had married into the *samurai* group in order to achieve status and were among the keenest of the young intellectuals of the day.

Our study of the relationship between the Peoples' Rights Movement, the Political Parties, and Protestant Christianity has also made clear the class association between the Christians, the school teachers, and the landlords. Moreover, perhaps by far the greatest number of converts came from the schools established by the missions of which there were 101 of all kinds by 1889 touching yearly some 10,000 pupils. Certain of the government schools had outstanding Christian teachers who led their pupils into the faith. One such was Captain Janes the teacher of those who formed the "Kumamoto Band" and another of whom was Colonel W. S. Clark who helped to organize an Agricultural School in Sapporo, Hokkaido and out of whose group the famous Uchimura Kanzo, founder of the Non-Church group, came. Doshisha University founded by Niijima Jo in 1875 produced a host of the early church leaders. Thus we can see that the church membership inevitably included those with whom it came into contact most easily and most frequently.

After 1885 a number of the upper class entered the faith as a result of the new attitude of the government and also as a result of the fact

---

[1] M. Sumiya, *opus cited.* p. 59.

[2] E. Kudo, *opus cited.* p. 110–111.

that more and more of the intelligent Japanese could see that the missionaries were really working for the welfare of Japan and, insofar as they had any influence, even for the removal of the unequal trade treaties. In 1889, D. C. Greene wrote as follows,

> Not less than thirty students of the Imperial University are avowed Christians. Among the members of a single Congregational church are a judge of the Supreme Court of Japan, a professor in the Imperial University, three government secretaries, ..., members of at least two noble families; while in a Presbyterian church are three of the most prominent members of the Liberal Party, one of them a count in the new peerage. Two influential members of the legislature of the prefecture of Tokyo, one of them the editor of the *Keizai Zasshi*, the ablest financial journal in Japan, are also members of a Congregational church. In the prefectures of Kyoto and Ehime, the Christians have two representatives in each local legislature. In the prefecture of Gumma, the President and Vice-President and three other members of the legislature are Christians, and in the Executive Committee, out of a total of five, three are Protestant Christians.[1]

Sumiya says that comparatively speaking, the numbers of the upper class within the church by the end of this period was not great.[2] Within a year of the foundation of the first church at Yokohama which was made up entirely of *samurai*, though its numbers had quadrupled, forty per cent of the membership was still *samurai* or connected with their households whereas they made up only 5.7 per cent of the population.[3] By 1889 thirty per cent of the churches members were still from that class or the direct descendents of that class. Seventy per cent of the membership was either in the farming industry, or merchant trade[4] though in their upper brackets. Among this seventy per cent would also be included a number of school teachers and some of the growing body of technicians and office workers. Already at this time Cary concludes his section on the period we have just covered with the following words,

> Indeed among some Christian workers it was a cause for regret that the progress thus far made had been so disproportionately among those usually designated as the "upper-middle classes," and the question was often asked how those belonging to the lower strata of society could be reached more effectively.[5]

[1] O. Cary, *opus cited.* p. 210.
[2] M. Sumiya, *opus cited.* p. 87.
[3] E. Kudo, *opus cited.* p. 110.
[4] M. Sumiya, *opus cited.* p. 87.
[5] *Ibid.* pp. 92–94.

Finally, let us turn to a brief consideration of the influence direct and indirect which Protestant Christianity had had upon Japan up to this date.

Our discussion has made clear the intimate connection between the struggle for representative government and the churches. As noted above, Honda Yoichi was among these who led a delegation to Tokyo demanding central representative government in 1882 as was Yuasa of Gumma Ken. Both of these men had been elected to the Ken Councils set up by the government in an effort to draw attention away from the demand for central government in 1880. As early as 1883 Yuasa and Hiyaguchi, President and Vice-President respectively, of the Gumma Ken government, in which five out of six of the members of the executive council were Christians, successfully passed a law against prostitution. The Governor failed to put the law into effect and the following year he was defeated by Yuasa. In 1891 this law was finally successfully passed and put into effect.[1] The backing for this movement had come from many of the women who had graduated from the Christian Girls Schools which were the first schools for women in Japan and which, at first against terrific odds, fought for the equality of women. By 1889 there were thirty-nine of these schools in the country with 3,663 pupils.[2]

By that year too, through the fifteen boys schools with 2,709[3] pupils the church was making a real contribution to Japan's need for trained leadership.

The early efforts of Dr. Berry and other medical men to aid in the modernization of Japanese medicine did not go unrecognized.[4] Today, Japan ranks with the other great nations of the world in the medical field.

The church had also become a pioneer in prison reform, education for the blind and the pioneering of modern nurses' training.

To measure, in any exact sense, the influence of Christianity in Japan in this period is obviously impossible but the story we have traced would indicate that its influence far exceeded the relation of its relatively small numbers to the forty millions of Japanese people.

We believe we have successfully answered the questions we set ourselves at the beginning of this chapter. We have traced the numeri-

---

[1] M. Sumiya *Kindai Nihon no Keisei to Kirisuto Kyo*, p. 93–94.
[2] O. Cary, *opus cited.* p. 209.
[3] *Ibid.* p. 209.
[4] M. Sumiya, *opus cited.* p. 92.

cal growth of the church. We have shown the influence and events in Japanese society which sometimes tended to encourage and sometimes to retard the growth of the church. Christians had been very influential in the struggle for representative government though they had not been successful in achieving their goal. The oligarchy had not only maintained but increased its strength as this period comes to a close. The Christian faith had indicated its "charismatic" nature in its ability to be determinative in the life of its followers in a period of persecution, namely, from 1881 until 1884. In other words, it had struck genuine roots within the country. We have also traced something of the relationship between the way in which Japanese Christians expressed their faith and sought to organize their churches in the context of the environment from which they had come and were still a part. We have been able to show the class orientation of the church and to explain, in some measure, the reasons why it should have been related to the middle class rather than to other classes in Japanese society. Finally, we have indicated something of its amazing influence achieved over so short a period of time.

As we enter the final period of the Meiji era the Meiji Constitution has been "given" as of February eleventh 1889 and the form of the new Japan has begun to emerge. More challenging days lay ahead for the church.

PART THREE

THE NEW NATION 1890-1911

CHAPTER SIX

THE STRUCTURE OF THE NEW NATION, ITS POLITICAL AND SOCIAL CONSEQUENCES

The promulgation of the Constitution which the Emperor "granted" to the people of Japan on February 11, 1889 and that of the Imperial Rescript on Education of October 30, 1890, were really two sides of the same coin. That coin was the consolidation in the socio-political-economic life of Japan of a highly centralized, authoritarian form of social organization based upon respect for the Emperor and the Confucian concept of filial piety. The ruling oligarchs were thereafter able to use both of these concepts, namely "respect for the Emepror" and that of "filial piety" or respect due to superiors, whether they be one's parents or one's Emperor, to further their aims. The oligarchs were traditionally convinced, along with Hamilton rather than with Jefferson, that the people as a whole could hardly know what was best for themselves or for Japan.

As we pointed out in Chapter III, the shape of things to come had already begun to emerge as early as 1879. After the death of Okubo in 1878 Ito and Okuma emerged as the two most powerful figures among the young "samurai" bureaucrats. Iwakura, however, who was the only figure of any note among the former ancient nobility who retained prominence in the Reform Movement, was definitely behind Ito for he feared the progressive ideas held by Okuma insofar as representative government was concerned.[1] Undoubtedly Iwakura expressed his concern to the Emperor over the "levelling ideas" abroad in the country. This was behind the Emperor's concern, after 1879, to strengthen traditional Confucian moral principles and to increase reverence for the Emperor Institution. Thus the Yogaku Koyo, the forerunner of the Imperial Rescript on Education, appeared in 1882.[2] From this point forward the emphasis in the educational system upon "moral" education became stronger and stronger. Up until 1880 the French educational system was followed by the govern-

---

[1] It will be recalled that Okuma had a close personal relationship with G. F. Verbeck, the early Dutch-American missionary who was a principal government adviser up until 1878.

[2] See Chapter III, p. 142.

ment. This gave way in 1880 to the American system based upon elected, local education boards. We recall that at this time it was the policy of those anxious to avoid strong representative government at the center to give some measure of it at the local and prefectural level in order to draw fire away from the idea of representative central government. However, in 1885 the whole department of education was reorganized along Prussian lines by the new Education Minister, Mori Arinori, and the American system was abolished.[1] After his return from Europe Ito Hirobumi in his commentary on the Constitution stated that though Christianity was the spiritual foundation of Western Civilization since Japan had no such strong religion commanding the allegiance of the whole people, the Emperor Institution was to be the basis upon which the new Japan was to be founded. It is for this reason that Hugh Borton calls the Imperial Rescript on Education, rather than the Constitution, the "nerve axis of the new order."[2]

Throughout the educational system the authoritarian, nationalistic note became increasingly strong. There was great stress on discipline and the cultivation of the virtues mentioned above. Teachers and students were encouraged to live together in dormitories and compulsory military drill was prescribed for all.

The Imperial Rescript on Education was the natural culmination of this whole movement.[3] It emphasized loyalty and filial piety, respect for the Constitution and readiness to answer any State emergency. It exalted the Throne as "coeval with heaven and earth."[4]

Meanwhile political events in relation to the outside world continued to strengthen the advocates of a strong nationalistic policy. We recall that Ito had determined to give the form, if not the essence, of western political structures to Japan after 1885. The western nations had made it clear that not until Japan had a modern legal and judicial system which made it possible for foreigners to reside safely anywhere in Japan, and a strict Commercial Code, which would guarantee rulings in favour even of foreign merchants, would the Trade Treaties with their provisions for extra-territoriality be revised.[5]

Thus, the whole movement to adopt western forms of government

---

[1] C. Yanaga, *opus cited.* p. 102.

[2] H. Borton, *opus cited.* p. 180.

[3] For a translation of the Imperial Rescript on Education see the Appendix.

[4] D. Brown, *opus cited.* pp. 103 ff. gives an impressive account of this development.

[5] C. Yanaga, *opus cited.* pp. 191–197.

was not only "pressured" from within by the liberal movements but was fostered from without as a result of the desire to remove the stigma of the unequal treaties.

The second motivation undoubtedly became stronger after 1887 since by this time the government had strengthened its position against the liberals. In that year the Peace Preservation Law was passed in an effort to stifle the opposition of over six hundred liberal leaders who were about to congregate in Tokyo to agitate peacefully for true representative government. By its ruling they were debarred from entering the city on pain of imprisonment. Thus was the Peoples' Rights Movement finally broken by a law which remained in force for over a decade and which was used from time to time whenever the authority of the bureaucrats was seriously threatened.[1]

Attempts to revise the Treaties failed repeatedly between 1865 and 1890 with the result that the hand of those who were for militarism and expansionism was strengthened. Expansionism was to prove to the western nations that Japan would take by force, if necessary, what she could not secure from them peacefully so long as she was regarded as a "second-rate" power. As Delmer Brown points out, it is from this time onward that the spirit of modern nationalism becomes a determinative force in the life of Japan.[2] Inoue Taoru had to resign in 1887 as Foreign Minister because public indignation at his unseccessful attempts to repeal the Treaties was so great. (There was an element that feared unrestricted residence of foreigners in Japan and which would have been against any revision suitable to the western nations). Okuma was then brought in in an attempt to succeed where Inoue had failed because it was thought that he would be looked upon with greater favour by the western powers in view of his progressive ideas. He was able to secure a temporary sharing of judicial powers over foreigners until such time as Japanese laws were completely modernized. But even this was so unacceptable to the people that a fanatic made an attempt upon the life of Okuma and he was forced to resign in October, 1889.

One of the important things for us to note here is that even the former liberals, who had been reorganized into one great coalition

---

[1] Kataoka Kenkichi, the lieutenant of Itagaki in the Liberal Party and a leading Presbyterian elder spent some time in prison during this period because he refused to obey and went on to Tokyo in 1887. He claimed he had a perfect right to do so since he was only interested in making a peaceful demonstration. He later became a Speaker of the House of Representatives.

[2] D. M. Brown, *opus cited.* p. 112.

known as the Daido Danketsu by Goto Shojiro, were opposed to the revision submitted by Okuma. Okuma's followers, who had formed a party known as the Kensei-honto, were alone loyal to him. This enables us to see that even those who were liberal in their ideas with regard to the organization of Japan internally were not necessarily so in their attitude to foreign powers. Itagaki, albeit reluctantly, had supported the attempt to deal forcefully with Korea in 1874 and his movement had always been strongly nationalistic. At this point the liberals were even less prepared to patiently negotiate the unequal treaties than were the oligarchs. We shall find that the leadership in the Christian Church was similarly affected by a deep nationalism. Undoubtedly it was this nationalistic sentiment which confused liberal leaders. Thus they were unable to oppose effectively the bureaucracy which, whenever its policies were threatened, was always ready to make an appeal to the Emperor and thus to the "spirit of nationalism."

A Privy Council was set up in 1888 in expectation of the promulgation of the Constitution. It is significant that its duties were to advise the Emperor as to the Constitutionality of laws and administrative actions. The doctrines of Judicial Review in accordance with British and American practice were not followed. Moreover, this council was subject to no one save the Emperor and its membership was dominated by the Satsuma-Choshu bureaucrats plus the militarists. This made it possible for both of these groups to resist any attempt to revise the constitution and to rule unconstitutional any laws which they did not approve even though they had been passed by the Diet.

So pervasive was the Prussian method of doing things that Dr. Albert Mosse, an expert on Bismarckian polity and the organization of local government in accord with it, was employed to prepare a draft for local municipal and town governments. Popular election was recognized only in principal. Three candidates for mayor were to be nominated by the people and one of them thereupon appointed by the Emperor. This continued to give the central Home Ministry strong control right down to the local level.

After the passing of the Peace Preservation Law of 1887 and the increasing control of the central government it became more and more impossible for those who peacefully advocated true representative government to make any headway. Thereafter reform movements tended to become more and more radical as they were driven underground.

In order for us to understand the political development of the next two decades it is essential that we have a clear understanding of the exact nature of the Meiji Constitution.[1] After a careful study of the Constitution, and of the period leading up to it, McLaren makes the following remark, "Beginning with the confusion characteristic of every transition stage, manifested in this case by the conflicting jurisdictions of the Imperial and feudal governments, it ended with a highly centralized organization, founded upon a divine-right theory of monarchy and operating through a bureaucracy."[2] Of it E. H. Norman says, "It was conceived in a spirit of benevolent autocracy and has remained as the inflexible instrument of absolutism."[3]

Outwardly the Constitution provided for what appeared to be a form of modern constitutional government. The Cabinet remained in charge of the administration. A House of Peers was established. It was made up of three groups, that is, Peers of the realm as appointed in 1885, representatives of the highest taxpayers in each prefecture, and those appointed by the Emperor for their outstanding services to the nation such as scholars, industrialists, and philanthropists. The Constitution also provided for a House of Representatives composed of three hundred members. In order to be eligible to vote one had to be a male, twenty-five years of age, and pay direct taxes amounting to 15 yen. This tax qualification meant that there were only 460,000 voters in a population of fifty millions. In other words, the voting privilege did not extend beyond the class of fairly well-to-do landlords and property holders. The peasants and the great new mass of wage-earners were completely left out. In 1900 the secret ballot was introduced and the tax qualification cut by one-third but, although this doubled the electorate, it still only represented 900,000 persons in a population nearing 60,000,000. It must be borne in mind, therefore, that the political parties formed after the promulgation of the Constitution were representing, not the country as the whole, but either business interests on the one hand, or the interests of the landed class on the other, since it was these groups which were responsible for their election.

---

[1] F. Brinkley, *opus cited.* A full translation of the Constitution can be found in the Appendix to this volume.

[2] W. W. McLaren, *A Political History of Japan during the Meiji Era*, (New York: Scribners, 1916), 380 pp. This is an excellent treatment of political factors during the period but it sometimes tends to oversimplify the complicated nature of historical developments.

[3] E. H. Norman, *opus cited.* p. 188.

The Privy Council retained the role given it by Ito in 1888. It will be recalled that it was responsible to the Emperor alone.

The Cabinet and its Ministers were also responsible to the Emperor rather than to the Houses. At first there was some confusion about this since Article 55 of the Constitution was so worded as to make it unclear as to which it was responsible. Ito soon made it clear, through his commentary, that the Cabinets were responsible to the Emperor alone.[1] This crippled the opposition hopelessly for no one dared attack a provision of the Constitution which rested upon the Imperial prerogative but which, at the same time, made responsible government an impossibility. In its frustration the Opposition often attacked the clan bureaucracy and even the Genro but it never attacked the Constitution, the revision of which could alone have effected any basic change in the status of the political parties. As a result the Executive branch of government remained free of any serious responsibility to the Administrative Houses. Though the House of Representatives could initiate legislation, according to the Constitution, this provision was nullified by the fact that the Privy Council could rule it out if it chose to and Ito was head of the Council. The small group under his direction who had prepared the Constitution had made certain that the political parties would prove little threat to the traditional Satsuma-Choshu clan government.

Even the provisions for civil liberties, including that granting religious freedom, were compromised by the fact that the Peace Preservation Law was still in effect and by what the government might deem as "public peace and order." McLaren says, "Generally speaking, all the provisions of this chapter are so stated as to avoid a categorical announcement of positive rights which appertain to the status of citizenship."[2] Failure to understand these weaknesses in the Constitution was to lead, time and again, to the defeat of forces in Japanese society aimed at true democratic equalitarianism and, on the part of the Christian community, at an effective social witness.

Another institution in Japanese government which is peculiarly Japanese, namely the *Genro*, must be understood to gain a full appreciation of the forces at work in the political scene for the remainder of this period. This institution was only semi-official. There was no legal provision for it but it nevertheless exerted great power. The *Genro*, or Council of Elder Statesmen, was made up of those men in the bureau-

[1] W. W. McLaren, *opus cited.* p. 192.

[2] *Ibid.* p. 194.

cracy who, during the Meiji period, had had great experience in government. Ito, Yamagata, Matsukata, Oyama and Inouye were among its members and all of them were from either Satsuma or Choshu. Both the Emperor and various cabinets from time to time called upon these men for their advice and they not infrequently interfered directly in political affairs.[1]

Even in the matter of finance the executive was not strictly responsible to the legislative branch. If the Diet could not be called, or had not dealt with a budget before dissolution, the Constitution stated that the government was to continue to function on the basis of the previous year's budget. Moreover, there were numerous fixed expenditures that did not require the consent of the Diet. Though it was possible for the Diet to obstruct Cabinet action through holding up a budget it could not bring the activities of a government to a halt.

Though the final Supplementary Rules appended to the Constitution provide for its revision, (in spite of the fact that the preamble speaks of its immutable laws), a two-thirds majority of both houses was required in order to do so, and since the House of Peers was at all times extremely conservative there was little chance that this might happen.

With the ability to dominate the Press and with the Emperor Institution to sanction its activities, the power of the ruling oligarchy could scarcely be threatened.

Even though the right to organize political parties was granted with the constitution, their old leaders Okuma and Itagaki could see from the outset that obstruction was the only policy they could follow since creative action had been frustrated by the provisions of the Constitution. It was possible for them to make their weight felt through refusing to pass the budgets presented by the Cabinet. This they proceeded to do.

The first Diet opened in July 1890. For the first year Yamagata Aritomo, the inveterate military leader from Choshu, was Minister President. He was unconditionally opposed by all the major parties—the Jiyuto, led by Itagaki, the Kaishinto led by Okuma, and the Daido Danketsu led by Goto. These parties attacked the budget but a compromise was reached before the house recessed. Prior to its next meeting in 1891, however, the Premiership was taken over by Matsukata Masayoshi.

---

[1] *Ibid.* pp. 176–7.

The Opposition did not appreciate the fact that the Premiership had regularly passed between Choshu and Satsuma leaders since 1885. Ito of Choshu was then followed by Matsukata of Satsuma. It was obvious to all that matters were entirely in the hands of the oligarchy despite the forms of representative government.

When the government convened, sweeping reductions in the budget were again recommended so that Matsukata secured the Emperor's assent to dissolve the House. In the election which followed, bribery and police force were used by the government in order to secure the election of members favourable to it. A great deal of life was lost and many were injured. The government failed to elect a majority, however, and Matsukata was so compromised by his action that he was forced to resign.

Ito again took over as Minister President. Yet the Opposition was as adamant as ever and slashed over Y8,000,000 from the recommended budget, cutting out completely the funds appropriated for building warships. Ito acted quickly. He resorted to a device which has never failed to be successful. He had the Emperor issue a rescript calling for the acceptance of the budget. No Opposition member dared to raise his voice in contravention of the Emperor's expressed will. The budget was passed. Ito could see, however, that he had strained matters to the breaking point so that he attempted to cut down the budget through various economies thus dulling the edge of the Opposition attack. He also arranged a compromise whereby he gained the cooperation of Itagaki and his party. This alienated both Okuma's Kaishinto and the Upper House, which hated all parties. The issue brought about the dissolution of the House.

Okuma's opposition was based not only on the defection of the Jiyuto and the matter of the irresponsibility of the government to the legislature but on the issue of Treaty Revision. The government had been quietly working at this question and was anxious to gain the popularity which would ensue as a result of successful revision. Indeed a promise for revision in 1899 was secured by the government in 1894. Okuma and all of the Opposition forces went to the country on a "strict enforcement" of the restrictions against the travel of foreigners inland in Japan as a means to force foreign governments to revision. The government could see that such a policy would simply disrupt their efforts which were aimed at ensuring security to foreigners.

The next diet lasted only seventeen days, when as a result of disorderly conduct, the Emperor dismissed it on June 2nd, 1894. Ito had engineered this since he could see no hope for the success of the system he had inaugurated and Japan was becoming discredited abroad. Before the next government could be convened the Sino-Japanese war had broken out and, since it absorbed the total concern of the people, the issue was postponed for the time being.

What happened when the government reconvened in October 1894 is extremely significant for the purposes of our study. Prior to the outbreak of the war the parties had determined to make a final fight for representative institutions. With the outbreak of the war all opposition ceased. McLaren says, "... in the brief session of the Diet convoked in October 1894 at Hiroshima, the war capital, each section of the Lower House vied with the others in enthusiastic loyalty to the Emperor and the government."[1] Just a moment before the great cry of the Opposition had been for economy. Now all sides were prepared to pass immense budgets for military necessities and expansion and also as gifts in recognition of military services. This was done without so much as a critical question, an abrogation of responsible government.

For some time the Opposition had clamoured for action on the foreign front. They were convinced that the agreements with China over Korea in 1885, granting equal rights to economic activity in Korea and including a non-intervention clause in Korean internal policies, were a sign of weakness. Shortly after these agreements had been reached other foreign powers made similar agreements with Korea which were detrimental to the interests of Japan. At that time, Ito was cautious concerning any involvement in foreign affairs which might threaten the power of Japan before she was strong enough to meet it successfully. Now all those pressing for foreign expansion were united in the war effort. The country closed ranks to bring the Sino-Japanese war to a successful conclusion. The spirit of nationalism was at its height and the period of expansionism had begun.

We need not go into any detailed account here of the causes of the Sino-Japanese war.[2] Suffice it to say that Japan had been given no encouragement by the example of the great Western powers to act in

---

[1] *Ibid.* p. 227.

[2] C. Yanaga, *opus cited.* Chapter 17 contains a detailed account of the events leading up to the conflict which appears to be factual and fair. Brinkley in his *History of the Japanese People* is completely biased in favour of the Japanese cause while McLaren in his *A Political History of Japan during the Meiji Era* gives the false impression that the war was a scheme of Ito's directed solely to considerations of Japan's internal political conditions.

any way other than she did. The actions of Britain and France in 1856 and 1857 in China, the Osaka event of 1865, and the Triple Intervention which occurred at the end of the Sino-Japanese war, were all to prove that Japan had entered a world of power politics in which military might appeared to be the decisive factor in a nation's destiny.

The actual occasion of the war was that Li, the representative of the Manchu Dynasty of China in Korea, in contravention of the agreement of 1885, had quite obviously interfered in the political affairs of Korea to the detriment of Japanese economic interests. Efforts were made to appease the situation but Li persisted and, counting on the internal political dissention in Japan, looked for an easy victory. Beyond this Japan was disquieted by the internal confusion in Korean political affairs. The inability of the monarchy in that country to bring about internal stability had for some time been the occasion of Japan's difficulties with China. This instability also held out a tempting situation to Russia to interfere as that country turned her attention more and more to Manchuria and to Korea. Japan felt that she could not stand by and see this territory taken over by powers which might not prove friendly to her. In any event, hostilities were entered upon and Japan with her small but well-trained and modern armed forces proved far superior to those of China. When the spring of 1895 arrived Japan had already defeated the Chinese forces and Ambassador Li, representing the Tsungli Yamen (the Peking government of the Manchu Dynasty), had been sent to Japan to negotiate a peace treaty. The Treaty of Shimonoseki was subsequently signed by China and Japan on April 17, 1895. By its terms China recognized the complete independence of Korea, ceded the Liaotung Peninsula, the island of Formosa, and the Pescadores, paid an indemnity of 200 million taels of silver, and opened the four cities of Shashi, Chungking, Suchow, and Hangchow to Japan for commercial and industrial purposes.

The worst suspicions of Japan concerning Russian intent were shortly to be confirmed. Less than a week after the Treaty of Shimonoseki had been signed Russia, France and Germany intervened, ostensibly on behalf of China, to insist that the ceding of the Liaotung Peninsula would make the independence of Korea meaningless and would disturb the peace of the Far East. What Russia was concerned for, however, was her own need for an ice-free port and her own plans for expansion in that area.[1] Japan was forced to accept the

[1] *Ibid.* p. 252.

"advice" in view of the fact that the war had exhausted her military and financial resources. In any case she would have been no match for the three major intervening powers. France and Russia had earlier concluded a Dual Alliance which allowed Russia to pursue her interests in the Far East without interference from Germany on her western borders. Germany was interested in expanding her interests in China so that she was prepared to take part in the intervention but England, concerned for the intent of Russia and of Germany and anxious to secure a friend in the Far East, was unwilling to take part. She was, before long, to conclude an alliance with Japan in an effort to protect her Indian and Chinese interests over against Russia. Yanaga has this to say concerning the significance of the Triple Intervention,

> The Triple Intervention was a bitter pill for the Japanese to swallow. It has been referred to as one of the most tragic chapters in the history of modern Japan. In the face of overwhelming odds there was nothing else to do but to yield. The people did not allow themselves or the government to forget the national humiliation for the next ten years, during which the whole country worked and lived for one consuming passion—namely, to even the score at an opportune moment. The intervention demonstrated to the Japanese that the course of their own national development could no longer be planned and followed independently of and unaffected by external factors and developments on the international scene. That Japan was being drawn inexorably into the vortex of European power politics had become unmistakably clear.[1]

Of course, Japan might have avoided the problem altogether by following what had become the acceptable method among western powers in exploiting China, that of carving out "spheres of influence" which the other powers recognized as invoilable and which the Chinese government had no alternative but to accept. Had she used this method with regard to the Liaotung Peninsula the western powers would have been in a more difficult position to object. Actually, in concert with Britain and, for a while with Russia, this did become the method of expansion on the Asiatic continent which she adopted. In summing up the affect of the Sino-Japanese War on Japan, D. M. Brown concludes, "In a real sense, then, the Sino-Japanese War was a product of the force of modern nationalism in Japan as well as a powerful stimulus for a further growth of the phenomenon."[2]

While the war itself had been a blow to the development of responsible government in Japan, since little critical responsibility was

[1] *Ibid.* p. 252.
[2] D. M. Brown, *opus cited.* p. 129 ff.

shown by any of the parties throughout it, the war had one consequence which was fatal to its future development. As a result of Japan securing Formosa, a Colonial Department had to be set up in the Administration and a Cabinet Member appointed to head it. Yamagata, who was then president of the Privy Council and had headed the armed forces in the war, arranged that the Governor-General of Formosa should be a high officer of the Army or the Navy and managed to add to the list of appointments to office a proviso that the Cabinet Members representing the Army and Navy should be high officers of the same.[1] With the spirit of nationalism and militarism at a high pitch in the nation this action went almost unnoticed and completely unchallenged.

Its result was two-fold. In the first place it meant that, in the future, the clan bureaucrats could give the parties considerable representation within the legislature without losing their own control over the Administration since all the high offices in the Army and Navy were held by the clansmen and they could henceforth wreck any Cabinet by simply resigning. The Cabinet could not reassemble without a Minister of the Army and of the Navy and these had to be appointed from the forces which, as we have said, were under the control of Satsuma and Choshu. In the second place it gave the military the upper hand over civil control. In actual fact this meant a victory for Yamagata over Ito for the former had traditionally stood for militarism and expansionism while the latter had sought to expand the power of Japan economically and politically on as peaceful and rational a basis as possible. He had avoided all foreign entanglements up until the Sino-Japanese war. From this point onward Ito found himself worsted again and again by Yamagata. Ito had to resign following the war since the acceptance of the "advice" of the western powers had proven so unpopular within the nation. Thus Yamagata's faction was further strengthened.

To what extent the government was controlled by the continuing power of the clansmen can be seen from a simple account of the Minister-Presidents who held power for the remainder of the period. Matsukata formed his second Cabinet in 1896 with Okuma as his Foreign Minister. The latter's reputation as a result of his strong foreign policy had made him extremely popular. Okuma soon resigned since it had been his consistent policy to stand for representative

---

[1] W. W. McLaren, *opus cited.* pp. 234–5.

government and he found no support within the Cabinet. This brought continued obstruction from the parties and the final collapse of Matsukata but not before he had corrupted a great many party men into cooperation with him through bribery. Matsukata had done the same thing during his first Ministry in 1891. Throughout the period, the military faction in particular, was ready to hold out money offers to party men who would support their policies. Since so many ministries fell and elections were frequent the only way the politicians could regain the expense of securing office was either in outright gifts from their supporters in return for which they would seek favours for them or through being willing to pledge support of the government in return for a price.

In any event Ito followed Matsukata and made a last attempt to form a Cabinet without the support of any of the parties. He knew, however, that he would fail and he was anxious to prove his point that the time had come when the bureaucracy had to cooperate with a party if a government was to succeed. This was, of course, more true for Ito than for Yamagata because the latter could rely more heavily on the arrangements he had made for the support of the Ministries of the Army and Navy. Ito soon failed and amazingly enough requested the Emperor to appoint Itagaki and Okuma to office since they had united their forces under the party name Kenseito (Constitutionalists) in order to oppose the oligarchy.

The Okuma-Itagaki coalition fell apart within six months, and this left a clear field for the military to reassert itself under another Cabinet headed by Yamagata. Yamagata found an ally in one Hoshi Toru who had taken over the leadership of the Kenseito and who was a notorious "spoils" man. In return for financial arrangements whereby Hoshi would gain certain concessions for the business interests he represented he supported Yamagata's budget which provided among other things for the expansion of the military. This was 1898.

Ito once again entered the fray and himself became leader of the Rikken Seiyukai a political party made up of the majority of the Kenseito and especially that part of it which had formally been the Liberal Party headed by Itagaki. As Norman points out,[1] the party which at one time had counted Ito its greatest enemy was now headed by him and on his terms. It had long since given up the struggle for liberalism and reform and had become the representative of the

[1] E. H. Norman, *opus cited.* p. 193.

wealthy rural landlords. Albeit it did stand on the side of civilian rather than military control. The Kensei-honto (Real Constitutionalists) under Okuma continued to stand in Opposition and to struggle for representative government. At this time Saionji, who was to become Ito's successor as head of the Seiyukai and who was a member of the old feudal aristocracy attached to the Emperor as Iwakura had been, was made President of the Privy Council and the Christian Kataoka was made Speaker of the Lower House, which he remained for a number of sessions. Ito's methods were not acceptable to the party men. He could not rely either on them or on the people and yet he was in a minority among the Elder Statesmen, that is, the Genro, who had become the Emperor's principal advisors and were dominated by Yamagata.

Katsura Taro, the protege of Yamagata became the next Premier Minister-President and remained in power until the close of the Russo-Japanese War in 1905. Whenever he was unable to pass a budget he dissolved the house and as a result the party politicians lost out financially. Thus he was able to break the opposition of all save the most recalcitrant. Katsura was discredited by the terms secured as a result of the Russo-Japanese War which made it impossible for Japan to secure any indemnity from Russia.

Saionji became Premier in 1906 but only with the cooperation of the bureaucrats who were ready to go along with his party so long as their own purposes were served. They were able to wreck his work when they chose through the Army and Navy Ministers. This they did in 1908. Although Saionji was re-elected by the people the Elder Statesmen had Katsura made Premier by the Emperor. They knew that the people had no liking for Saionji since his party secured a great deal of their support through bribery of the electorate and represented only the rural landlord class. Katsura remained in power until 1911 when he turned over the government to Saionji whose regime lasted until the close of 1912.

We have gone into this somewhat detailed yet superficial account of the political developments within the country in order to illustrate the extent to which power remained in the hands of the small coterie of oligarchs and failed to reach down to the people. Actually it was impossible for the political parties under the Constitution, and especially with the special provision for the Ministers of War and the Navy in the Cabinet, to achieve representative government. Their frustration led to their demoralization while, at the same time, the military were able to dominate the policy of the country during a period of external expansion. In any case, the Seiyukai could hardly lay a claim to representation of any save the rural landlords while the Kenseito and Okuma's party (which eventually was named the Kokuminto) broadly speaking represented the merchants, the manufacturers and the higher salaried class, who alone could vote since they met the property qualifications. These were reduced at the turn of the century yet left the electorate at less than a million in a population fifty five times as great.[1]

Before we turn from internal politics during this period we ought to say a word concerning that small group which continued to struggle for what they believed was a more democratic Japan. Oi Kentaro and his "Soshi" were mainly malcontents who were ready to use any measures whatever in order to overthrow the bureaucracy. The great majority of the reformers, though sometimes driven to extremes by the repressive measures of the government, were, on the whole, ready to obey the law when they could conscientiously do so. It is not surprising that we find a number of Christians such as Abe Isoo, Katayama Sen and Tokutomi Soho among the leaders in this early Labour and Socialist movement. Unfortunately, their desire for reform and the price they had to pay for it eventually led them away from the church for reasons with which we shall deal in Chapter VIII.

Because of the Peace Preservation Law and other restrictive measures employed by the government after 1888 the reformers turned to literature and the arts to express their ideas which were relatively new in Europe let alone in Japan. Periodicals like "The Nation's Friend," founded by Tokutomi had the express purpose of "helping the country toward political and economic democracy through political liberty, economic equality, and Christian morality."[2]

The social Democratic Movement was launched in March 1901. Its founders included Katayama Sen, Kawakami Kiyoshi, and Abe Isoo. It advocated a strong peace policy, the abolition of class, the public ownership of both land and capital, the state ownership of communications, the equitable distribution of wealth, free education, and the equality of political rights.[3] However, the Home Minister ordered its

---

[1] For a more detailed account of the political struggles and intrigues of the period see W. W. McLaren, *opus cited.* Part II, and U. Iwasaki, *opus cited.* Chapter 7.

[2] C. Yanaga, *opus cited.* p. 230.

[3] For an excellent discussion of this movement see Takenaka, Masao, *Relation of Protestantism to Social Problems in Japan* 1901–1941 (Yale University: Unpublished Doctoral Thesis, 1954).

dissolution within three hours of its formation! This event enables us to see a common phenomenon in Japanese political life. The great majority of Japanese are traditionalists and conformists. The government can count on this. Those who do advocate change are therefore most exceptional, their numbers are few and the government can easily resort to stern measures against them. All of this leads such reformers to extremes so that they advocate grandiose policies which have little chance of realization rather than to adopting a strategy of progressive advance, a step at a time.

Interest in Labour problems began with an Association for the Study of Social Problems in 1890 just as the factory system began its development. Katayama Sen and Rev. Charles Garst, a Unitarian missionary, were active in this movement. By 1897 the former had helped to organize the first official labour union in the country known as the Workmen's Society. Its numbers had grown to 5,400 by the turn of the century. This, in spite of the fact that during the depression of 1897, following the Sino-Japanese War and the consequent inflation, the government, using police methods, had done its best to suppress the movement.[1]

Through the newspaper the Yorozu Choho, Uchimura Kanzo, from the Christian point of view, and Kotoku and Sakai, from a Socialist point of view, expressed strong opposition to the Russo-Japanese War and the whole expansionist program of the militarists. This was the only real opposition to the government within the nation. These men were opposed to the whole concept of power politics as a threat to the peace of mankind. Their opposition continued throughout the war though they were forced to resign from the periodical mentioned above and the Heiminsha (Commoners' News) which they later established was suppressed by the government in January 1905.

The conditions in the mines of Japan were extremely bad.[2] As a result two strikes in which a great deal of violence occurred took place in 1907. One of these was at the Ashio copper mines and the other at the Beshhi Copper mines. The authorities and the press in general blamed the Socialists for the violence. Thereafter the Socialists themselves were divided over the methods they should use whether those of direct or parliamentary action, or a combination of the two. So great became the dispute between Kotoku, Tazoe, and Sakai, repre-

[1] C. Yanaga, *opus cited.* p. 233.
[2] *Ibid.* p. 240.

senting respectively the three different positions, that the interests of the labourers and the peasant groups, whom they were supposed to serve, were completely lost sight of. During 1907 the government banned ten books on Socialism and Kotoku as well as Sakai and a number of their followers were arrested after a demonstration known as the "red Flag Incident." The press supported the government which thus emboldened arrested one after another of the Socialists and kept a strict account of them whenever they were freed. Kotoku and his anarchist followers were involved in a plot to assassinate the Emperor in 1910. This came as such a shock to the Japanese people that the Socialist movement was doomed. Even more moderate men such as Katayama Sen had to flee to the United States to seek refuge from the government. For some years both the Labour and the Socialist movements were unable to make any progress as a result of the extremism of some of its following and the suppression so easily resorted to by the government.

Since this was a period of economic and political expansion in many ways what happened in the external relations of Japan during the period is even more important than her internal political development which, as we have seen, was more retrogressive than progressive. Let us turn then to two major factors in the relations of Japan with other nations, namely, the events leading up to and including the Russo-Japanese War of 1904–5 and the final revision of the unequal treaties.

Within a year of the conclusion of the Sino-Japanese War, Russia had renewed her interests in Korea and through the Li-Lobanov Treaty of 1896 Russia gained privileges both within the Chinese economy and within Manchuria. Russia was determined, if possible, not to allow the Japanese to become the protectors of Korea. Thus when Yamagata and Lobanov signed a Protocol in 1896 guaranteeing the independence of Korea the Russians to all practical purposes ignored it in view of the fact that they were still in search of their ice-free port. By 1898 they had gained that objective through the leasing of the Liaotung Peninsula from China, the prize formerly sought by Japan at the conclusion of the Sino-Japanese War. Russia was now free to turn her interest to the development of the Manchurian Railroad and to other interests in Manchuria. Pressure from Russia was for the time being released on Korea though she was exposed to Russia on her northern boundary.

In March 1900, since the United States and England, were concerned over the rivalry between Russia and Japan vis-a-vis their interest in

Korea and China, Secretary Hay announced his "Open Door" policy which was to maintain the "spheres of influence" in China while recognizing the latter's political autonomy. Japan agreed to this but Russia did not.

Just at this time the Boxer Rebellion broke out. This was an attempt of forces in China to wrest the control of their country from foreigners and a protest against the inept Manchu dynasty which did nothing to stop the massacre of a number of foreign missionaries and merchants. Japan was asked to step in since the United States and Britain, indeed none of the other European powers, could place sufficient forces on the spot to quell the uprising. Japan did so and displayed such military proficiency in the process that all of the western powers were impressed. Clearly a new power to be reckoned with had arisen in the Pacific. England was quickest to see this and hastened to conclude an Alliance with Japan in 1902 which not only greatly enhanced the prestige of the latter but secured an ally for England against Russia. It also meant that Japan could not enter a struggle with Russia without the fear of intervention from a third power.

Meanwhile, Russia had used her troops to quell the Boxer uprisings in Manchuria but contrary to agreements among the powers, and unlike Japan, she did not withdraw her troops. Japan felt they posed a direct threat to her interests in Korea. She made various attempts to negotiate with Russia but the latter ignored her. As a result Japan broke off diplomatic relations with Russia on February 6, 1904. Russian forces then crossed the Yalu River into Korea and Japan considered this an act of war.

We need not go into the details of the war. Japan worsted Russia on both land and sea. She was enabled to do this with funds borrowed from New York and London since both the United States and England were sympathetic to the Japanese cause. By the summer of 1904 Russia was sending out peace feelers but the Japanse were not yet sure of their position so that it was not until she had inflicted further humiliating blows upon Russia that in the summer of 1905 she accepted the good offices of President Roosevelt to intercede between the belligerents. Russia was in trouble at home with a revolution on her hands and, though not completely defeated, she saw little hope of possible victory. Japan, on the other hand, was exhausted financially and her military resources were in danger of exhaustion. It was therefore in her interest to negotiate. She did not feel in a position to insist too strongly on all the terms of peace in spite of her victories because her government knew, though her people did not, just how close the nation was to bankruptcy. For this reason Japan did not insist upon the indemnity she sought from Russia because to do so might have prolonged the war. The people of Japan did not understand this since it had been the announced policy of the government to secure such an indemnity. Failure to do so led the people to believe that Japan once again had been "sold out" by the western powers and thus the Katsura government fell in spite of the successful prosecution of the war.

Nevertheless Japan secured a great deal from the Treaty of Portsmouth which concluded the war. These terms included:

1. Recognition of Japan's paramount political, military, and economic interests in Korea.
2. Transfer to Japan of the rights enjoyed by Russia in the Liaotung Peninsula.
3. Ceding to Japan of the sourthern half of Sakhalin.
4. Ceding of the southern half of the Manchurian railway.
5. Withdrawal by Russia and Japan of troops from Manchuria save for railway guards which were to be maintained.
6. Noninterference by Russia and Japan in any measures which China might take for the development of Manchuria.
7. Exploitation of railways purely for commercial, and not strategic purposes except in the Liaotung peninsula.

The Russo-Japanese War greatly increased the military prestige of Japan throughout the world and the whole cause of militarism and expansionism at home. Following the war the Japanese militarists set out to build a still greater army and navy. This was done in spite of the economic needs of the nation.

As a result of the Russo-Japanese War, Japan now had a free hand in Korea. Shortly after the war Ito was sent to Korea as Resident-General and until 1909, when he was assassinated by a Korean fanatic, he sought to modernize the country and to give her an ordered economic and political life. The Koreans resented being "made over" and resisted many of the reforms which Ito sought to institute. Japan was reluctant to annex Korea outright since she was afraid of world opinion which had begun to suspect her strength and her military tendencies. The Japanese government under Katsura used the occasion of Ito's assassination to send Terauchi, the Minister of War, as the new resident-general but with the intent of annexing the country which she did on August 22nd, 1910. Japan had finally secured a firm foothold on Asian soil and the temptation to expand further was thereby increased.

The Anglo-Japanese Alliance which was first entered upon in 1902 and then further strengthened in 1905 was renegotiated with less enthusiasm in 1911. This was owing, not only to suspicion of the growing military power of Japan, but to the fact that in the revision of tariffs on the basis of equality in that year Japan had shown little concern for British economic interests. However, England overlooked these factors in view of the fact that she needed Japanese friendship over against Germany.

Only one matter, of greatest importance so far as Japan's international relations were concerned in this period, remains for our consideration and that is the revision of the unequal treaties. Actually the Japanese government had reached an agreement for their revision with Britain prior to the outbreak of the Sino-Japanese War. The result of that war convinced Britain that she had done the right thing and brought the other western nations to the place where they felt it would pay to follow suit. By the terms of the negotiations with Britain all extra-territoriality rights were to be given up in Japan by 1899. The five year period was to give the Japanese government more time to bring her judicial and commercial codes fully into line with those existing in the west. However, as a result of her willingness to give up extra-territorial rights the Japanese government conceded to Britain a continuing low tariff, ranging from five per cent especially on the goods which Britain exported in quantity to Japan such as cottons, woolens, iron, steel and machinery. The upshot of this was that other nations claimed the same rights under most-favoured-nation clauses. Japan had agreed that she would not revise these tariff schedules until 1911. By that time these had become as unpopular with the Japanese people as the full unequal treaties had been. Japan gained full tariff autonomy by the Treaty of Commerce and Navigation of 1911 thereby finally erasing what she had considered a humiliating mark of inferiority and discrimination which had been with her for almost forty years. She had secured through economic and military prowess what had not been granted to her otherwise. She had "arrived" as a power among powers in the world of that day.

A summary of the two decades between 1890 and 1911, then, reveals that though Japan had adopted the forms of western representative government she actually had fastened upon her a system of state absolutism. This was reflected in both the Constitution and the Imperial

Rescript on Education. The struggle between government and the political parties for popular, responsible government ended in defeat for the political parties which, by the very nature of the Constitution, were able to be little more than obstructionist. The Sino-and Russo-Japanese wars encouraged those who were for militarism and expansionism. Though government in general was still largely guided by the Satsuma-Choshu clique the essential struggle in government circles changed from that between the clans to one between Ito and Yamagata, the former representing a predominantly civil interest and the latter a definitely military one. Radical reform groups were easily suppressed in view of the overwhelming power of the state. While revision of the unequal treaties gave Japan a sense of acceptance among the great powers, the fact that they came so late and only after Japan had proven herself from a military standpoint encouraged both militarism and a growing nationalism.

CHAPTER SEVEN

THE DEVELOPING ECONOMY

We are concerned in this chapter, as we were in Chapter IV, not so much with economic facts and phenomena in themselves as we are with the effect which they had upon the changing social structure of the Japanese nation. We are, for example, concerned with such questions as the following:

1. What was the net increase in the national product and how did this increase affect the life and customs of the people?
2. In what way was increased income distributed and how did it influence class structure in this period?
3. How did the developing economy affect population growth and movement?
4. What was the relationship between the technological needs of the new economy and the consequent changes in class structure?
5. What was the relationship between public and private ownership of the means of production and how did these affect the class and power structure within the country?
6. How was this reflected in the tax system?
7. What attempt was made to deal with the social problems created by the new economy?
8. What was the relationship between Japan's growing international trade and her relations with the peoples of other nations, especially with those who lived within her own borders?

We are interested in each of these questions relating to the Japanese economy because we are convinced that they have some real bearing upon the development of Christianity within Japan during our period.

The two decades from 1890 to 1911 were ones of amazing economic as well as military expansion. Even McLaren, whose interest was overwhelmingly political, admits this when he says, "During the first decade of the parliamentary regime the interest in constitutional progress had flagged, and the struggle for commercial development and military expansion absorbed all attention."[1] And the following

[1] W. W. McLaren, *opus cited.* p. 277.

quotation from Lockwood indicates the nature of the period into which we are moving,

> The decade of the 1890s marked a turning point in the evolution of the Japanese economy. The assimilation of machine technology, the accumulation of banking and industrial capital, the expansive influences of world prosperity and rising prices—all facilitated a rapid rise of industrial output. Two victorious wars at an interval of a decade, gave additional impetus to the development of transport, banking and strategic industries, under the leadership of the state and the nascent zaibatsu. By 1914 Japanese industrial capitalism was still weak in comparison with the advanced economies of the west. But it had now emerged from its formative stage.
> The basic patterns were established which were to characterize it for the next quarter century.[1]

We have indicated that with the stabilization of her currency by 1885 a period of economic prosperity set in for Japan which, save for two brief recessions in the after math of the booms which followed the Sino- and the Russo-Japanese wars, lasted throughout the whole period.

The amazing growth of the economy can be marked all along the line. By the end of the period farmers were spending $ 80,000,000 on fertilizers alone and until the turn of the century the improvement in agricultural methods was able to support the growing population. Japan's merchant marine which in 1871 had consisted of 46 ships aggregating 17,948 tons by 1910 had grown to include 6,436 ships aggregating 1,564,443 tons. Whereas a good sized factory had scarcely existed at the time of the Restoration by 1912 there were 11,000 such employing 700,000 operatives. Joint stock companies which had not previously existed now numbered 9,000.[2] Imports and exports each increased eight times between 1880 and 1913 which was at twice the rate of international trade in general.[3] "Total production and real income" says Lockwood, "may have increased 80 to 100 per cent between 1890 and 1914."[4] While there may have been a modest improvement in general well-being the increasing national product and expanding home market was largely absorbed in new industrial plant and military expansion.[5]

---

[1] W. W. Lockwood, *opus cited.* p. 18.
[2] F. Brinkley, *opus cited.* pp. 694–5.
[3] W. W. Lockwood, *opus cited.* p. 312.
[4] *Ibid.* p. 20.
[5] *Ibid.* p. 88–9.

We have indicated above that a great deal of this was also absorbed by a growing population. E. H. Norman contends that since the Japanese population was taxed so heavily to provide the new industrial plant there was no home market to absorb the new production, therefore, Japan had to search for foreign markets or perish and this was one of the forces motivating her military as well as economic expansion.[1] W. W. Lockwood claims that this is far too facile an account of things and is able to substantiate his argument with statistical material which shows that the Japanese home market continued to fabsorb a larger share of the net product than did the foreign though the latter was a major consideration.[2] Population growth accounted for by far the greatest amount of this consumption but it also went to support a small though growing middle class of technicians and salaried officials. The home and foreign markets grew together.

Both the Sino-Japanese and the Russo-Japanese War had an expansive influence on the economy and this in turn stimulated militarism.[3] For example, as a result of the Sino-Japanese War and the indemnity received from China, Japan was able to go on the gold standard.[4] This made it possible for her to borrow much more easily in foreign capitals and she in turn used these borrowings, to a very large extent, for military equipment. The Japanese merchant marine doubled in the two years following the Sino-Japanese War and countless new banks as well as small industries were established.[5] As a result of the Russo-Japanese War, Japan was able to establish her economic hegemony in Korea and to expand it in South Manchuria. This in turn stimulated the establishment of new financial and industrial plants and increased technological development.[6]

At the same time, this type of expansion increased government expenditure enormously. It tripled from 1893–1903 to reach Y 289,000,000. By 1909 it had doubled again to Y 600,000,000. To finance this expenditure the tax burden fell most heavily on the peasants who really paid the land tax rather than the landlords and to some extent upon the merchants and the industrialists though a very large part of it came through new taxes on consumption which, of course, both the rural and the city populations paid. The farmers in Japan have to sell

[1] E. H. Norman, *opus cited.* p. 165–6.
[2] W. W. Lockwood, *opus cited.* p. 307 ff.
[3] C. Yanaga, *opus cited.* p. 314.
[4] W. W. Lockwood, *opus cited.* p. 19.
[5] *Ibid.* p. 19 and p. 35.
[6] *Ibid.* p. 20.

almost their whole produce in order to realize a necessary cash income to buy fertilizer etc.[1]

Before we move on to a consideration of the questions we have posed one further great change in the nature of the Japanese economy ought to be noted. We have already pointed out that the Japanese bureaucrats were anxious to build the new industry, insofar as possible, upon Japanese rather than imported capital. Until 1895 they succeeded remarkably well in doing so for at that time the national debt stood at only Y 30,000,000. Between 1895 and 1913, however, it leaped to Y 1,600,000,000. Japan was in danger of financial bankruptcy but World War I, in which she scarcely had to participate as a belligerent but which gave her an opportunity to sell widely, made it possible for her to re-establish herself.[2] Thus Japan passed from a state of relative national independence to a profound dependence upon the international economy. In every respect she had entered the international scene.

Let us turn now to answer specifically the questions we have set ourselves in this chapter.

In the first place, "What was the net increase in the national product and how did this increase affect the life and customs of the Japanese people?"

All the evidence suggests that there was a net increase of 100 per cent in the national product in the period we are considering. The following figures give a conservative estimate.

	Net National Product
1883–1887	Y 2,854,000,000
1908–1912	5,593,000,000[3]

It is estimated that not only the production of food and of industry in this period doubled but that this also happened all along the line in the area of primary production as well.[4] This very great increase in production also indicates an increase of at least 50 per cent in the output per gainfully employed person.[5] That increase is accounted for in the main by technical improvements and methods of all kinds.[6] Lockwood says,

[1] *Ibid.* p. 35.
[2] *Ibid.* p. 36.
[3] *Ibid.* p. 135.
[4] *Ibid.* p. 88–9.
[5] *Ibid.* p. 168.
[6] *Ibid.* p. 169.

> Behind these curves of expansion lies a complex interaction of forces: the growth of population in urbanized, industrial employment; the extension of markets enlarging the circuits of exchange both at home and abroad; the accumulation of capital in new and diversified forms of plant, inventories and equipment; the introduction of new technological skills and modes of business organization.[1]

A very small fraction, indeed, of this increase in production went into raising the standard of living for the great mass of Japanese people. This standard, even by the beginning of World War II was below "the minimum requirements of health, comfort, and security, even by Japanese standards."[2] The conclusion is that for the great masses of the people their living and spending habits remained unchanged right up until World War II.[3] This accounts for the fact that while a great modern industrial and financial plant has arisen in Japan life as lived by the average Japanese has not greatly changed so far as the way in which he satisfies the basic needs of his life is concerned.

If the net national product did not accrue to the benefit of the average Japanese where did it go? The answer is, of course, that in the main, it provided the major share of the savings and tax revenues which laid the foundations of industrial and military expansion during the Meiji period.[4] And here we have to note the fact that conspicuous consumption is not, on the whole, a characteristic of the Japanese middle and upper-middle classes. Many of those who became industrial leaders, as we have already suggested, were *samurai* or sons of the *samurai*, and were inspired by the code of *bushido* which enjoined a discipline of the outward life. Japanese taste in art also enjoins economy of word and action especially in poetry, drama, and the visual arts. Saving came naturally to such people and they invested what they earned. The joint-stock company, with its sharing of risk, also came naturally to a people in the habit of working collectively rather than individually. Within this class at least traditionalism served the purposes of capital accumulation much as the Protestant ethic did in western capitalism.

We turn to answer our second question, "In what way was increased income distributed and how did it affect the class structure of the nation?"

As we have already seen, a great proportion of the increase in

[1] *Ibid.* p. 119.
[2] *Ibid.* p. 148.
[3] *Ibid.* p. 420.
[4] *Ibid.* p. 88–9.

income as a result of the enlarged net national product was absorbed in greater government expenditure for the expansion of heavy industry, for expansion of the merchant marine, and for outright military expenditure. Government expenditure equalled one-ninth of the value of the net national product at the end of our period and 40 to 50 per cent of that expenditure was for military purposes.[1] While, on the positive side, this expenditure was a stimulus to employment and technical progress on the whole it diverted attention away from advance in industries not related to the military and, in a marginal economy, took enormous sums from educational and welfare projects. These would have increased the efficiency of the economy through further technical advance and a decrease in employee absenteeism.[2] Moreover, if the tax burden had been lower, increased savings might have gone into industrial and manufacturing plants which would have expanded the economy even more rapidly than was the case.

What increase in income did reach the people did not fundamentally change the class structure of the nation. The following quotation fully illustrates our point,

> In approximate terms we find that over half of Japan's 12.6 million households received incomes below 400 yen in 1930. These incomes accounted for about a quarter of aggregate household income. The second quarter went to 28 per cent of the families in the 400–800 yen range. The remaining half accrued to the most prosperous 16 per cent of the nation. Over 10 per cent was actually appropriated by the 0.2 per cent, of the people at the apex of the pyramid. The great mass of the population, therefore, was below the 1,000 yen level, while some 1,739 families enjoyed incomes of 50,000 yen or more. The true income distribution was probably even more concentrated than these figures indicate. For this household distribution does not include corporate savings, which accrued mainly to the well-to-do class. Probably, too, incomes in the upper brackets are understated.[3]

The chief cause of this inequality was the size and concentration of property incomes relative to incomes from labour.[4] During the thirties, (close statistics are not available for Japan during our period) whereas Britain and the United States used 40–44 per cent of the cost of production for wages, Japan used only 27 per cent, and Germany, the economic structure of which Japan most closely resembled, only 32

[1] *Ibid.* p. 35–7, p. 292, p. 577.
[2] *Ibid.* p. 35–7, p. 292, p. 577.
[3] *Ibid.* p. 273.
[4] *Ibid.* p. 274.

per cent.[1] At the lowest level of the middle class, that is to say, among the majority of the families with incomes from 400–800 yen there was no excess of income over expenditure.[2]

The over-all picture then is that little change in the class structure of the nation was brought about during our period, or even up until World War II, by the change in the Japanese economy and the increase in net product which resulted. As in feudal times there was an excessively wealthy but tiny minority at the top of the pyramid. Below them was another 16 per cent of the nation represented, as we shall see, by small entrepreneurs and landlords. This strata can be said to have enjoyed a decent standard of living. The landlords held land upon which the peasant paid taxes largely in kind, while they paid in cash. The tax burden fell back upon the peasant, however. The other half of the aggregate income was shared by some 2,000,000 persons in the labour force and the peasants who, economically speaking, must be considered the lower class.

Save for a change, to some degree, in the personnel at the top of the pyramid the structure remained much as it had in feudal times. The families at the very top were *zaibatsu* who had been either great merchants in feudal times, such as the Mitsui, or successful *samurai*, such as Iwasaki, who headed the Mitsubishi interests. Says Lockwood, "Thus the inequalities of wealth and power which characterized the ancient feudal system, with its territorial magnates, were now superseded by corresponding inequalities in the new regime of private property and corporate business enterprise.[3]

In 1930 there were 30,000,000 gainfully occupied persons in Japan. Half of these were in farming and fishing. Of this total force 32.2 per cent were classed as entrepreneurs; 3.7 per cent as large and 28.5 per cent as small entrepreneurs. Among the latter are all those who owned their own land as farmers and countless landlords who also carried on small business establishments either linked to larger industrial plants or supplying needs locally, such as bean paste and fertilizer. Among the remaining 67.8 per cent of gainfully occupied persons who were classed as employed workers, 2.7 per cent were of the managerial

[1] *Ibid.* p. 276.

[2] *Ibid.* p. 423.

[3] *Ibid.* p. 279. From page 272 ff. Lockwood gives a detailed statistical base for the conclusions which I have reached above which are also supported by E. H. Norman in his *Japan's Emergence as a Modern State*, *opus cited.*, but with much less detailed support.

group.[1] This included corporation officials down to department heads, all technicians, engineers, doctors, dentists, teachers, priests, and other professionals requiring a higher school education or better. The remaining 65.1 per cent were peasants, members of farm families who spent part of their time working on the land and part in industry and who made up a great pool of cheap labour. It also included members of the armed forces who were only .8 per cent of the population. Thus when we speak of the middle class we certainly cannot consider them to have comprised 34.9 per cent of the population though the strict Weberian, economic, definition of class would force us to that conclusion. This is so because a great many of those who were small entrepreneurs were those who either had small businesses which just made ends meet or were small landowners who lived scarcely above the subsistence level. It would be closer to reality to consider the 16 per cent of the nation which lived on half the national income as comprised of the lower-middle through the upper-upper classes and all others as forming the lower classes.

Even though the class structure of the country was not greatly changed by the economic revolution which took place as Japan became a modern industrial nation, obviously its social structure could not remain unchanged.

Our third question is, "How did the economic revolution affect population growth and movement within the nation?"

Between 1894 and 1914 there was a 25 per cent increase in the population. During the Tokugawa period the population had remained in the neighborhood of 30,000,000 persons. By 1885 it had risen to 39 millions, in 1894 to 41.6 in 1914 to 52.8 and in 1935 to 69 millions.[2]

During the period with which we are concerned here the enlarged population was supported by increased efficiency in fishing and agriculture. This is reflected in the fact that in 1914 Japan imported only 5.5 per cent of her rice consumption.[3]

The increased pouplation was absorbed in expanding industry so that by 1913 there were over 2 million workers in mining and industry out of a total labour force of less than 30 million.

In 1895 only 12 per cent of the population lived in cities of over 10,000 persons but by 1935 46 per cent lived in such. In fact by 1920 one in four persons lived in a city of over 400,000 per sons whereas

[1] These figures are taken from Lockwood, *opus cited,* Table 17, p. 208.
[2] *Ibid.* p. 21, 137.
[3] *Ibid.* p. 21.

the agricultural population remained stationary.[1] This great movement took place during and after the turn of the century. Whereas in feudal Japan nine out of ten persons were probably directly related to agriculture by 1914 three out of five families were thus related and one-third of them not only carried on their work on the land but, at the same time, provided a part of the labour force for small scale and even large scale industry.[2] In the Japanese family system the eldest son succeeds to the ownership of the land but as families grew the other members of the family moved to the cities to find work in industry.

Farmers who owned their land, landlords, and small scale entrepreneurs strove to provide an education for their children so that they might enter the new salaried and managerial class.

A great many of the "daughters of the land" were hired out to great textile plants. In 1896 261,000 out of 435,000 operatives in the mills were women. Labour conditions in the mills were so unbearable that there was a 50 per cent turnover in the labour force every six months. A good many of these young women, some of them kept in the mills in virtual slavery, returned to the land broken in body.[3]

As was the case in eighteenth century England, there was a very great deal of occupational and social mobility as men and women moved from one end of the country to the other in search of new economic opportunities.[4] Lockwood concludes, "The rise of great cities was the most striking outward feature of the population movement within Japan. Urbanization also extended social and occupational mobility still further by exposing great numbers of people to the new ideas and new habits of living which went with city life."[5] It is natural that we should find an earlier breakdown in the strength of the family system, for example, within the growing cities than at the village level and a greater openness to new ideas as well as a collapse of traditional religious faith and customs.

Our fourth question deals with the technological needs of the new economy and the consequent changes in class structure.

Obviously this great change in the economic structure of the country could not take place without new skills being learned by all of those who took part in the new industry. While the managerial and pro-

---

[1] *Ibid.* p. 21, 441, 187.
[2] *Ibid.* p. 21.
[3] *Ibid.* p. 485–6.
[4] *Ibid.* p. 159.
[5] *Ibid.* p. 482.

fessional classes made up only 2.7 per cent of the population their technical skill was a major factor in the modernization of the country one so vital that obviously the whole process could not have taken place without it. Those who were trained in the new skills, ranging all the way from engineering to setting up modern commercial and judicial codes, were either educated in the new schools of the nation or sent abroad for study. For example, in 1885 only 9 per cent of the import-export business in Japan was handled by her own nationals but by 1913 the number of foreigners in the trade was a mere fraction of the whole.[1] The same process took place in the merchant marine for at the turn of the century the great majority of Japanese ships were manned by foreign officers, mainly British, but by the end of World War I the vast bulk of the fleet was commanded by the Japanese themselves. The new skills were not confined to new groups alone. As a result of new techniques a practically stationary agricultural force was able to supply the growing food needs of the population. This, however, did not affect the class structure of the nation. On the other hand, the new technicians and the managerial class were an essentially new phenomenon in the class structure.

Our fifth question is, "What was the relationship between public and private ownership of the means of production and how did these affect the class and power structure within the country?"

The formation of an association known as the Association for the Study of Social Policy in 1895 reflects the prevailing theory concerning the economy in Japan not only at that time but right up until World War II. At the outset the Association made three basic statements. The first was that it was opposed to "laissez faire" on the ground that it produces selfishness and widens the gap between rich and poor. Its second point was that it was opposed to socialism because it would tend to destroy the influence of the capitalists whose help was needed if the country were to be strong. Its third stand was that the prevailing structure of private enterprise should be preserved while, at the same time, efforts should be made to ensure harmony between government and business as well as between the classes.[2] Each of these points reveals the way in which a people accustomed at once to placing the interests of the group prior to those of the individual and yet of recognizing, at the same time, an essential inequality in rank among men, would think. Even the person with no more than a passing

[1] *Ibid.* p. 329.
[2] C. Yanaga, *opus cited.* p. 74.

acquaintance with Japanese economic life knows of the great concentrations of wealth in the hands of the *zaibatsu* families prior to World War II and of the tremendous inequalities in wealth which were characteristic of the nation's economic life. Japan, however, was neither a corporate Fascist state in the formal sense of the word such as prevailed in Italy, nor a Nazi state in which political considerations without question prevailed over economic, such as was the case in Germany.

There were at least four major forces at work in the Japanese economy all intimately, though not formally, related. These were first, the state; second, large scale enterprise as represented by such *zaibatsu* as the Mitsui, the Mistubishi, the Sumitomo, and the Yasuda; third, the host of small scale enterprise which were linked to, and frequently directly or indirectly dependent upon, the large scale enterprises; and fourth, the growing labouring class and the traditional peasant class. Power at the top was only informally shared by the civil and military bureaucracy and the families which controlled the great holding companies. There was no official link between them and while in times of emergency such as the Sino-Japanese and the Russo-Japanese Wars they served as one much of the time there were great differences between them. Indeed for all their power and their intimate, if informal relationship to government, the great capitalists never did have places of determinative power so far as the decisions which affected the total destiny of the nation were concerned. For this reason the military were able to gain the upper hand over them in the 1930s.

Nevertheless, there was an intimate relationship between government and business. As we have already related, the government got out of most of the major businesses it had begun in an effort to modernize the country. This they did by selling the enterprises to such families as the Mitsui and Iwasaki. Nevertheless, through subsidies as well as direct control the government continued to have an interest in banking, shipping, heavy industry such as steel, and colonial enterprise. The government built the great Yawata steel works in 1901. Private enterprise, on the other hand, continued to have basic control in agriculture, the traditional industries such as silk and textiles, and in the production of consumer goods though even here large scale industry was helped by the government.[1] Lockwood says that,

> In addition to a preoccupation, with strategic industries, it may be

[1] W. W. Lockwood, *opus cited.* p. 22.

> noted here simply that State policy in Japan reflected a consistent bias (1) in favour of industry as against agriculture, (2) in favour of exports to finance Japan's external requirements and (3) in favour of large propertied interests and employers, as reflected in discriminatory tax policy, hostility to trade unions, and the absence of protective legislation for factory workers.[1]

Government activity in business during our period then was far greater than in Britain or America, for example, though save for industries such as steel and the railways, the government was not formally in business as it had been at an earlier stage.

As Lockwood points out, someone had to take the initiative in developing large scale industry and this could not be done without large capital resources. Had the *zaibatsu* not taken on this responsibility the State would have had to do so since small scale enterprise was unable and unwilling to take the risk. What did happen was that when a real element of risk was involved, the government stepped in to give guarantees through subsidies. While the *zaibatsu* were most active in the field of heavy industry, of shipbuilding, mining and the like, which actually accounted for less than 10 per cent of the national product, through their interests in the textile industry and the banks, there was scarcely any avenue of economic life over which they did not have some control.

Here we ought to say just a word about the silk and textile industries lest the impression be given that Japan became a modern nation solely as a result of the development of new industries. This is far from the truth. Both the silk and the textile industries were traditional in the country and it was these and their growth which during our period account for the development which was made in the newer areas of the economy. The output of silk, for example, between 1889 and 1893 was 7.5 million pounds, but by 1909–1913 it had increased four times to 27.9 million pounds.[2] From 1900 to 1913 the spinning mill output rose 150 per cent. While much of the silk industry was still carried on at the farm home level, tremendous plants had also developed as had the textile mills.[3] China and Korea became more and more important to Japan for the export of these materials, especially since by World War I Japan had to rely less on Britain for the import of heavy machinery and thus did not have to export so heavily to the west.

---

[1] *Ibid.* p. 22.
[2] *Ibid.* p. 27.
[3] *Ibid.* p. 28.

These traditional industries did not only make development in other areas of the economy possible, but they absorbed 40 per cent of the industrial labour force, while another 40 per cent was engaged in such traditional small industries as Japanese paper making, braids, and mats.[1]

As a result of the fact that the traditional industries still absorbed 50 per cent of the manufacturing labour force in 1910 and that these industries were concentrated in establishments of five workers or less, we discover a large part of the gainfully employed working force calling itself entrepreneur. Twenty per cent of the working force called themselves "employers" as late as 1930.[2] These establishments, some of them no more than a farm family in size, were linked in turn with the larger mills if, for example, they were engaged in the silk trade. Thus small industry was to a very great extent dependent upon large and even where these industries were not directly dependent they had to apply for credit through the existing banking structures, many of which were owned by large enterprise and who loaned at rates that were discriminatory of small, as opposed to large-scale industry.[3] Moreover, as a result of the monopoly which the large enterprises enjoyed, it was almost impossible for new financial forces to challenge the great families.[4]

On the other hand, Lockwood expresses very clearly the close relationship which existed between the *zaibatsu* and the government in the following terms,

> The combines, as they grew in power, came in turn to exercise pervasive influence in the government itself. They contracted close family and business affiliations with leading bureaucrats. They financed the major political parties. Their top executives moved in and out of official agencies like the Bank of Japan or the Ministry of Commerce. And they operated as virtual partners of the government in developing the semi-official institutions like the Yokohama Specie Bank, the South Manchuria Railway, and other 'national policy companies' at home and abroad.[5]
>
> One may say that the modern Japanese economy was developed mainly by private enterprise, operating with a framework imposed by social tradition and a good deal of conscious political manipulation.[6]

---

[1] *Ibid.* p. 33.
[2] *Ibid.* p. 207.
[3] *Ibid.* pp. 210–11.
[4] *Ibid.* p. 221.
[5] *Ibid.* p. 221.
[6] *Ibid.* p. 200.

Corporate enterprise came naturally to a people who were accustomed to close cooperation under strict obedience to superiors. There was no mistrust whatever of concentrated capital as there has been in the United States and England and therefore no such thing as legislation to curb it. A traditional orientation to a hierarchical system plus the deep sense of group solidarity throughout society worked in favour of the kind of economic organization which developed. A minimum of actual government coercion was necessary in order to keep the system going because of this natural support which grew out of cultural orientation. This concentrated socio-economic-political power worked against the development of a strong middle class. It also worked against the establishment of strong protective trade unions as did the over supply of labour itself.[1]

We may say that power as represented by both political and economic factors was shared by three groups whose interests did not always coincide during the years 1890–1911. Those three groups were the bureaucrats whose interest were mainly of a civil nature led by Ito and then by Saionji; the military bureaucrats dominated by Yamagata and Katsura; and the great financial magnates, the *zaibatsu*.

Let us turn to our next question, a brief consideration of the way in which the class and power structure we have outlined above was reflected in the tax system.

As we pointed out above, tax on land was made to bear the brunt of modernization right up until 1890. This continued to be the case. In 1908 the farmer paid approximately 28 per cent of his income out in land, income, and business taxes as compared with 14 per cent in the case of the merchant and industrialist.[2] This was another force which impelled people to move to the cities. As late as 1913 taxes on business income and property provided less than 15 per cent of tax revenue.[3] These taxes fell heaviest on small and medium incomes derived from business.[4] Moreover, what could not be raised through taxes on land and business was, of course, raised through indirect taxes on consumer goods. These taxes which, next to real estate, accounted for more revenue than any other source fell heaviest on the great bulk of the people who could least afford them.[5] The tax structure was a reflection

---

[1] *Ibid.* p. 234.
[2] *Ibid.* p. 26.
[3] *Ibid.* p. 522.
[4] *Ibid.* p. 285.
[5] *Ibid.* p. 522.

of the interest of those who held power and influence. The very extension of the suffrage in 1900 was an attempt to make it possible for more persons in the city to vote. Previously the rural areas had held far greater voting power and it was therefore difficult to increase land taxes without a great struggle in the Diet. With a larger vote coming from city interests this end could be achieved more easily.

What attempt was made to deal with the social problems created by the new economy?

All the evils attendant on a new development of industry were characteristic of the Japan of our period. Child labour, widespread slum conditions, raw abuses in dormitory life and in sweatshops exacting long hours of work, these were the rule rather than the exception. One of the highest rates of tuberculosis in the world was the fate of Japan and especially of its workers. The accident rates were excessively high.[1] The turnover in the labour force was as high as 40 to 50 per cent a year as late as 1925. Concern for efficiency alone would have moved a nation more concerned for human welfare. There was little excuse for much of this suffering, for other countries such as the United States and Great Britain had been all through this before and had by this time developed machinery to mitigate its worst evils. That some Japanese did know of this and were concerned is indicated by the fact that as early as 1898 a draft factory law was introduced in the Diet, though it was hopelessly voted down. Throughout the period child labour was practised and from 1900 until the end of our period, it was a crime to agitate for a strike. A Mining Act was passed in 1905 and a Factory Act in 1911 but neither of them were enforced until 1916 and then in an emasculated form. If even a small fraction of the enormous sums spent on armaments had gone into efforts to eradicate these conditions and to raise the general living standard much could have been done. It will not do to say that some measure of social justice for the labouring classes was just then being entered upon through a strengthened labour movement in the western world because basic welfare laws had been passed in England and elsewhere decades before. The leaders who went abroad to observe techniques of industry also had an opportunity to study these laws which had grown out of the painful transition to an industrial economy elsewhere. We can only conclude that they chose to ignore them. It did not soon occur to a people used to thinking in terms of "high" and "low" to rebel against these conditions or to do

[1] *Ibid.* p. 486.

anything save accept them. Moreover, had wage scales been higher and conditions in the dormitories better so that the young women operatives could have returned decent sums to their peasant parents the latter might have been able to free themselves readily from the grip of the landlords upon them. Could it be, as Norman suggests, that there was collusion between the country landlord, who was himself frequently a small entrepreneur and thus understood the requirements of the sytsem, and the great mills and factories, with the intent of making impossible what might have become a peaceful, economic, revolution in Japan redounding to the welfare of all?

Finally, "What was the relationship between Japan's growing international trade and her relations with the peoples of other nations?"

As we have seen, in spite of the fact that there was a growing home market in Japan which accounted for the consumption of four times as much of the national product as did her export trade, Japan's export-import business quadrupled between 1890 and 1913.[1] Asia became Japan's major trading area after 1900 and, so far as the west is concerned, Europe receded in importance and the United States and the British Dominions, especially India, increased.[2]

Added to these facts is a further one of great significance and that is that while in 1885 only 9 per cent of the export trade was in the hands of the Japanese, and that British firms predominated until after the turn of the century, by 1913 the bulk of overseas trade was handled by Japanese firms and over half of it carried in Japanese ships. It had not taken them long to learn the ways of the market and the unequal treaties did not make them feel kindly toward the foreign trader. The almost virtual disappearance of the latter, was a spur to chauvinistic nationalism.

We have traced, then, the main outlines of the Japanese economy as it influenced the social structure of the nation between 1890 and 1911. That structure was, as it had been in the feudal period, in the shape of a pyramid with the ruling coterie at the top headed now, at least formally, by the Imperial Household, and then by the bureaucrats and the capitalists. The latter were a new class to share power and reflect the phenomenal interest of the Japanese nation after 1890 in industrial and commercial pursuits. The *samurai* who did not go into government service went into business and the professions. A perfect example of this is Iwasaki, who headed the Mitsubishi interests. It is interesting

[1] *Ibid.* p. 312, 339–45.
[2] *Ibid.* p. 395–97.

to note that Iwasaki was close to Okuma and each served the other in their particular spheres, Okuma aiding Iwasaki politically while the latter helped Okuma to considerable wealth. A similar relationship existed between Inouye, the Elder Statesman, and the Mitsui interests. It ought to be clear, that the pyramid of which we speak had little height and a broad base. At the top were clustered the Imperial Household, and the Peers of the Realm, all of whom had by now considerable wealth. In association with them were the bureaucrats and the *zaibatsu* with the latter representing far more wealth though the former had risen from men who were almost poor until they were, by any standards, wealthy. Beneath them was a very small middle class made up of technicians and professional men as well as entrepreneurs owning at least moderately sized enterprises, and a group of wealthier landlords. The great base of the pyramid was filled with the labouring and farming classes.

Geographic factors were also of importance in forcing Japan as a modern nation into an industrial role with expanding world trade. She was fortunate to have developed at a time of general expansion in the world economy. While there were factors against her in that she was small and mountainous her ability to use sea travel and the fact that she did not need extensive railways and communications made it easy for her population and her goods to be mobilized.

Throughout our period the motto was, *jukoku kyohei*, "a rich country, a strong army." Military considerations, as we have seen, played a large role in the economy although not the decisive role that they did after 1930. Conflict as well as cooperation was the nature of the relationship which existed between the three major power groups the military bureaucrats, the civil bureaucrats, and the great industrial leaders. Economic forms were taken from the west, as were political forms, but the spirit which infused the whole was one of authoritarianism and of group solidarity; a spirit characteristic of traditional Japanese culture.

This was a period of great expansion for Japan. By 1910 her colonies nearly equalled the area of the home islands themselves. We cannot agree with Lockwood when he concludes, "The quest for Empire in East Asia was impelled by no single motive, except as most Japanese were indoctrinated in varying degrees with a mystical faith in the Imperial destiny."[1] One certainly cannot justify Japan's aggressive acts but one must understand that she had had practically no encouragement

[1] *Ibid.* p. 534.

to take any other course. Power had forced her to open her own gates; power had forced her to submit to unequal treaties; power had exploited the great land mass China, which lay beside her, and had long since subdued India. Power in the form of Russian interests seemed to be threatening her both in 1894 and in 1904. One can agree, that in taking the course she finally took Japan not only destroyed her own natural Asian market, and the web of international trade she had built up with the west, but eventually had her own industrial power destroyed as well. But one must also agree with the thesis of R. K. Scalapino, that Japan was adrift in an world of power politics and that the treatment she received during our period played into the hands of the military faction and appeared to justify its ultimate course.[1,2]

---

[1] R. A. Scalapino, *Democracy and the Party Movement in Pre-War Japan*, Berkeley: Univ. of Cal. Press, 1953).

[2] I have used W. W. Lockwood, *The Economic Development of Japan*, almost exclusively in this chapter not because it is the only book on the subject, but because it is one of the most recent and perhaps the most comprehensive of its kind. G. C. Allen, *Japanese Industry: Its Recent Development and Present Condition* (New York: I.P.R. 1940), and his *A Short Economic History of Modern Japan* 1867–1937 (Toronto: MacMillan, 1951) are both excellent works. John E. Orchard's *Japan's Economic Position* (New York: 1930), though older is still an authoritative source of information, especially for our period. E. H. Norman, *opus cited*, though not so detailed, nevertheless possesses incisive and authoritative insights.

CHAPTER EIGHT

THE NEW FAITH AND THE NEW ORDER IN TENSION

The years between 1890 and 1911 may be divided into two periods so far as the development of Protestant Christianity is concerned. The first period, which all agree was a generally retarded one, ends with the century itself.[1] The second period, which was one of relatively rapid growth, takes up the intervening years between 1900 and 1911.

The period opened, as our discussion has already mede clear, in a spirit of intense nationalism. Success in the Sino-Japanese and the Russo-Japanese Wars only increased this. Yet the increasing opportunity it gave her for acceptance among the more powerful nations of the west inclined her to attempt to maintain peace in the interest of the "status quo" which was favourable to her following the Russo-Japanese War.[2] The sting of extra-territoriality had been removed by 1899 and though the government, following the revision, first acted to make it more difficult to propagate Christianity through the Christian schools, this order was modified in a few years. The government had been willing to tolerate the revolutionary impact of Christianity if it meant treaty revision, but the moment revision was achieved those in authority could afford to move against Christianity. To do so, however, they had to pass a law that would be restrictive of all religious faiths since the Constitution had committed them ostensibly to religious freedom. To this restriction the Buddhists objected and the bill was defeated in the Diet. Nevertheless, Christianity grew apace especially among the rising salaried and intellectual classes. As our sketch of the economy of the nation has made clear, this group developed in size and significance only after the turn of the century.

The growing spirit of self-confidence and nationalism was reflected in the desire of the churches to be increasingly free from any dependence upon foreign help and even foreign thought. Especially after the Russo-Japanese War an increasing number of churches launched out and supported themselves financially.

---

[1] O. Cary ,*opus cited.* p. 212 ff. C. Yanaga, *opus cited.* pp. 127–8, M. Sumiya, *opus cited.* p. 96 ff.

[2] D. M. Brown, *opus cited.* p. 168.

While there was a general tolerance toward Christianity as late as 1907 such men as Kato Hiroyuki, whose point of view toward Christianity had changed with whatever happened to be in the national interest, declared openly that Christianity was opposed to true Japanese patriotism.

There were a few Christians, such as Kataoka in the Diet, Admirals Uryu and Serata in the Navy, who were in high places and the fact that the Christians had from 13–20 members in the Diet through most of the period indicates an influence far beyond what numbers would suggest. Yet neither Christians nor the values they represented were ever decisive in the policies adopted by those in control of the economic and political life of the nation.

At the outset let us consider the numerical growth of the church between 1890 and 1911. In 1888 there were 25,514 full members in the church and by 1891, 31,000 members. For 1894 the figures are 35,000, for 1897, 36,000 and for 1900 37,000.[1] When one considers that, at this time, there were almost 500 missionaries and over one thousand professional workers connected with direct evangelism alone, within the Protestant movement, the painfully slow growth of this period can be seen at a glance. Moreover, there were over 125 schools with more than 12,000 students in them supported by the Protestant movement.[2] However, a sharp change is shown in the rate of growth after 1900 so that the numbers of Christians had risen to 60,000 by 1902, and to 75,000 by 1907.[3] This growth increased markedly to the end of our period.

Sumiya is able to show that there was a remarkable falling off in the increase in membership in particular churches in the first decade following the granting of the Constitution. In one typical city church, between 1882 and 1901 only ninety persons were baptized.[4] Moreover, during this period a great many of the churches in the countryside were closed. Sumiya states from the Records of the United Church of Christ

---

[1] Sumiya, *opus cited.* p. 105–106.

[2] O. Cary, *opus cidet.* p. 296. There is some discrepancy between the figures shown by Sumiya and Cary for similar years. This is probably because Sumiya is reading from Japanese records established at one date and Cary from Missionary Records of a slightly later date. Taken over a period there is general agreement.

[3] M. Sumiya, *Chusan Kaikyu no Seiritau to Kirisutokyo*, (Christianity and the Establishment of the Middle Class), No. 6, 1954 of the periodical *Fukuin to Sekai*, (Tokyo, Shinkyo Shuppansha), p. 24.

[4] M. Sumiya, *Kindai Nihon no Keisei to Kirisutokyo*, (Tokyo: Shinkyo Shuppansha, 1950), p. 105.

that almost all of the churches closed during this period were either in the countryside or in the smaller cities.[1]

On the other hand, the churches established after the turn of the century were in the capital cities of prefectures such as Fukuoka and Okayama and in large industrial and commercial centers.[2] Sumiya claims that, in this interval, the following change had taken place both within society and within the church. As we know, industrial expansion on a large scale did not take place until after the Sino-Japanese War. The period which then set in was one of unusual economic expansion, not only in traditional industries such as silks and textiles but also in heavy industry. At the same time, government offces of all kinds were expanding as Japan sought to modernize her commercial and legal system in order to dispense with the unequal treaties by 1899. As a result, there was a large movement of population to the centers of industry and government. In the meantime the old *samurai* class had passed away and the Peoples' Rights Movement had not only dissolved but the landlords who had supported both it and, to some extent Christianity, were now opposed to any movement of an equalitarian kind as inimical to their real interests. Thus while Christianity met with new opposition in the countryside and with general opposition during the 1890s by 1900 the new class of salaried officials was well established. The great majority of these were sons of the *samurai*, of petty bourgeoisie, or of country farmers and landlords who could manage to raise enough to send their sons on for higher education. It was from this group that the Protestant Churches drew most of their members.

It was to these young men that the churches directed their efforts at mass evangelization from 1900 on. It had taken the church a decade to realize what was happening but she was quick to see where her new opportunities lay. From 1900 on the great increase in church membership took place among this group and from among students who were studying at the higher schools and universities in order to enter this class.[3] Most of those who belonged to this new status-group had a freedom which did not belong to the lower classes because they had to learn new techniques. As they did so they absorbed new ideas of all kinds. Since the bureaucrats needed their help, without which the new system could not operate, they could not oppress them as easily as the lower classes nor could traditional Confucian values be imposed upon

[1] M. Sumiya, *Chusan Kaikyu no Seiritau to Kirisutokyo*, p. 24.

[2] *Ibid.* p. 24.

[3] M. Sumiya, *Chusan Kaikyu no Seiritsu to Kirisutokyo*, p. 26.

them without a critical response. That the new growth in Christianity was taking the direction indicated above was realized by those at work at the time.[1]

However, there was a problem occasioned by the fact that growth was among that part of the population which was on the move. According to statistical reports there had been a 65 per cent leakage in church membership in the decade prior to 1902. This would indicate that while the net increase in membership during those years was scarcely over 1,000 per year until the turn of the century the gross increase had been greater. Yet there was this very great loss. As we shall see later, there were other reasons for it. None the less the fact that many of those who became new members were forced to move frequently from one plant to another, or on graduating from school moved to another part of the country and thus were lost to the church, is undoubtedly one of the factors accounting for this great numerical loss. One church is cited as having members all the way from Hakodate to Kagoshima. One of the reasons they were lost is that the denominations had no way of recommending their members to those of another denomination.[2] We have already mentioned the geographical sectionalism of the various denominations partially caused by comity agreements and partially by the fact that the missions had been separated from one another because missionaries were confined to the ports and certain major cities until 1899. Thus certain denominations grew up in one place, others in another. The fact that this was permitted to happen is a clear example of the way in which denominationalism can work against the growth of the church. The Church in Japan would have been more alert to what was occurring had there been a stronger ecumenical concern among the missionaries.[3]

We turn now from a consideration of the numerical growth of the Protestant Christian community to the much more complicated matter of the influences and events in Japanese society during the period which tended to retard or to encourage the growth of the faith.

---

[1] *The Christian Movement in Japan*, 1903–1906. The annual reports of the missionary and Protestant Christian Movement in Japan, established by the General Conference of Missionaries 1900, Tokyo, p. 41. (See Biblio. p. 360)

[2] *Ibid.* p. 63.

[3] Another reason given for the retarded growth of the church, which seems reasonable, is that given by Dr. Cary, opus cited, when he says that the church was simply exhausted by the growth which had taken place in the preceding decade and that whereas, in earlier years, all Christians had accepted a responsibility to bring others into the faith it was now left largely to the professional ministry. p. 215.

It is scarcely necessary for us to bring forth more evidence to show how strong was the growth of nationalism, especially during the first years following the promulgation of the Constitution and prior to the agreements for the removal of the unequal treaties which were reached in 1894. Many of the fomer *samurai* had gone into education and the enforcement of the new educational system along German lines which was established after 1885 came naturally to them as they instilled the code of *bushido* (code of the warrior) into their pupils.[1] After 1892 the conflict between Christianity and Shinto intensified.[2] Professor Inouye Tetsujiro claimed that since Christianity insisted on the equality of all men it could not, at the same time, hold true respect for the Emperor. He accused Christianity of having no concern for the State. The Buddhists also formed a major society, the Sonno Hobustsu Daido Dan, for the express purpose of counteracting the infuence of Christianity. Borton says, "In reality, Christianity and a strong nationalism coexisted and tolerated each other. The government was confident, however, that the universal dissemination of morals and ethics based on traditional nationalism would more than counteract any subversive effect of Christianity."[3]

On the one hand, Christianity rejoiced at Article 28 of the Constitution which read, "Japanese subjects shall, within limits not prejudicial to peace and order, and not antagonistic to their duties as subjects, enjoy freedom of religious belief." This appeared to promise religious freedom, even if somewhat circumscribed. This the government was more or less forced to grant, especially if Japan was to wrest herself free of the unequal treaties. On the other hand, the Imperial Rescript on Education was a clever device to deepen state absolutism and to counter any revolutionary movement, especially Christianity.

The very preoccupation of the country with the concerns of political life which surrounded the granting of the Constitution, the holding of the first elections, and the issuing of the Imperial Rescript on Education took general interest away from matters of religious concern.

The Education Department continued to make it difficult for the Christian schools and the fact that the government schools were gradually attaining an excellent standard, supported as they were by the tax system, made it almost impossible for the Christian schools to compete.

---

[1] *Bushido, the Soul of Japan*, by I. Nitobe, Teibi, Tokyo 1914, is an excellent treatment of Bushido and its content.

[2] D. M. Brown, *opus cited.* p. 119.

[3] H. Borton, *opus cited.* p. 184.

Difficulties were placed in the way of Christian students seeking entrance into government higher schools. Uchimura Kanzo was discharged from his position as a professor at the First High School in Tokyo for allegedly showing disrespect to the Imperial House during a reading of the Meiji Rescript.

The Army appeared to discriminate against Christians and higher government offices were closed to them.[1] When Christians made representations to the government regarding discriminatory action against them, citing the constitution, they were told that the government did not have any interest in religion so long as the Imperial Rescript on Education was taught and followed.[2] Thus the government could appear to be neutral in religious matters while at the same time promoting a religion of state absolutism.

Cary displays exceptional insight into the situation so far as it affected many of the Christian leaders when he says, "Doubtless the charge laid against them charging lack of patriotism led them to be more earnest in displaying their patriotism, and the morbid nationalism thus fostered increased friction between them and the foreign missionaries."[3] Reverend Yokoi Tokio advocated a "Japanese Christianity" independent of all foreign influences. There was a increasing demand for freedom from all ties with the foreign missionary movement. Insofar as this was a genuine attempt to be independently responsible before God as the Church of Christ in Japan, both of these movements were to be welcomed but the strained relationships between missionaries and Japanese Christians were just as frequently an attempt of the latter to indicate their patriotism as much as, if not more than, their Christian faith.

This spirit was reflected, for example, in an attempt by a number of Japanese Christians to divest Doshisha University of its Christian orientation so that it would be more acceptable to the Education Department. It was also reflected in the insistence of even such leaders as Kozaki that it was their interest in Confucianism which had led them to Christianity rather than influences from the west. Ebina Danjo, another outstanding leader, was strongly nationalistic in his approach. Indeed, as we shall see in greater detail later, the influencc of a radical "liberal" theology as represented by Unitarianism, naturalism and extreme rationalism, which was just then coming to Japan, was seized

[1] O. Cary, *opus cited.* p. 238.
[2] *Ibid.* p. 239–40.
[3] *Ibid.* p. 243.

upon as being more in accord with a type of faith which an intelligent Japanese might accept. The more orthodox and pietistic theology of the missionaries was rejected. One outstanding Christian leader, Kanamori Tsurin, was so deeply influenced by the "new theology" that he left the pastorate and advised his followers that they had been misled. Those who were most radical theologically were also the most nationalistic suggesting that there was a real connection in motivation between the two movements. An acceptance of the "new theology" meant that one was simply accepting that which was obvious to the Japanese mind while at the same time it provided an opportunity to assert independence from the missionaries.

Sumiya points out that the weakness of Japanese Christianity was that it possessed a strong ethical and moral orientation without, at the same time, possessing a deep sense of both personal sin and responsibility to a personal God. By personal sin is meant the inherent tendency of all men to assert their freedom over and against God. This was most apparent in its inability to overcome more successfully the desire for social acceptance.[1] Even the United Church of Christ in Japan, the most conservative theologically, ceased to use the Heidelberg and Westminister Confessions.[2] Had the church had more time to adjust to the pressure that was exerted against it, it would doubtless have countered such more effectively; but a church still young in years, which has to face a nationalism native to it and a disturbing new thought at one and the same time, can scarcely be condemned when the churches of the west have, from time to time, displayed the same confusion down through the centuries.

Undoubtedly the patriotism which Christians expressed during the Sino-Japanese and the Russo-Japanese Wars, plus the activities of compassion carried on by such organizations as the Y.M.C.A. during them, led many Japanese to a greater tolerance of the faith.

After 1900 the government attempted to use Christianity for its own purposes. That is to say, recognizing the need for a strengthening of the moral fiber of the country which was suffering under the stresses and strains of modernization, the government called upon the Christian and other faiths, both in 1908 and again in 1911, to cooperate in a movement for the strengthening of national morals.[3] To some this

---

[1] M. Sumiya, *Kindai Nihon no Keisei to Kirisutokyo*, p. 110, 116.

[2] *Ibid.* p. 116.

[3] *Ibid.* p. 120 and *Japan Christian Year Book*, Tokyo 1912–1913. (See Biblio. p. 360)

was a sign of the final acceptance of the Christian faith in Japanese society; to others it was an attempt of the government to fasten a new feudalism upon the people. So far as both the Christian faith and the government were concerned it was an uneasy alliance. The latter was prepared to use the Christian faith where it could and to suppress it when it threatened the interests of the country according to its interpretation. Article 28 of the Constitution gave them perfect freedom so to do. Because the faith continued to grow persistently, and among a class of men which the government needed, it could scarcely take any other attitude.

Apart from Uchimura Kanzo, who from the time of the Russo-Japanese War was radically opposed to Japanese expansionism, and a few of the Christian Socialists, the great majority of Christians were completely confused as to their relationship to their own society. They failed to understand the pressures which their own culture was exerting upon them and upon the expression of their faith. Sumiya cites the fact that whereas the greatest rate of growth had taken place in the Congregational Church prior to the granting of the Constitution, it was the first to show signs of decline.[1] Many of the upper class who had taken an interest in the faith fell away since it was no longer the thing to do. Another section of that church, as we shall see, became involved in the struggle for social justice and, influenced by the "new theology" as well as by the indifference of the church as a whole, grew away from the roots from which it had sprung.

The development of the economy had a two-fold effect upon the growth of the faith. On the one hand, owing to the development of the middle class and its relative freedom from traditional authority and its search therefore for a new inner authority, Christianity was given an opening into which it entered with some success. On the other hand, the increase in economic and commercial activity drew many young men away from an interest in the ministry or a teaching career in Christian schools. A number of men were lost to the ministry who were actually in it, because they could find more remunerative employment in business. Moreover the general decline during the nineties in the numbers becoming Christians had also discouraged them. There was as well a marked decline in the number of students entering theological colleges.[2]

We have already observed how the Peoples' Rights Movement was broken when the landlords discovered that genuine democracy was not

[1] M. Sumiya, *Kinda Nihon no Keisei to Kirisutokyo*, p. 106.
[2] O. Cary, *opus cited.* p. 254, C. Yanaga, *opus cited.* p. 128.

in their interest vis-a-vis the peasant group and how their sympathies turned rather to supporting the government in its attempt to promote absolute loyalty to the Emperor based upon traditional Confucian authoritarianism. This was not really difficult to accomplish because Christianity was as yet far too young a movement to have made any deep impression upon rural Japan, the stronghold of conservatism. Because the government could rely upon a spontaneous obedience on the part of the great majority of the lower classes it seldom had to use overt force to achieve its ends. Economic considerations, therefore, reinforced the resistance to Christianity in the countryside. Moreover, such was the force of traditionalism that the "hands" in the factories, who had come from rural backgrounds, were imbued with it. This combination among others made it difficult, even for the radical element in the Christian community, to gain any following among the masses. Thus the church lost touch with them both in the rural areas and in the cities.[1]

A further point ought to be made here. As Sumiya points out,[2] the development of Japanese capitalism was, prior to 1899 of necessity, and after that by choice, very nationalistic, as witness the dominance of Japanese in a short period of time in the export-import business. This was a natural, human reaction to the treatment received as a result of the unequal treaties which had made it difficult for the Japanese to enter international trade. When this force was combined with the rise in militarism after the Sino- and Russo-Japanese Wars and we add to this the vertical structure of the Japanese economy dominated as it was by the *zaibatsu*, there was little room left for the development of a large middle class. Had such a class developed, it would have traded beyond national boundaries. Thus a movement in the direction of economic internationalism would have arisen which, to some extent, did take place in the west. Because there did not grow up in Japan a bourgeois middle class penetrated extensively by Christianity as it was in the west, the Christian movement did not develop a very great sense of internationalism, or even of its own ecumenical nature.

There appears to be no evidence that Christians were ever in primary decision-making positions within the economy during this period. Those who were in such positions were former *samurai* with the exception of the Mitsuis, who had been great merchants for centuries. While benevolent paternalism had been one characteristic of feudal

---

[1] M. Sumiya, *opus cited.* p. 112–13.

[2] M. Sumiya, *Chusan Kaikyu no Seiritsu to Kirisutokyo*, p. 25.

times in the relations between lord and peasant, and while there were examples of such in the great factories which grew up during the decades between 1890 and 1910, mercy was not a particular quality of the *samurai.* In business as in politics those who became enemies were implacable in their hatred and would move against each other with ruthlessness. This was, for example, the case in the struggle between Ito and Yamagata. Similarly in business, those in control were ready to use any methods to achieve their ends such as the harsh anti-strike legislation of 1901. In all fairness it must be said that, even in the west, labour unions still had many of their major battles ahead of them before they achieved acceptance and the word "socialism," whether associated with democratic methods or not, had the connotation which the word "communism" does today. It is true, as Lockwood claims, that other nations did have factory and welfare laws worked out after much suffering on the part of the labouring population of the west. But it is also true, that even here, those laws were only imperfectly applied as witness the very poor mining conditions in such places as Wales and Pennsylvania. Nevertheless, the fact that the Christian faith failed to make greater gains than it did in this area is indicative of the fact that in the economic life of the nation, as in the political, while it had some influence at secondary levels it failed to exert such at the primary, policy-making level.

"What, if any, evidence is there that the 'charismatic' quality within the Christian faith was able to surmount, even though it may have been conditioned by Japanese society as a whole?"

This is a much more difficult question to answer for the decades between 1890 and 1911 than for the two decades prior to them. In the latter we were able to point to the striking "revival" of the years 1883 and 1884. Here we saw the faith making headway in spite of a hostile environment. We were able to point out that just as the pressure against the faith increased, the first generation of men who had prepared themselves for the ministry were at the height of their youthful vigor and enthusiasm. Speaking theologically, we would say that God had raised them up for such an hour. Yet the amazing growth in the church which took place between 1900 and 1911, especially at the turn of the century, is no less an evidence of the ability of the faith to root itself in a new culture. It is quite striking that the church was as alert as it was to that group in society which was most responsive to the gospel, the new managerial and intellectual class. As we have seen, its major evangelical effort was toward this group and it was probably wisely placed. When has the Christian faith ever entered a new culture and not been influenced by it? Witness the thought of Clement of Alexandria or even of Brunner and Reinhold Neibuhr in our own day. There is evidence in the thought of each of them of the particular environment with which they are most familiar.[1] It was more difficult for the faith in these decades to free itself from the pressures of a society which had taken on greater stability and rigidity than was characteristic of it in the two previous decades. What is rather amazing is that, all things considered, it made the advances it did so that the church was firmly rooted in a new culture.

One striking evidence of the ability of the Christian faith to raise up men prepared to stand in determinative judgment of their own society was the role which Uchimura Kanzo played. We find that from the beginning he sensed the idolatry that appeared to be implicit in the Japanese emperor-institution. He was willing to carry this to the place where he was forced to oppose the entry of his nation into the Russo-Japanese War on the ground that it was contrary to the spirit and teachings of Jesus Christ.[2] Moreover, Uchimura could not be accused of being either particularly internationalist in spirit or of lacking in love for his country. His thinking was moulded not only by his allegiance to his Lord but also by his conviction that Japanese Christianity ought, in many ways, to be peculiarly Japanese and his friends took him to task for the fact that he showed so little interest in cooperating with like-minded people in other lands. He is known most widely as the founder of the famous non-church group in Japanese Christianity.

We turn now to a consideration of the institutional life of the church in the final period of our study. "In what terms did the Protestant Christian Movement express its faith and in what organizational forms? What if any purely Japanese influences were expressed through these?"

Confronting the new resistance to Christianity in Japan, the Church of Christ in Japan proposed union to the Congregational churches. We will recall that almost inadvertantly, actually in part because of their physical isolation from each other, separation had grown up between two bodies which had originally been united in the church formed at Yokohama in 1872. The Apostles' Creed, and the Articles of the Evangelical Alliance were to form the basis of faith for the proposed new

[1] In the case of Clement, I have reference to such writing as *The Instructor* and *The Stromata*. Brunner's *Justice and the Social Order* shows deep evidence of his western, and particularly, Swiss background. Neibuhr's *Faith and History*, shows evidence of the thinking of one accustomed to the counterplay of American power politics.

[2] *Japan Christian Year Book*, (Tokyo: 1916), p. 217. (See Biblio. p. 360)

church. The Westminister Confession and the Heidelberg Catechism were to be held in veneration. There were to be presbyteries and a General Conference though much was to be left in the hands of the local congregations. Many Japanese Congregationalists were frightened of the tight organization involved and some of the Congregational Alliances in America were also averse to them. As a result this effort failed.

In 1890 the Church of Christ adopted the following statement of faith which was followed by the Apostles' Creed:

> The Lord Jesus Christ, whom we worship as God, the only begotten Son of God, for us men and our salvation was made man and suffered. He offered up a perfect sacrifice for sin; and all who are one with Him with faith are pardoned and accounted righteous; and faith in Him working by love purifies the heart.
>
> The Holy Ghost, who with the Father and Son is worshipped, and glorified, reveals Jesus Christ to the soul, and without His grace man being dead in sin cannot enter the kingdom of God. By Him the prophets and Holy men of old were inspired; and He speaking in the scriptures of the Old and New Testaments is the supreme and infallible judge in all things pertaining unto faith and living.
>
> From these Holy Scriptures the ancient Church of Christ drew her conconfession; and we holding that faith once delivered to the saints join in that confession with joy and thanksgiving: THE APOSTLES' CREED.[1]

It can be seen at once that this statement is deeply reminiscent of that of the earliest church which was based in turn, in part at least, upon the creed of the Evangelical Alliance.

Sumiya claims that this statement, with its disregard of the Confession which had been earlier recommended by the missionaries, was an evidence of the increased nationalism of the time.[2] On the other hand, Cary presents convincing evidence that all connected with the church, especially the missionaries were concerned that such a statement, brief and concise as it was, though surely not easily understood by those who stood outside of the faith, should be prepared in the face of the onslaughts of "Buddhism, Confucianism, Agnosticism, Rationalism, and radical Unitarianism."[3]

The spirit of which Sumiya speaks was more evident in the attempt of the Congregational churches in 1891 to state their faith afresh. They said,

---

[1] O. Cary, *opus cited.* p. 233.
[2] M. Sumiya, *Kindai Nihon no Keisei to Kirisutokyo.* p. 116.
[3] O. Cary, *opus cited.* p. 233.

> We believe in One God, infinite, perfect, who is made known in the Bible as Holy Father, Holy Son and Holy Spirit. We believe in Jesus Christ, who, being God became man; who suffered and died and rose again that He might save sinners. We believe in the Holy Spirit who bestows the new life. We believe in the Bible which was given by the inspiration of God and makes us wise unto salvation. We believe in the Holy Church, baptism by water, the Lord's Supper, the Holy Lord's Day, eternal life, the resurrection of the dead and in just rewards and punishments.[1]

There is much to be said for this statement and it has the distinction, while not being unique, of being a statement which appears to have arisen out of the life of the Japanese church, since it was not an established creed but a declaration of faith arrived at out of common discussion.

A statement that is a radical reflection of the spirit of the times is that prepared by a Congregational Conference in 1895. It said,

> We who, believing and revering Jesus Christ as Saviour, are called of God, do greatly mourn over the present condition of the world, and assembled here in prayer unto God and in the rich enjoyment of the Holy Spirit's gracious influence, we determine to proclaim the Gospel and to establish the kingdom of God according to the following principles:
> 1. That all men should repent of all sin, and through Christ should return unto obedience to the Heavenly Father.
> 2. That all men being the children of God, the great principles of love and sympathy should be upheld among them.
> 3. That the home should be purified by maintaining the principles of monogamy; and the mutual duties of parents and children, elder and younger brothers, should be fulfilled.
> 4. That the nation should be elevated and the welfare of mankind promoted.
> 5. That the hope of eternal life should be perfected through faith and righteousness.[2]

Cary goes on to say,

> By many, especially by those who desired to see a Japanese form of Christianity, this declaration was hailed with great enthusiasm. A Japanese professor of the Doshisha wrote of it as being by far the most influential document yet issued by the Christians of Japan and said, 'Viewed from the standpoint of conciseness, of absence of dogmatism or theocratic tendency, and of the prominence given to morals and ethics based on the personal instruction of Christ, the instructions forming the

---

[1] *Ibid.* p. 236.
[2] *Ibid.* p. 259.

> basis of this creed must be considered as the best of their kind since the establishment of the Christian Church in Japan.' By some others, who considered the document a production of those who were trying to combine Christianity with Confucian and Shinto elements, it was thought unsatisfactory because of what it omitted rather than what it contained.[1]

As we have mentioned in an earlier chapter, in the 1870s and the 1880s the American Episcopal Church, the Canadian Methodist Church, and the Methodist Church South, had established missions in Japan. They united in 1907 and adopted both the traditional statements and forms of government of the Methodist Churches in the west. Some difficulty was experienced with those in the United States and Canada who opposed the union but it was overcome. Bishop Honda, an outstanding Christian from the time of his baptism in 1872, an alumnus of Drew University, was elected the first bishop of the new church.

At the end of our period, then, we have the following four major churches among Protestant Christians each with their own separate polities and creeds, the Church of Christ (Presbyterian), the Congregational, the Episcopal, and the Methodist.

No consideration of the way in which the Japanese Church expressed its faith during this period would be complete without a more detailed account of the influence of the "new theology" and of higher criticism in general upon the life of the Japanese church. The important thing for us to note here is that this disturbing element in the young church's history took place just at a time when that church was under great pressure from the rising spirit of nationalism within the country. We have already mentioned the strongly moralistic note characteristic of Japanese Christianity and the tendency present in it to use Christianity as a base for the moral and ethical life of the nation. This note was often struck, especially in the decade following the turn of the century.[2] *Bushido*, which was the background of many of those who were still the church's leaders as well as their background in the ethical school of Confucianism both helped this non-reflective, ethical emphasis and the relation which it took to the interests of the nation. One hears Christianity recommended in Japan today for the same reasons. This practical, rationalistic background made it easy for the young church to accept an interpretation of Christianity which de-emphasized its transcendent character. This in turn made the faith more acceptable

---

[1] *Ibid.* p. 259–260.
[2] *Ibid.* p. 305.

to those among the intellectuals who could not countenance a faith beyond reason. Since religious faith in Japan is traditionally suspect for its irrational character, (for example, Shinto, as well as many of the Buddhists sects), this was a further reason to reject suprarational elements in orthodox Christian faith. But it was also true that those who embraced the new theological radicalism were also the most conservative nationalists.[1] This would indicate that both positions were related through the spirit of nationalism. Ebina Danjo, who was one of the most popular preachers to the young university students of Tokyo, at this time, is a case in point. His thinking is revealed in his estimation of what happened to the Christian community during the Russo-Japanese War. He wrote:

> The Statesmen of that time were all men of intelligence, and though we had no connection with them, yet they and we alike were animated by the same spirit of love of country. Men of high official standing had watched us narrowly and they approved our attitude, and thus they gave us freedom for evangelism.[2]

His emphasis was service to Christ through service to the nation.[3]

Insofar as a striving for independence and creativity in the expression of faith is concerned, as in striving for independence of church organization, the motive which matters is whether this striving is an attempt under the guidance of the Holy Spirit to relate Christ to one's own life and responsibilities or is simply an attempt to be self-assertive. The motivation in the case of the church in Japan at this time was probably mixed. Undoubtedly it had something of self-assertiveness in it. This is one of the reasons why the relationships growing out of the ecumenical church are so necessary. These relationships alone can resist the temptation for any church to become parochial and to that degree less than Christian.

Another way in which the thought-life of the church during this period sought to answer the needs of the day was the way in which it met the emergence of self-consciousness among the displaced intellectual and salaried class with whom it was working. So long as one is a firm part of family relationships in Japanese society he is submerged in the group. The very idea of individuality and personality fails to become important in such a context. Now, however, tens of thousands of young people were cast adrift from their habitual moorings and

---

[1] *Japan Christian Year Book* (Tokyo: 1904), p. 191. (See Biblio. p. 360)
[2] *The Christian Movement in Japan,* 1910. p. 324. (See Biblio. p. 360)
[3] M. Sumiya, *opus cited.* p. 115.

forced to find their way alone. In the process they found "the self." The literature of the time, as evidenced in the writing of Takayama Chogyu, a Buddhist, and Kitamura Tokoku, a Christian, is repleat with the struggle which ensued. Sumiya claims that Uchimura Kanzo alone really understood this conflict because he insisted upon the reality of the encounter between God and the individual.[1] Thus many thousands of intellectuals turned to his teaching.

When we turn to church government we find that almost from the beginning there were problems over who should control what in the Church of Christ in Japan. It is perhaps natural that these debates should be sharpest in this church as distinct from the others for it being Presbyterian in polity showed a greater concern over church administration than did the other denominations. Moreover, they had as their leader from the first Uemura Masahisa a man who was both deeply Christian and yet strongly nationalistic. He expressed himself as follows:

> Japan needs an independent Christianity. An independent Christianity cannot exist without an independent church. Apart from Christ and the Spirit Japanese Christianity has no need to rely on anyone whatever. Sufficient unto itself, resolved to stand alone, it must advance along the whole line towards the realization of this ideal...Those who set before themselves the ideal of church independence must not forget that the same importance attaches to independence in theological interpretation.[2]

It is not strange that problems and differences should develop as a new church grows from seed implanted by those outside the culture in which it develops. Tragedy stalks only where these are not overcome in a spirit of Christian forgiveness and understanding. By 1904 a tense situation had developed within this body. The Japanese brethren felt that the church in Japan should have complete control over all work done in relation to it whether that work was supported by them or not. The missionaries felt that they had a responsibility to the church in the United States and elsewhere for the funds which were coming to them and thought that the work ought to be carried on on the basis of mutual agreement. As Cary points out, it is difficult for men brought up in the

---

[1] M. Sumiya, *Chusan Kaikyu no Seiritsu to Kirisutokyo*, p. 26–28.

[2] Hiyane Antei, *Shukyoshi* in the Gendai Nihon Bunmeishi edition of that work. pp. 262–63. This passage is also cited in M. Takenaka, *Relation of Protestantism to Social Problems in Japan*. 1901–1941. Unpublished Yale University doctoral thesis. p. 176.

tradition of leader-follower relationships to think of cooperation in terms of mutual responsibility. Cooperation is rather thought of as the willingness to follow a leader as his faithful *deshi* (disciples).[1] Japanese politics can only be understood in this way for men did not follow policies but personalities such as Ito, Itagaki or Okuma. Be that as it may, the Church of Christ in Japan worked out principles for recognizing churches which it hoped would make as many of them financially independent as possible. Such churches were to be under the direct control of the presbyteries of the church, as is to be expected. Those that could not become self-supporting, which usually meant those which were being started by missionary enterprise, were also to fall under the full jurisdiction of the church as soon as they raised 50 per cent of their budget locally. Even this arrangement did not suit many of the Japanese churchmen and from 1907 on, save where local arrangements were worked out between local missionaries and their brethren in the local churches, and in spite of the fact that an action had been taken by the Synod in 1906 which voted in favour of a resolution presented by the Council of Missions indicating its willingness to work under the Church of Christ, no official relationship existed between that church and the Council after 1907.[2]

A healthy spirit of independence, which was also a manifestation of the spirit of the times, was indicated in the Congregational churches too. Organized as they were in accordance with Congregational polity, though maintaining an alliance among themselves throughout the country, they established complete financial independence by 1906. New enterprises alone were helped with foreign funds.

In 1889 the Canadian Methodists formed a Quarterly Conference. Ordained ministers and laymen had a one-for-one vote. Each missionary also had a vote. In 1907 the three branches of Methodism were united under a Bishop and declared themselves as follows:

> In policy the church follows again Methodist standards being Episcopal, with presiding Elders nominated, in double the number necessary, to the bishop for his appointment of the proper number for a period of four years each, and with an itinerant ministry without time limit to the pastorate. That is, pastors receive their appointsments annually.[3]

Missionaries were to work under the Bishop in consultation with the Mission Boards involved.

---

[1] O. Cary, *opus cited.* p. 275–76.
[2] *Ibid.* p. 338.
[3] *Ibid.* p. 340, as quoted in *Japan Evangelist,* June, 1907.

The Episcopal Church in Japan was promised the appointment of a bishop from among its own numbers immediately after the Russo-Japanese War, providing it could raise the necessary funds to support his responsibilities. This was not accomplished until 1923.

The spirit of unity among both missionaries and the Japanese churches in general was manifest in the great Tokyo Missionary Conference of 1900 and the meeting of the Japan Evangelical Alliance in 1906. At the former, a standing committee was established to work on a greater degree of comity, the production of an annual yearbook, and the setting up of joint evangelistic campaigns in cooperation with the Japanese brethren. Native pastors and the missionaries combined their efforts in the Forward Movement which was largely responsible for the rapid rate of growth in church membership right after the turn of the century. The Japan Evangelical Alliance eventually became the National Christian Council of Japan.

We need say little of the churches constituency. We have already dealt with the nature of its numerical growth which was extremely slow during the decade after the promulgation of the constitution but increased rapidly after the turn of the century. By 1908 there were approximately 75,000 baptized children and full members of the Protestant churches. Of these, four-fifths were in the four major Protestant bodies. Of them, 33 per cent were Church of Christ, 30 per cent Congregational, 23 per cent Methodist, and approximately 14 per cent Episcopalian. These figures do not account for the growing numbers who were influenced by Uchimura Kanzo's non-church group and who, therefore, could not be included in the statistics.

We have already indicated the class orientation of the Protestant churches.

Between the end of the period of flux and that of our present period, a whole new generation had arisen in the church. Up until the end of the first period, the majority in the church had been former *samurai*-related to the Shogunate. They were the intellectuals. They were also the rejected ones. They gave leadership to the Peoples' Rights Movement. However, with the coming of the constitution and the increased strength of the bureaucracy, plus the reaction of the landlord group in the countryside, that movement broke down. The political-economic combination of the bureaucrats and the *zaibasu* was far too strong for any movement from the "grass roots" to the top which is what the Peoples' Rights Movement sought to be. When it was added to the new strength given to State Shinto through the increase of nationalism, and the confusion which nationalism, shared by both opposition and conservative forces alike, brought into the situation the movement for the reform of the whole of Japan from the bottom up, of which the first small Christian group had dreamed, no longer seemed a remote possibility. As a result men like Uemura Masahisa turned their attention to the inner life of the church and its organization. Had the ground swell of evangelism continued as it gave promise of doing in the 1880's it is unlikely that there would have been time for the Christian community to give so much time and concern to the questions of autonomy after 1890. To some extent this was undoubtedly an expression of frustration.

Another reason why so many Christians no longer took up their responsibility for political reform was the corruption which seemed to engulf the political parties after 1890. We have shown that this was caused by the fact that the House of Representatives was without any real power save that of obstructionism. The House was, therefore, frequently dissolved. This meant that election costs were extremely high for those taking part and they sought to recoup their losses through their remunerations as representatives. Frequently, these were not sufficient and so they were easy prey to the administration's offer of funds to secure passage of the legislation it desired.

The church, then, did not find new territory to conquer until, following the Sino-Japanese War, the new salaried class began to appear. The great majority of these were petty officials in government, technicians, and managers in industry, and professional persons who, as our economic survey showed, were a very small proportion of the gainfully occupied populace. They were a new generation of intellectuals and of "displaced persons". They were uprooted from their traditional surroundings and were freer than any of the other groups in society from the necessity to conform. It was here that the church made its great advance.[1]

The picture, at the close of our period is of a very stratified church. Though there were a few members of the upper classes, a great many of these fell away with the reaction against the church in the early nineties. There remained a few in positions of importance, though secondary influence in the armed forces, the government, even in the judiciary and in the press. The church had lost almost all contact with the labouring and peasant classes save for a group of radical, Christian

---

[1] M. Sumiya, *Chusan Kaikyu no Seiritsu to Kirisutokyo*, p. 24.

intellectuals, whom we shall discuss shortly, and those who were carrying on philanthropic work. By far the great majority of its membership lay in the small middle class.[1]

We come finally to the question, "What influences, if any, had the Protestant Christian Movement exerted upon Japanese society in the final two decades of our period?"

It can be shown very clearly that Protestant Christianity did have a very real influence in this period as it had almost from the beginning of its existence. This influence was far greater than its numbers would indicate. When this has been said, however, we must also recognize that Protestant Christianity was never a decisive movement so far as the destiny of the nation was concerned. Its leaders were not in positions of primary power within the Japanese power structure. Even those who were to some extent its friends, and who were in such positions, of whom Count Okuma may be considered one, were prepared to bless Christianity in the interests of the moral welfare of Japan.

In the first elected House of Representatives, for example, thirteen out of the three hundred representatives were Christians. The first Speaker was a Christian, Nakashima Nobuyuki, as was the Chairman of the Committee of the Whole, Shimada Saburo,[2] In 1908 there were fourteen Christians out of three hundred eighty members of the House, seven of these were Presbyterians, five Congregationalists, and two were Methodists.[3] This represented a number far in excess of the proportion of Christians in the country. Moreover, Kataoka Kenkichi for example, up until his death in 1903 was more than once made Speaker of the House. Shimada Saburo, as editor of the powerful Mainichi Newspaper of Tokyo, and as a member of the House, together with Okuma carried on an unrelenting battle against political corruption, especially that represented by Hoshi Toru who controlled the Kenseito and the Tokyo City political machine. Even Okuma, however, with all his personal power was unable to effect the development of truly re-

[1] That this is still the class orientation of the Protestant Christian Church in Japan is illustrated from the following statistics taken from an article entitled, "Japan's Spiritual Situation" by Theodore Jaeckel in the July issue of *The Japan Christian Quarterly*. They are for 1953. (See Biblio.)

Farmers	50% of Japan's Population –	2.00%	of Prot. Chris.
Labourers	27% ,, ,, ,,	3.00%	,, ,, ,,
Fishermen	3% ,, ,, ,,	.05%	,, ,, ,,
Middle Class	20% ,, ,, ,,	94.05%	,, ,, ,,

[2] O. Cary, *opus cited.* p. 229.

[3] *Japan Christian Year Book*, Tokyo, 1908, p. 38. (See Biblio. p. 360)

presentative government within the land. Even less so were the small minority of Christians who were active as elected representatives of the people. They nevertheless held out the hope of a better day.

If it was true that the Christians were unable to affect decisively major political decisions within the country they were more successful in making a faithful witness on a less grandiose scale. Christians were most influential in the movement against licensed prostitution. They were largely instrumental in the passing of the Cessation Act on October 2nd, 1900, which made it possible for prostitutes to cease their occupation without the consent of their masters.[1] The influence of this movement went far beyond the issue of prostitution itself. It brought the whole question of the worth of individual human personality before the people of the nation.

Certain of the missionaries in particular were quick to attempt to do something for the young women who were crowded into the dormitories of the great textile mills. We have noticed the amazing growth which took place in these plants during the period. Living conditions were extremely bad and the girl operatives were frequently sent as indentured labour to them. They were the daughters of farmers who needed funds in order either to retain their land, or to pay their debts. Frequently there was a twenty-four hour shift in the mills so that girls got into the bedding which had just been left by those who had gone on shift. The girls had little, if any privacy, immorality was rife and few of them lasted a year before they were broken in health. There was a 50 to 60 per cent turnover in labour each year. Often the girls whose health was broken or who could not stand the conditions of the factory, yet could not return home, became prostitutes or maids in tea houses. As early as 1903, Christian homes alongside the factories were established.[2] An attempt was made to give the girls some degree of education and to teach them to sew. Honesty in all relationships of life was emphasized especially toward employers. No mention is made of a reciprocal responsibility! A tone of hostility toward those who were engaged in the political agitation for factory laws and the creation of labour unions can be noted in the report of those who were carrying on this work. However, in a 1908 report by J. M. Holland this attitude is changed and there is an understanding not only of the necessity for a general uplift among the poorer classes but of the necessity both for the acceptance of social responsibility by the employers and the en-

[1] *The Christian Movement in Japan*. 1903–1906, Tokyo, p. 35.
[2] *The Christian Movement in Japan*, 1903–1906, Tokyo, A 1903 report.

actment of good factory laws.[1] A factory law was achieved in 1911 though it was not put into force until 1916. It called for the abolition of labour in the mills of children under 12 years of age and set a 12 hour day for women workers. However, it provided loopholes for the employer even at that![2]

The Christian movement also led in the establishment of philanthropic organizations such as orphanages, homes for the blind and for lepers, and work for the rehabilitation of prisoners. It was estimated that one quarter of all philanthropic effort in the country was under Christian auspices in 1902 and that by far the greater part of private social work was Christian, Protestant and Roman.[3] This work stimulated the Buddhists to renewed activity in this field and also the government to establish welfare departments. Insofar as this work was inspired by a spirit of paternalism, it can hardly be called an expression of Christian love, either on the part of Christians or of non-Christians. More often, however, it was a genuine respect for human personality which, for example, reached out to break down the caste barriers against the *eta*, an outcast group. In general, it was recognized as such by the people of Japan and they were thus enabled to see the very close relationship between Christianity and the responsibilities of everyday life, a dimension of religious faith neglected by the traditional faiths of the country.

A further expression of the influence of the Christian faith was the activity of some of its members in the early labour movement. Among its pioneers were Abe Isoo and Katayama Sen, as well as Yamaji Aisan, Kinoshita Naoe and Kawakami Kiyoshi. Each of these was also active in the early socialist movement.[4] However, many of the earliest unions organized around Katayama Sen, as early as 1888, became the victims of the dishonesty of some of their officers and had to dissolve as a result. Christians were very active in the Engineers' and Firemen's Union of the Japan Rail Company. Within it they formed a strong Temperance Society and the Union was well organized. However, they were forced to strike in 1898. Five of the ten leaders in the strike

[1] *Japan Christian Year Book*, Tokyo, 1908, p. 186 ff. (See Biblio. p. 360)

[2] *Ibid*, 1914, p. 138.

[3] *The Christian Movement in Japan*, 1903–1906, Report on Elecmosynary Work for 1902.

[4] An article entitled, "The Labour Movement in Japan" in the Japan Christian Year Book for 1917, p. 314 ff. is one of the best available sources for information on the relationship between Christianity and the Labour movement during this period.

were Christians who felt it was their duty to sacrifice their positions for the sake of the uplift of labour in Japan.[1] The government acted quickly since the strike threatened to become general. The press, on the whole, rallied to the government and the reaction of the public as well as the government was so repressive that by the time an anti-strike law had been passed in 1901 most of the unions had dissolved. This tended to drive the movement to greater extremes. This was furthered by events after the mining strikes of 1904, which we mentioned in Chapter VI. No further attempt was made to organize anything resembling a union until Suzuki Bunji, a Christian and a Unitarian, organized his Labourer's Friendly Society which, while extremely effective in lifting the level of life among the labourers themselves, was more a labourer's mutual aid society than what we might consider a union for the purpose of collective bargaining with employers. Nevertheless, it was a distinct step forward.

Perhaps one of the unfortunate things about this movement, which was really the extension of the Peoples' Rights Movement of earlier days in that it sought to reform Japan from the "grass roots" rather than from the top down, was that it was led by men whose theology, when they had any, was as radical as their social application of the gospel ethic. They were deeply affected by the "new theology". This made the more orthodox Christian leaders, such as Uemura Masahisa, skeptical of them. As a result such leaders were driven farther away than ever from the church while the church, on the other hand, lost touch with them. Uchimura Kanzo found common cause with them in opposition to war but his emphasis was so individualistic that he failed to appreciate their concern for social problems.

Christianity also had its representatives in the creation of western art forms, such as the novel, in Japan. Shimada Saburo, the editor of the Mainichi newspaper was a leader in the literary, as well as the political, field. Tokutomi Soho although he later gave up his Christianity in favour of nationalism, who founded "The Nation's Friend" a literary and political journal modelled after "The Nation" in the United States, was another of these. So were Kinoshita Naoe and Nakamura Kichizo, both of them novelists of note.

Almost all of the major critical journals of the time of both a political and literary type were either edited by Christians or had a close relationship to the Christian fellowship. Among them were such journals

---

[1] M. Sumiya, *Nihon Shakai to Kirisutokyo*, (Tokyo: Daigaku Shuppansha, 1954), p. 74.

as the *Kokumin no Tomo*, the *Rikugo Zasshi*, the *Jogaku Zasshi*, and the *Bungaku Kai*. In many ways these had a Christian influence on society far in excess of the theological writings of men like Uemura and Uchimura. They suffered from two shortcomings. One of them was that they usually lacked theological depth; the other was that the literary style of a man like Shimazaki Toson tended to be tinged with the western approach to writing and because the genre had as yet not found itself authentically related to Japanese culture at any profound level it tended to be as much imitative as creative.

The Protestant Christian Movement was foremost in the promotion of education for women from its earliest beginnings in the small schools gathered together by missionaries in Nagasaki in the 1860's, to the establishment of the Ferris Institute in the early 1870's until by the close of our period it had 51 schools for girls with a total of 4,762 pupils.[1] While it cannot be proven that by this time the conception of home life had been very deeply influenced certainly respect for womanhood in general had increased and the influence of these young graduates as mothers upon their children cannot be overestimated.

In these and other ways, which penetrated the framework of personal relationships in the country and yet which cannot be placed on record, Christianity definitely influenced the life of Japan. These influences were significant insofar as they went. That they were not determinative for the whole culture is not surprising. Nor is it surprising that this is still not the case. One must be naive in the extreme to expect that a country, displaying the cohesiveness characteristic of the social life of Japan, as well as possessing a high form of indigenous culture, would become permeated with Christian values within the short space of sixty or even one hundred years!

Granted that Christianity accomplished all that we have outlined above it is easy to claim far too much for it. Thus we hear Dr. D. C. Greene, a great Christian missionary, then resident in Japan for almost forty years, making the following statement:

> However, this may be in recent years, as has been indicated in previous numbers of the Christian movement, Japan has given clear evidence of a warm sympathy with the western conception of the relation between government and people, a conception which had its roots in Christianity. The progress of the new civilization is really based on this new conception, and its progress has been stimulated at almost every stage

[1] *Statistics from the Christian Movement in Japan*, 1912. Appendix. These figures include children of Kindergarten age.

> by almost complete freedom of thought and an approach to equality of opportunity hardly surpassed in the freest countries of the west. The state of mind which has thus been created has proved, as it was bound to do, responsive to the appeals of Christianity, and the growth of the churches and the increasing spirit of independence which they exhibit are convincing proofs that Christianity is already naturalized in Japan.[1]

In the report for the year 1903, Dr. Greene cites the change in the rights of the individual which had taken place since 1869. Then a *samurai* could cut down a beggar without question but now the Prime Minister cannot do it without making himself liable to arrest.[2] He goes on to say:

> There may be a recrudescence of the old thoughts and feelings now and then; but the universal condemnation which it receives shows that the old order has passed away and the nation has thoroughly accepted the new order founded upon essentially the same conceptions of the value and rights of the individual which lie at the base of the social fabric of the nations of Western Europe and America.[3]

Dr. Greene can be forgiven for his enthusiasm over the great changes which had certainly taken place since his arrival in Japan. But it is hard to see, in view of our study of the actual situation in both the political and economic order of Japan, how he could have reached the conclusions he did. Had he not mistaken the "forms" for the "reality"? If it was true that the Prime Minister could not cut a man down without being liable before the law, which in itself was a revolutionary change, it must be said that even here one of the basic motivations of those who instituted these laws was that the country might rid itself of the unequal treaties. In the sense that such humane laws were the product of Christian influence in western culture these too can be said to have been inspired indirectly by that spirit but to claim that they were basically motivated by an appreciation of Christian values is to misread the situation. Had those with the power of decision in Japan really accepted a view based upon "the value and rights of the individual"? Our evidence and the tragic events of history which have transpired in the meantime would lead us to a contrary view. Indeed as late as 1909 a writer in the Christian Yearbook says, "In the present period of public admission, the attitude of the government toward Christianity is not at all settled. At one time it might be favourable and at another time

---

[1] *Japan Christian Year Book*, (Tokyo: 1907), p. 4.
[2] *The Christian Movement in Japan*, (Tokyo: 1903–06) p. 14.
[3] *Ibid.* p. 15.

quite unfavourable; it changes as change the opinions of the officials in power."[1]

When the Home Minister called together the Christians with the Buddhists and Shintoists in 1908 and again in 1911 to ask their cooperation in serving the moral ends of the nation many of the most observant Christians were cautious concerning the implications of such meetings. Surely it was a mark of the "arrival" of Christianity, a far cry from the conditions of 1859. On the other hand, it involved dangers of compromise apparent to many who cared most.

Far from Japanese leadership accepting western democratic procedures they had established a political and economic structure which made it impossible for such procedures to make any appreciable headway in Japanese society. This state of affairs was threatened slightly during the twenties of this century but for all intents and purposes it remained unchanged until the end of World War II.

While Mikio Sumiya may have oversimplified the situation he appears to this writer to have properly summed up the situation in the church at the end of the Meiji period in the following manner. Uemura Masahisa, he says reflects the reaction which one group of Christians made to their situation. Uemura declared himself thus:

> The church today, first of all, needs to clarify the idea of church and needs to lift it up. The church is the Kingdom of God where the will of God is fulfilled perfectly, and where Christ Jesus exists and His Spirit is acting. Through this ideal the church lives and should live...If this is true I believe the church is able to guide society and also to fulfill the needs of society. Ultimately society will be swallowed up in the church.[2]

Frustrated in their ability to make any vital impression upon society they turned their attention almost exclusively to the life of the church. They neglected their social witness. Uchimura Kanzo, on the other hand, decided that the institution of the church, which to maintain meant compromise with the state, was unessential to a vital Christianity. Personal religion alone mattered. He is quoted as saying, "Society is no more than a collection of individuals"[3] and "social reform must start with the individual."[4] And further, "We should cultivate man and train

[1] *Japan Christian Year Book* (Tokyo: 1909), p. 142.

[2] M. Takenaka, *Relation of Protestantism to Social Problems in Japan*, (Yale University, Unpublished Doctoral Thesis, 1954), p. 184, as quoted from Uemura Masahisa, *Zenshu*. Vol. V. pp. 110 ff.

[3] M. Takenaka, *opus cited*. p. 119 as quoted from Uchimura Kanzo, *Zenshu*, Vol. V. p. 276.

[4] *Ibid*. p. 119 as quoted from Uchimura Kanzo, *Zenshu*, Vol. XIV. p. 117–18.

man. After building up man then we should reform society. Putting this method aside it is nonsense to discuss the social problem. Just like one who talks about strategy without training the rank and file."[1] Abe Isoo is singled out as an illustration of another fundamental reaction. He along with his colleagues struggled for social justice but with little concern for Christianity as much. In each of these there is a fallacy which meant nothing short of tragedy for the Japanese church. The first reaction left Christianity devoid of its proper social witness, the second undermined the strength of the church, the third ended up with little element of transcendental faith within it in order to judge aright the situation which it faced.[2]

A brief review of the period then reveals the following. In the first decade of the period the growth of the Protestant faith was slow and discouraging. Part at least of this was due to the increased nationalism within the nation, bringing with it reaction to the west, and part was a result of the preoccupation of the nation with internal political and economic concerns. The church by the second decade displayed her "charismatic" nature in reacting swiftly to the situation created by the appearance of a new middle class, a product of the changed economic structure, and won her following chiefly among this group.

The growing spirit of nationalism was reflected within the life of the church. It was at least one of the motivating factors in the church's struggle for independence from foreign ties of both an administrative and theological kind. Japanese Christians were, on the whole, confused by the issue of nationalism. They did not understand the nature of the economic and political power structure of which they were a part. This made it difficult to present a Christian faith which was radically transcendent and which therefore demanded total obedience.

While Protestant Christians did have an influence far out of proportion to their numbers in the population, the fact that they did not share economic and political power to any significant extent had a very limiting effect upon their influence. On the other hand, the Christian faith was so deeply rooted in the nation by 1911 that those who did hold political power could not afford to oppose openly the faith but were forced to recognize, and, insofar as they could, use it in what they conceived to be the interests of the nation.

---

[1] *Ibid.* p. 119 as quoted from Uchimura Kanzo, *Zenshu*, Vol. XIV. p. 15.

[2] M. Sumiya, *Kindai Nihon No Keisei to Kirisutokyo*, pp. 119–120.

CHAPTER NINE

CONCLUSION

In conclusion let us hastily review the ground we have covered and then set forth clearly the insights which have emerged from our study.

The relationship between the political structure of Japan and the development of Protestant Christianity ln the period between 1859 and the Restoration of the Emperor was clearly one which worked against the rapid growth of the faith. The nature of Japan's new relationship with the outside world did not dispel her distrust of Western intentions and therefore did not prove any help to an acceptance of the faith by the Japanese. Seen from its positive side the relationship of the faith to Japanese society during this period made it possible for those who were pioneering the movement to dig their roots deep, to gain an understanding of the language and the culture and thus to be better prepared for what lay ahead.

The decade of the 1870's brought a permissive attitude toward Christianity on the part of the authorities as a result of their desire to find acceptance among the western nations and to right the unequal treaties. A period of relatively rapid growth of the faith took place. Japan was exposed not only to Christianity but to all manner of new ideas from the west. These concepts covered the whole gamut of human experience from those of personal relationships to those of a new political and economic order. It was a period of flux, of crisis and of change for Japan. Anything might have happened within the nation at this time. Protestant Christianity shared in the great repercussions set up within Japanese society. In its relationship to the Peoples' Rights Movement Protestant Christianity found access, as it has not before or since, into the Japanese countryside. Protestant Christianity found itself related to the *samurai* of the former Tokugawa government more than to any other group in Japanese society. They were the *disinherited* who were looking for a totally new way of life both for themselves and for their nation. Their religious background in the Wang Yang-Ming school of Confucianism and their intellectual background were among the factors which made them exceptionally open to the new faith.

In the 1880's Protestant Christianity displayed its "charismatic" quality in that during the first half of the decade it grew in spite of intense opposition from powerful groups within Japan. In the latter half of the decade the faith was accepted to some extent superficially as were the forms of other western institutions. Its consequent growth did not necessarily indicate permanent allegiance on the part of many who embraced it. By the end of the decade both the Peoples' Rights Movement and the political parties which grew out of it were suppressed. The alliance between those who were struggling not only ceased to make headway in the countryside but was cut off from any basic relationship to the lower classes. The clan bureaucracy had fastened its hold firmly upon the country by the end of the decade. It had been aided in this not only by a nationalism based upon traditional Japanese values but upon an intensification of it as a result of modern methods of communication plus a modern conscript army. But it was the unequal treaties and the failure to revise them which helped to draw out Japanese nationalism and brought it to the fore to play the prominent role it did in modern Japanese history. The reforming zeal of the early Christian *samurai* leaders was broken by the overwhelming opposition against them while, at the same time, their allegiance in common with their Japanese brethren to the *welfare of Japan* swept them up into the rising tide of nationalism and broke their will toward fundamental reform.

In the 1890's Protestant Christianity appeared to have "lost its public" altogether. People were preoccupied with economic and political activity. Nationalism engulfed the nation including the church. The increased power of the bureaucrats made it almost impossible for any new, reforming movement to gain a foothold in the country. Internal problems arose in the church as a result of the spirit of nationalism and the "new theology" both of which tended to be embraced by the same group indicating a relationship between them. Christians in general tended to be confused by the turn things had taken.

Yet by 1900 Protestant Christianity had sought out a new following. Economic growth plus a new civil service required to conduct a modern government had created a new group of salaried officials within the small middle class. The demands which society made upon this group often required those who made it to leave the traditional family life to which they were accustomed. Thus, they were exposed to fresh ideas which came streaming to them from the outside world. Because the bureaucrats needed this group for the services they provided to the new order, they could not be as easily controlled as were the lower classes through economic pressure or appeals to traditional custom. It was among this group that Protestant Christianity continued to make its greatest headway.

Throughout the years Protestant Christianity continued to exert an influence in the fields of education and social welfare in particular; but because it failed to influence in any essential way those who held positions of decisive authority within the power structure of the nation, its influence was never determinative for the society as a whole. Instead the *welfare of Japan*, as that was conceived by the oligarchy, was the fundamental, determinative factor in the new order.

There were at least three major reactions to this situation within the life of the Protestant churches, as Mikio Sumiya has so clearly pointed out. The one was to disclaim any responsibility for society because it could be changed only after individuals were changed. The second was to forego responsibility for society because it could be changed only after the Christian church was itself first established and built up. The third was to become so involved in the struggle for social change that that became the end rather than the product of Christian concern. Each of these produced confusion in the minds of those who held them as to their full Christian responsibility and as to where they stood in relation to their social milieu. There were, of course, variations of these three positions but had they been held together in a whole conception of Christian obedience the future for the Japanese church, and perhaps even for the new order in Japanese society, might have been less tragic than it was.

A study of this period then clearly reveals the intimate relationship between economic and political forces and events in Japanese society and the development of Protestant Christianity within it. Obviously the Christian faith had to deal with other forces in Japanese society as well, which at times made it easier, but usually made it more difficult, to enter effectively into the life of the nation. Nonetheless, it was the success of the oligarchy as it sought the *welfare of Japan* through reestablishing Japanese society along traditional lines after 1880 that gradually effected the closure of the nation's life against the winds of fundamental social changes and which, therefore, frustrated the hopes of the leaders of the Christian church that the faith would grow rapidly. The tension between the political, social and economic power of the oligarchs and the life of the church while it conditioned the growth of the latter did not, however, absolutely determine it as the rise in its membership during an adverse period between 1880 and 1885 and the fact that it continued to gain ground after the turn of the century demonstrates.

Underlying the power of the oligarchy a motivation has been disclosed, namely the *welfare of Japan*, which was the spiritual force providing meaning and guidance for their leadership. Obviously other motivations played their part but time and again it is this consideration which proved determinative for their action. This motivation was there prior to the events in which it became manifest. For example, in the refusal of either side to call in outside help which might have been disastrous for the autonomy of the nation in the struggle for power prior to the Restoration. It was there in the Osaka Event of 1865 in which a decision was made clearly in the long range interest of the nation and in which chauvinism was rejected. It was there to motivate the removal of the edict boards against Christianity after 1873. It frustrated the attempts of Saigo in the Korean Affair and again in the Satsuma Rebellion of 1877 when to have followed Saigo's course of action, dictated as it was by considerations of military chauvinism, would probably have made it impossible for the nation to gain time to acquire the economic strength necessary for Japan to become later on a modern power. It prompted the rise of a deepened nationalism after 1888 and it stood behind both the Sino- and the Russo-Japanese wars. In each case it provided unity of action and it acted to reinforce reliance upon traditional patterns of behavior largely because outside nations, acting in their own self interest, had made any other course of action unthinkable. It was the underlying appeal of this concern for the *welfare of the nation*, albeit increasingly expressed through the Emperor institution, upon which the oligarchy was able to rely in order to solidify its own power as well as to advance the interest of the nation as it understood it.

But it was the power of this concern for the *welfare of Japan*, legitimate from the Christian point of view when held under the sovereignty of God, which rendered confused the leadership of the Protestant Christian community as it sought to play a creative role in the life of the nation. Only a very few Christians were able to maintain a constructive, critical, prophetic relationship to their own society in the face of this competing loyalty. As tension mounted in relation to the western nations the ability of any liberal forces to effect change in Japanese society became more and more restricted. Japan became a modern industrial and military power but except for external political dress she remained essentially traditional.

Over against the "charismatic" power of the *welfare of Japan* as expressed in the activity of the oligarchy and the emperor institution must be set the "charismatic" power of the Christian faith to break into Japanese society in defiance of accepted patterns of behavior. Thus during the "revival" of 1883–84 the devotion of the young Christian *samurai* leaders to their new Lord was carried out in the face of strong opposition within society at large. This force was at work not only in the ability of the young church to find a new following after the turn of the century but also in the sustained day by day witness of both the Japanese Christian community and its leaders such as Uemura and Uchimura. Nor were the more radical Christian leaders without this quality which enabled them to maintain their struggle against insurmountable odds. After all the Protestant Christian community was no more than a small *sect* in the surging sea of Japanese culture.

Finally, the following important though secondary findings emerge from our study.

In the first place the faith tended to find acceptance among that group in society which had some understanding of the ethical sense which Christianity itself produces.

In the second place it was adopted by those who stood over against the accepted order or by those who were least secure in it.

In the third place, the background of those who did accept the faith was definitely reflected in their interpretation of it.

In the fourth place, when Japanese society was relatively "open" and its old structures most threatened, Christianity had its greatest opportunity.

In the fifth place, when the re-integration of the social structures within Japanese society began to take place, on an other than Christian basis, the Protestant Christian faith continued to grow but the rate of growth was much slower than had been anticipated. Moreover, it was confined to that group which had the greatest freedom from the pressure of the new social structure.

In the sixth place, though the Christian faith had some influence in mitigating social evil, its influence was never decisive over the whole of society because it failed to engage the loyalty of those in major decision-making positions.

In the seventh place, we have discovered that the great majority of Protestants failed to understand fully enough where they stood in relation to their own culture. They lacked an understanding of the nature of man as man-in-society. As a result their theological interpretation of their predicament did not make it possible for them to respond as creatively as they might have done to their situation.

Generalizations with application to other areas of rapid social change which may have resulted from our study must be accepted only as helpful insights for possible guidance certainly not as rules for action since each culture obviously presents its own peculiar problems. With this proviso in mind, the Japanese case does suggest that the Christian churches bear certain considerations in mind.

It would appear that state absolutism in any guise is as inimical to the Christian faith and to the spread of its influence in society as it has always been. The present intensity of nationalism in many of the nations in process of rapid change may well indicate that the faith to which Christianity has to relate itself in these nations is an unconditional loyalty to national self-interest rather than to the traditional faiths within them the revival of which in many instances is a manifestation of new cultural pride rather than faith in the faiths as such. It was not without significance that the Christian faith in Japan found acceptance among those who were previously conditioned to the possibility that the national interest might best be served through loyalty to a higher moral order.

The Japanese experience would seem to bear out the contention of Troeltsch and others that new *sects* usually find their following among "the disinherited". It is true that those who first took up the new faith had been deprived of all power in the new order. On the other hand, the young bureaucrats of Japan while they used the role of the emperor institution in Shinto as the centre around which to organize the new Japan, if they did not reject, nevertheless neglected both traditional Shinto and Buddhism. It is true that they relied heavily upon an authoritarianism inculcated by centuries of the practice of one school of Confucianism. Yet there is no reason to believe that had Japanese society remained *open* for more than a few decades the Christian faith might not have become the adopted faith of a significant number of those who might then have given political and economic leadership to the nation.

The latter consideration would suggest that the Christian churches should be concerned as to whether societies remain *open*. A society may remain open for a time and then through a realignment of social structures old or new, or a combination of both, may close again. The history of the past century in Japan would suggest that:

> "There is a tide in the affairs of men
> Which taken at the flood, leads on to fortune;

Omitted, all the voyage of their life
Is bound in shallows and miseries.

(Act iv, Scene iii, *Julius Caesar*)

Obviously an *open* society where Christianity, along with other faiths, may complete for the ultimate loyalty of men is most favourable. Such a condition exists, however, only in a small part of the world. Through discerning social analysis the Christian churches ought to know when a society is in flux and thus most likely to find those within it eager and ready to accept the Christian faith as a creative alternative. It ought to know not only where individuals are who need such an alternative but where whole groups and classes of men are searching for new approaches.

The Japanese case makes forcefully clear that the fact that the Christian enterprise is inextricably bound up with every phase of human life. The fact that Japan was rebuffed again and again in her effort to adjust the unequal treaties acted to make her reject the western world and with it the essence of her political institutions. She turned her face away from new cultural values and this meant that the door was almost closed upon the growth of the Christian church. A wise Christian strategy must be alert to every act of social injustice at every level of human society including that of international relations.

Yet the experience of Japanese Christians within the period we have studied demonstrates that even a minority can make some significant difference to the establishment and maintenance of social justice over a significant period of time. Whether such efforts may or may not succeed in determining the direction of the society as a whole they are nevertheless of the greatest importance for those whose lives may be affected at any given time.

Finally, we must not claim too much for social analysis, imperative as we believe it to be for the planning of a Christian global strategy. While it may be very helpful in assisting understanding and thereby promoting the Christian faith the course of the faith itself is not predetermined. In one major instance at least we have seen that the faith deepened inwardly and spread outwardly at the most rationally inauspicious time.

Post-war Japan remains in a state of flux and of rapid social change. Recent reports would suggest that a new alignment of political, economic, and social forces reminiscent of the old oligarchy may well be consolidating its powers while using the old basic appeal to the loyalty of the Japanese as Japanese in its service. Whether this be the case or not, the lessons of the Meiji period remain of first rate importance not only for the Christian community but for society at large as Japan continues the search for a new way to meet the challenge of the contemporary world.

APPENDIX

EXHIBIT A

Some Results of a Questionnaire sent to Japanese Christian Leaders on Matters related to the Content of this Study

(NOTE: In September, 1954, when this study was first under preliminary consideration by the writer, 185 questionnaires were sent to Japanese Christian leaders to gain their reaction to some of the problems with which the study seeks to deal and to suggest problems yet unnoticed. The selection of those to whom it was sent was made with reference to positions of leadership within the church and interest in the problems with regard to which we sought an expression of opinion. The actual selection was not made by the writer but by Reverend Ando Hajime, a graduate of Union Theological Seminary in Tokyo, who has held a special interest in this study from the beginning. It must be emphasized that what we have here is merely an expression of opinion. Thirty-six replies were received. Thirty-five of them were from Japanese leaders at various levels and one was from an American missionary leader whose long residence in Japan qualified him as one whose opinions were worthy of consideration. What does make the replies significant is that three of them were from able Japanese sociologists who are also Christians and who have given a great deal of thought to the problems of our study; nine were from Christian ministers who are, or have been, national leaders; ten were from Christian ministers who might be considered area leaders and thirteen were from local ministers all of whom have made an effective witness at that level. The replies which showed the greatest degree of deviation from the general opinions expressed were from two Christian leaders who have been outstanding evangelists and who felt that the questions asked had little relevance to the concerns of the Christian faith. Those questions answered most readily and frequently had to do with the class orientation of the Christians in Japan, the relationship of Christianity to the emperor institution, the effect of persecution, whether it was easiest to become a Christian in the country or in the city and whether democracy or feudalism were most favourable to the development of Christianity. The greatest hesitation was displayed in answering the questions with relation to the economic order. The questions were divided into four sections, those dealing with the Social Order, Politics, Economics, and the Faith and Life of the Church, respectively. The results of the questionnaire have been worked out statistically by the writer and further details may be obtained from him. It must be stressed that while the replies to this questionnaire were helpful in suggesting preliminary problems for investigation, they had no determinative influence upon conclusions reached in the study.)

A. *The Social Order*

Without exception there was complete agreement that Christians had come from the middle class and have continued to do so. The reasons most frequently given were that this class could most readily understand and that they were most interested. The missionary leader replied, "The evangelistic effort was directed to this class. There is nothing in Christianity which orientates it to a particular class."

There was a wide measure of agreement that the Kyodan (United Church of Christ in Japan) was related to the middle class. Where there was any orientation to the other classes the Roman Catholic and the Episcopalian were related to the Upper and the Salvation Army and Holiness sects to the lower classes.

There was the widest agreement that it was easier to become a Christian in the city than in the country. The reasons given were that life is freer from custom and family obligation in the city than it is the country and that missionary and church personnel have been concentrated in the cities.

Those who expressed an opinion were convinced that Protestant Christianity had had an effective influence on the following reforms in modern Japanese society (they are arranged according to the frequency with which they were mentioned), social work, monogamy, abolition of licensed prostitution, democracy, temperance, respect for personality, education, literature and general culture. One of the sociologists felt that Christianity had had no decisive influence in any area.

B. *Politics*

There was wide agreement that the emperor institution had had a negative influence upon the development of Christianity, but some of the replies had significant qualifications. The reasons given were that the Emperor had taken the place of God for many Japanese, that the institution weakened the right of the church to speak to society, that it confused the people and gave them a servile attitude. However, one outstanding leader made the point that it was the use made of the institution, not the institution itself, which was at fault.

The majority were convinced that democracy was most favourable to the growth of Christianity though feudalism had a few advocates. Yet there was significant qualification of the approval given to democracy. Most objected to the tendency to stress individualism at the expense of the group.

The majority felt that both the Constitution of 1889 and the Imperial Rescript on Education were unfavourable to the growth of Christianity although some felt that while the Rescript was bad the Constitution was good. The reason given for the unfavourable reaction was that they forced Christianity to work within severe limitations, though it was the interpretation given to them which was most to be deplored.

The majority felt that the laws restricting the Press and Association had an adverse effect upon the growth of Christianity, while some felt that they had little influence and that what influence they did have depended upon the attitude of the local authorities.

The question was asked, "What has been the nature of the influence which politics in general has had upon Christianity since the Meiji Restoration?" Typical replies were as follows: the ruling class flattered the church and gave it a servile attitude; the church lacked courage and strength to engage those in political power; the government has been oppressive in its attitude to

Christianity and when this was not possible it has used it; religious freedom made Christianity possible but the state doctrine of the Emperor's divinity made entry into the lower classes most difficult; the superficial acceptance of constitutional government had an undesirable effect upon the development of Christianity; the opposition of the government enabled the church to see God as central.

C. *Economics*

Most agreed that capitalism was favourable to the growth of Christianity in Japan in the days of its earliest development, that is, from 1868 to 1889. The general reaction was that as it developed more fully capitalism had an unfavourable effect upon the growth of the faith. A significant number felt that it had no relation to the development of Christianity.

The great majority thought that the close link between government and the economic order had had an adverse effect upon Christianity. However, the opinion was expressed that the church was not really aware of the nature of the relationship and thus took no stand in relation to it. Two contrary opinions found expression more than once, the first said that the church had no responsibility here, the second said that the church must accept more responsibility here.

The majority were convinced that "paternalism" in the structure of Japanese society, especially within the economy, had affected the development of Christianity. The reasons given were that it prevented the growth of Christian liberalism, individualism, and the labour movement; it always worked in favour of the employer enjoining hard work and respect for property but condemning socialism and labour unions. Its influence could be felt in the life of the church giving the minister an authoritarian view of his position in relation to the people and thus preventing the young, who rebelled against this, from entering the church.

D. *Faith and Life of the Church*

Almost all were agreed that the spirit of evangelism within the churches is weaker today than it was in the early Meiji period. The reasons given were as follows: the church has become pastor-centred; liberal theology took away the sense of urgency; there is no persecution, while at the same time, there is satisfaction with the "status quo;" there is general discouragement; faith has become mere knowledge.

Most were agreed that the church had made no attempt to approach the different classes in Japanese society according to their needs. The sociologists claimed that this accounts for the fact that the faith is orientated to the intelligentsia since they alone have understood it.

The majority agreed that materialism had had a most adverse effect upon the development of the faith throughout the period but a significant number were convinced that its influence was strongest in the closing days of the Meiji era.

There was a wide measure of agreement that the "revival" of 1883–84 had occurred because of the depth and simplicity of the faith. Some, however, attributed it to the critical nature of the times and to the popularity of western culture. Most felt that a "revival" of similar intensity did not occur again because faith has tended to become mere knowledge, or because its emotional excesses brought about a reaction to it, or that the hardening of the social structures of Japan prevented it.

The majority were agreed that persecution had had a good effect upon the life of the church, though one-third of those who so replied qualified their statements recognizing that it had had an adverse effect upon numerical growth. One prominent leader said there had been no persecution.

When asked how existence in a predominantly Buddhist society had affected the thought and practice of the Japanese church, several significant replies were received. Among them were the following: Buddhist habits of meditation, their abstract ideas, and their general religious attitude has affected the approach of Japanese Christians to their faith; through tradition and custom Buddhism has had a negative influence upon the development of the Christian faith; the pantheism of Buddhism has made an understanding of Christianity difficult; its emphasis on emotionalism has had a negative influence. One-quarter of those who replied said it had had no important influence whatever.

To the question, "Did the influence of Chinese Philosophy and Culture in Japan have a favourable or unfavourable effect upon the acceptance of Christianity?" two-thirds replied that it had a favourable effect and one-third that it had an unfavourable effect. Among the opinions expressed were the following: its strong interest in ethics created a strong initial interest in Christianity; it acted for the Japanese as the Old Testament does to the New for the western Christian; the ethical interest it created blocked an understanding of revealed religion.

When asked to name churches that had been particularly successful in weathering the storms which successive crises throughout the years had brought to them the same churches in Tokyo, Sapporo, and Kochi ken on the island of Shikoku, were named a significant number of times. Few could give examples of those which had failed but the ones which were given were in the countryside.

Finally, the question was asked, "What lessons ought to be learned as a result of the church's experience in Japanese society over the past one hundred years?" The following are some of the replies based on a consensus of opinion: the church must approach the labouring classes; it must approach all classes; it must understand social conditions which prevented growth and seek to overcome them; there must be less absorption in theology and more practical expression of the faith; the church needs a theology which the common man can understand; it cannot proceed in defiance of the national character; a Japanese theology is required; the church must stress evangelism rather than the building of institutions; it must cease to rely upon foreign capital; it must learn a finer spiritual discipline while understanding the appeal of materialism.

EXHIBIT B

The Imperial Rescript on Education

Promulgated October 30, 1890. A translation by the Imperial Department of Education 1907.

Know ye, Our subjects: Our Imperial Ancestors have founded Our Empire on a basis broad and everlasting, and have deeply and firmly implanted virtue: Our subjects ever united in loyalty and filial piety have from generation to generation illustrated the beauty thereof. This is the glory of the fundamental character of Our Empire, and herein also lies the source of Our education. Ye, Our subjects, be filial to your parents, affectionate to your brothers and sisters; as husbands and wives be harmonious, as friends true; bear yourselves in modesty and moderation; extend your benevolence to all; pursue learning and cultivate arts; and thoroughly develop intellectual faculties and perfect moral powers; furthermore, advance public good and promote common interests; always respect the Constitution and observe the laws; should emergency arise, offer yourselves courageously to the State; and thus guard and maintain the prosperity of Our Imperial Throne coeval with heaven and earth. So shall ye not only be Our good and faithful subjects, but render illustrious the best traditions of your forefathers.

The Way here set forth is indeed the teaching bequeathed by Our Imperial Ancestors to be observed alike by Their Descendants and the subjects, infallible for all ages and true in all places. It is Our wish to lay it to heart in all reverence in common with you, Our subjects, that we may all thus attain to the same virtue.

BIBLIOGRAPHY

(NOTE: This bibliography is divided into two parts. The first division has to do with those studies related to the methodology used and the second to the subject matter of the study. These in turn are divided into two parts. The first part contains those works which are basic to the argument of both methodology and subject matter. The second part contains those works which are either supplementary to, or have a bearing upon them. This bibliography is intended to be intensive, not extensive. There is a list of doctoral dissertations which have appeared over the past twenty years and which have some bearing upon this study or are relevant to the questions which it raises for future study. The footnotes are fully annotated and therefore the bibliography is only annotated where the nature of a work is either not implied in the title or does not appear annotated within the body of the work.)

I

A. Basic Works related to the Methodology of this Study

Aron, Raymond, *German Sociology*. Trans. by Mary and Thomas Bottomo re London: Heinemann, 1957. 141 pp.

Gerth, Hans H., and Mills, C. Wright, *From Max Weber: Essays in Sociology*. London: Oxford, 1946. 490 pp.

Parsons, Talcott, *Essays in Sociological Theory*. Glencoe, Ill.: Free Press, 1951. 459 pp.

——, *The Structure of Social Action*. New York: McGraw-Hill, 1937. 817 pp.

Pfister, Bernhard, *Die Entwicklung zum Idealtypus*. Tubingen: Mohr, 1928. Especially pp. 138–175 on Weber's "ideal-type."

Sorokin, Pitrim A., *Contemporary Sociological Theories*. New York: Harper, 1928. 785 pp.

Shils, Edward A., and Finch, Henry, *Max Weber: The Methodology of the Social Sciences*. Glencoe, Ill.: Fee Press, 1949, 188 pp.

Weber, Max, *The Protestant Ethic and the Spirit of Capitalism*. Trans. by Talcott Parsons. New York: Scribner, 1930. 292 pp.

——, *The Theory of Social and Economic Organization*. Trans. by A. M. Henderson and Talcott Parsons. Edited and with an introduction by Talcott Parsons. Glencoe, Ill.: Fee Press and Falcon Press, 1947. 436 pp.

——, *The Religions of China*. Glencoe, Ill.: Free Press, 1951. Trans. by Hans H. Gerth. 308 pp.

——, *Ancient Judaism*. Trans. by Hans Gerth and Donald Martindale, Glencoe, Ill.: Free Press, 1952. 484 pp.

B. Secondary References

Ballard, Lloyd V., *Social Institutions*. New York: Appleton-Century, 1936. 514 pp.

Barnes, H. E., and Becker, H., *Contemporary Social Theory*. New York: Appleton-Century, 1940. 947 pp.

Bendix, Reinhard and Lipset, Seymour M., Ed., *Class, Status and Power*. Glencoe, Ill.: Fee Press, 1953. 725 pp.
Brunner, Emil, *Christianity and Civilization*. New York: Scribner, 1949. 2 Vols.
Herskovits, Melville L., *Man and His Works*. New York: Knopf, 1952, 678 pp.
Linton, Ralph, *The Study of Man*. New York: Appleton-Century, 1936. 503 pp.
Mayer, Kurt B., *Class and Society*. New York: Doubleday, 1955. 88 pp.
Neill, Stephen, *The Christian Society*. London: Nisbet, 1952, 334 pp.
Niebuhr, H. Richard, *The Social Sources of Denominationalism*. New York: Holt, 1929. 304 pp.
——, *Christ and Culture*. New York: Harper, 1951. 259 pp.
Nottingham, Elizabeth K., *Religion and Society*. New York: Doubleday, 1954. 84 pp.
Panunzio, Constantine, *Major Social Institutions*. New York: MacMillan, 1939. 609 pp.
Pope, Liston, *Millhands and Preachers*. New Haven: Yale University Press, 1942. 369 pp.
Schumpeter, Joseph, *Social Classes: Imperialism*. New York: Meridian, 1955. 182 pp.
Studies in Quaker Thought and Practice. London: Friends Press, 1931. 3 Vols.
Sutherland, Robert L., and Woodward, Julian L., *Introductory Sociology*, Philadelphia: Lippincott, 1937. 720 pp.
Tawney, R. H., *Religion and the Rise of Capitalism*. New York: Harcourt Brace, 1936. 309 pp.
Troeltsch, Ernst, *The Social Teachings of the Christian Churches*. New York: MacMillan, 1931. Trans. by Olive Wyon. 2 Vols.
Wach, Joachim, *Sociology of Religion*. Chicago: University of Chicago Press, 1944. 418 pp.
Weber, Marianne, *Max Weber: ein Lebansbild*. Tubingen: Mohr, 1926. 719 pp.
Yinger, J. Milton, *Religion in the Struggle for Power*. Durham, N. C.: Duke University Press, 1946. 275 pp.

II

A. Basic Works related to the Content of this Study

1. *In Japanese*

Sumiya, Mikio, *Kindai Nihon no Keisei to Kirisutokyo* (Christianity and the Formation of Modern Japan). Tokyo: Shinkyo Shuppansha, 1950. 124 pp.
——, *Nihon Shakai to Kirisutokyo* (Christianity and Japanese Society). Tokyo: Tokyo Daigaku Shuppansha, 1954. 179 pp.
——, "Chusan Kaikyu no Seiritsu to Kirisutokyo" (Christianity and the Formation of the Middle Class) in *Fukuin to Sekai*. Tokyo: Shinkyo Shuppansha, June, 1954. pp. 23–28.
Kudo, Eichi, "Shodai Nihon Protestanto no Shakaizo" (The Class Structure of Early Japanese Protestantism), *Meiji Gakuin Ronsetsu*, No. 30. 28 pp.

Hiyane, Antei, *Nihon Kirisutokyoshi* (History of Japanese Christianity). Tokyo: Kyobunkan, 1949. 422 pp.

——, *Nihon Kinsei Kirisutokyo Jinbutsushi* (History of Christian Personalities in Modern Japan). Tokyo: Kirisutokyo Hakkosha, 1935. 558 pp.

2. *In English*

Beasley, William G., *Great Britain and the Opening of Japan*. London: Luzac, 1952. 227 pp.

——, *Select Documents on Japanese Foreign Policy*, 1853–1868. London: Oxford, 1955. 359 pp.

Borton, Hugh, *Japan's Modern Century*. New York: Ronald Press, 1955. 524 pp.

Brinkley, F., *A History of the Japanese People*. New York: Encyclopedia Britannica 1915. 784 pp.

Cary, Otis, *A History of Christianity in Japan*. New York: Revell, 1909. 2 Vols.

Christian Movement in Japan later bound as *The Japan Christian Year Book*—1903–1912. Tokyo and Yokohama: Standing Committee of Cooperating Christian Missions.

Cosenza, Mario, E., *The Complete Journal of Townsend Harris*. New York: Doubleday Doran, 1930. 616 pp.

Iwasaki, Uichi, "The Working Forces in Japanese Politics." *Studies in History Economics and Public Law*. Vol. 97. No. 1. New York: Columbia University Press, 1921. 135 pp.

Lockwood, William W., *The Economic Development of Japan*. Princeton: Princeton University Press, 1954. 603 pp.

McLaren, Walter W., *A Political History of Japan During the Meiji Era*, 1867–1912. New York: Scribner, 1916. 380 pp.

Murdoch, James, in collaboration with Yamagata Isoh, *A History of Japan*. London: Kegan Paul, 1926. 3 Vols.

Nitobe, Inazo, Bushido, *The Soul of Japan*. Tokyo: Teibi, 1914. 129 pp.

Norman, E. Herbert, *Japan's Emergence as a Modern State*. New York: Institute of Pacific Relations, 1940. 254 pp.

Proceedings of the General Conference of Protestant Missionaries in Japan held at Osaka, Japan, 1883. Yokohama: Meiklejohn, 1883. 468 pp.

Proceedings of the General Conference of Protestant Missionaries in Japan, 1900. Tokyo: Methodist Publishing Co., 1901. 1048 pp.

Report of the Evangelical Alliance held in London, 1846. London: Partridge and Oakey, 1847. 509 pp.

Ritter, H. A., *History of Protestant Missions in Japan*. Trans. by G. Albrecht and revised by Dr. C. Greene. Tokyo: Methodist Publishing Co., 1898. 446 pp.

Ryder, Stephen W., *A Historical-Educational Study of the Japan Mission of the Reformed Church of America*. York, Pa.: York Press, 1935. 172 pp.

Sansom, Sir George G., Japan, *A Short Cultural History*. New York: Appleton-Century, 1943. 554 pp.

——, *The Western World and Japan*. New York: Knopf, 1950. 504 pp.

Scalapino, Robert A., *Democracy and the Party Movement in Pre-War Japan*. Berkeley, Cal.: University of California Press, 1953. 471 pp.

Takenaka, Masao, *Relation of Protestantism to Social Problems in Japan* 1901–1941. Unpublished doctoral thesis. Yale University, 1954.

Verbeck, Guido, *History of Protestant Missions in Japan, From the Opening of Japan until* 1883. A report which may be found in the proceedings of the Osaka Conference, 1883, mentioned above, or on microfilm from the Missionary Research Library, Union Theological Seminary, New York.

Yanaga, Chitose, *Japan Since Perry* (New York: McGraw-Hill, 1949).

B. Secondary References

1. *In Japanese.*

Kuyama, Yasushi, Ed. *Kindai Nihon to Kirisutokyo* (Christianity and Modern Japan). Nishinomiya: Kirisutokyo Gakuto Kyodaidan, 1956. 382 pp. A discussion among a group of Christian leaders in Japan, some of whom answered the questionnaire which appears in the Appendix of this study.

Hiyane, Antei, *Nihon Shukyoshi* (History of Japanese Religions). Tokyo: Kyobunkan, 1951. 424 pp.

Matsumiya, Kazuya, *Nihon Kirisutokyo Shakai Bunkashi* (A Social Cultural History of Japanese Christianity). Tokyo: Shinkigensha, 1948. 346 pp.

Namae, Takayuki, *Nihon Kirisutokyo Shakai Jigyoshi* (A History of Christian Social Work in Japan). Tokyo: Kyobunkan, 1931. 311 pp. A full account of the role which Christianity played in Japanese Social work from the Tokugawa era until the present.

Oguchi, Iichi, *Nihon Shukyo no Shakai Teki Seikaku* (The Social Character of Japanese Religion). Tokyo: Tokyo Daigaku Shuppansha, 1953. 213 pp. Examines the factors which are peculiar to Japanese religion in general.

Nihon Kirisutokyodan Shakai Iinkai Ed. *Kirisutokyo to Shakai Henkaku* (Christianity and Social Change). Tokyo: Naigai Kyoryokai, 1953. A discussion among Christian leaders referring in the main to contemporary conditions but with some relation to the content of our study. 203 pp.

2. *In English*

Allen, George C., *A Short Economic History of Modern Japan*, 1867–1937. Toronto: MacMillan, 1951. 200 pp.

——, *Japanese Industry: Its Recent Developments and Present Condition.* New York: Institute of Pacific Relations, 1940. 124 pp.

Anesaki, Masaharu, *History of Japanese Religion.* London: Paul, Trench, Trubner, 1930. 423 pp.

Benedict, Ruth, *The Chrysanthemum and the Sword.* Boston: Houghton Mifflin, 1946. 324 pp.

Borton, Hugh, *Peasant Uprisings in Japan of the Tokugawa Period.* Tokyo: Transactions of the Asiatic Society of Japan. Second Series, Vol. XVI, May, 1938.

Boxer, Charles R., *The Christian Century in Japan* 1549–1650. Berkeley: University of California Press, 1951. 535 pp.

Bunce, William K., *Religions in Japan.* Rutland, Vt.: Charles Tuttle, 1955. 194 pp. An account of the religious situation in post-war Japan.

Copeland, Luther, *The Crisis in Protestant Missions in Japan* 1889–1900. Yale University: Unpublished doctoral thesis. 1949.

Embree, John F., *The Japanese Nation, A Social Survey*. New York: Farrar and Rinehart, 1945. 308 pp.

Encyclopedia of the Social Sciences. New York: MacMillan, 1935. 15 Vols. Article on *Max Weber* by Hans Speier, Vol. XV pp. 386–388. And on *Sociology* by R. M. MacIver. Vol. XIV. pp. 243–246.

Gubbins, J. H., *The Making of Modern Japan*. London: Seeley Service, 1922. 316 pp.

Hall, John W., *Japanese History: A Guide to Japanese Reference and Research Material*. Ann Arbor: University of Michigan Press, 1954. 165 pp.

Haring, Douglas G., Ed. *Japan's Prospect*. Cambridge: Harvard University Press, 1946. 474 pp. Contains an article by Talcott Parsons on *Population and Social Structure* which is particularly relevant.

Holtom, Daniel C., *The National Faith of Japan*. New York: Dutton, 1938. 329 pp.

——, *Modern Japan and Shinto Nationalism*. Chicago: University of Chicago Press, 1943. 226 pp.

Jaeckel, Theodore, "Japan's Spiritual Situation." *The Japan Christian Quarterly*, Vol. XXI, No. 3, July, 1955.

Japan Evangelist. Vol. 1–33, Tokyo: 1893–1925.

Japanese Religion in the Meiji Era. Trans. by John F. Howes in Vol. 2 the Centenary Cultural Council Series. Tokyo: Obunsha, 1956. 377 pp. Essays on Japan's Three Major Religions.

Kaempfer, Engelbert, *The History of Japan*. Trans. by J. G. Scheuchzer, London: Woodward Davis, 1727. 612 pp. An original account by a Dutch doctor resident in Nagasaki during the Shogunate of conditions in Japan at that time.

Katayama, Sen, *The Labour Movement in Japan*. Chicago: Kerr, 1918. (Out of Print)

Latourette, Kenneth, *The Development of Japan*. New York: MacMillan, 1920. 237 pp.

——, *The History of Japan*. New York: MacMillan, 1947. 290 pp.

——, *A History of the Expansion of Christianity*. Seven Volumes. See Vol. III, Chapt. 13 and Vol. VII, Chapt. 14. New York: Harper, 1937–45.

McGovern, William M., *Modern Japan*. New York: Scribner, 1920. 280 pp.

Mitsui, House of, *A Record of Three Centuries*. Tokyo: 1937.

Miyaoka, Tsunejiro, *Growth of Liberalism in Japan*. Carnegie Endowment for International Peace; Division of Intercourse and Education. No. 16, 1918. 24 pp. An Interpretation of "democracy."

Nida, Eugene, *God's Word in Man's Language*. New York: Harper, 1952. 191 pp.

——, *Customs and Cultures*. New York: Harper, 1954. 306 pp.

Nitobe, Inazo, *Western Influences in Modern Japan*, Chicago: University of Chicago Press, 1931. 532 pp.

Norman, E. Herbert, "The Genyosha," *Pacific Affairs*. Sept. 1944. pp. 261–64.

Okuma, Shigenobu, Ed., *Kifty Years of New Japan*. London: Smith Elder, 1909. 2 Vols. Extremely interesting articles by the leaders of Meiji Japan.

Oliphant, Laurence, *Narrative of the Earl of Elgin's Mission to Japan.* New York: Harper, 1860. 645 pp.

Ono, Yeijiro, *The Industrial Revolution in Japan.* Baltimore: American Economic Association. Vol. V, No. 1, 1890. 121 pp.

Orchard, John E., *Japan's Economic Position.* New York: McGraw-Hill, 1930. 504 pp.

Paske-Smith, "Japanese Traditions of Christianity," *Reports of Persecutions.* London: Kegan Paul, 1930. 142 pp.

Pooley, A. M., *Japan at the Crossroads.* New York: Dodd Mead, 1917. 362 pp.

Quigley, Harold S., Japan, *Government and Politics.* New York: Century, 1932. 432 pp.

Reischauer, August K., *Studies in Japanese Buddhism.* New York: MacMillan, 1925. 361 pp.

Reischauer, Edwin O., *The United States and Japan.* Cambridge, Mass.: Harvard University Press, 1950. 357 pp.

——, *Japan Past and Present.* New York: Knopf, 1952. 292 pp.

Saito, Soichi, *A Study of the Infiuence of Christianity Upon Japanese Culture.* Tokyo: Japan Council of the Institute of Pacific Relations, 1931. 71 pp.

Sato, Shosuke, *Some Historical Phases of Modern Japan.* New York: Japan Society, 1916. 164 pp.

Scalapino, Robert A., "The United States and Japan" in *The United States and the Far East.* New York: Columbia University, 1956. 239 pp.

Stead, Alfred Ed., *Japan by the Japanese.* New York: Dodd Mead, 1904. 697 pp. This volume contains valuable articles by a number of those who participated in the making of modern Japan.

Treat, Payson J., *Japan and the United States*, 1853–1921. New York: Houghton Mifflin, 1921. 283 pp.

Trewartha, Glenn T., *Japan.* Madison, Wisc.: University of Wisconsin Press, 1945. 607 pp. The best available geography on modern Japan.

Tucker, Henry, *The History of the Episcopal Church in Japan.* New York: Scribner, 1938. 228 pp.

Uyehara, G. E., *The Political Development of Japan*, 1867–1909. New York: Dutton, 1910. The introduction has particular reference to our study.

Walworth, Arthur, *Black Ships Off Japan.* New York: Knopf, 1946. 278 pp.

Appendix

(NOTE: The Doctoral dissertations which appear below have been written within the past twenty years and include only those which do not appear in the body of the bibliography. They have some bearing upon the methodology or the content of this study and they are listed in *Doctoral Dissertations* used by American Universities. Trotier, Arnold H., and Harman, Marian, editors, New York: Wilson, 1938–1955, now listed in *Dissertations Abstracts.* Ann Arbor: University of Michigan, 1955–1957.)

Baer, Theodore S., *Max Weber's Methodology of Social Science; A Critique.* Harvard University, unpublished thesis, 1952.

Baker, Wendell D., *A Study of Selected Aspects of Japanese Social Stratification.* Columbia University, 1956.

Bellah, Robert N., *Religion in Society in Tokugawa Japan*, Harvard University, 1955.

Cody, Cecil Earl, *A Study of the Career of Itagaki Taisuke* 1837–1919, a Leader of the Democratic Movement in Meiji Japan. University of Michigan, 1955. On Microfilm at the University of Michigan, Ann Arbor, Michigan

Floyd, Arva C., *The Founding of the Japan Methodist Church*. Yale University, 1939.

Munakata, Peter Francis, *The Application of Western Sociological Theory to the Analysis of Bureaucratic Structure in Japan*. A Pilot study and its interpretation. Fordham University, 1956.

Nahrendorf, Richard O., *Origins and Interpretations of Selected Sociological Concepts of Max Weber*. University of Southern California, 1948.

Noss, George Sherer, *An Inquiry into the Background of and Interpretation of the Critical Issues Confronting the Japanese Church in its Struggle with the Japanese Totalitarian State: Some Suggestions for a Solution*. Union Theological Seminary, 1943.

Pelzel, John C., *Social Stratification in Japanese Urban Economic Life*. Harvard University, 1950.

Yoshino, Roger I., *Selected Social Changes in a Japanese Village*, 1935–1953. University of Southern California, 1955.

The Journal of Asian Studies formerly *The Far Eastern Quarterly*, the publication of the Far Eastern Association each year in its September issue publishes an excellent bibliography of all works appearing in western languages on Japan.

INDEX

Abe Isoo, 119, 165, 170
Albrecht, Paul, "The Churches and Rapid Social Change," IX
Act: mining (1905), 140
  factory (1911), 140
Agricultural School in Sapporo, 98
America, 21, 49, 137
American, 11, 14, 20, 21, 23, 80
  consul, 10
  embassy, 13
  navy, 13, 27
  Reformed mission, 80
  vessel, 13
American Baptist Free Mission Society, 28
American Episcopal Church, 81, 157
Ando, Hajime, 179
Anglo-Japanese Alliance (1902), 124
Aomori Ken, 43
Ashio Copper Mines, 120
Association, 60
  laws restricting, 84, 180
  for study of social problems, 120
Association for study of social policy, 135
Awadzu, Komei, 89

Bakufu, 3, 4, 5, 6, 7, 8, 9, 10, 11, 12, 13, 14, 15, 16, 18, 19, 21, 35, 36
  anti-Bakufu, 5
Ballagh, Rev. J. H., 28, 29, 88, 89
Bank of Japan, 138
Berry, Dr., 100
Beshhi copper mines, 120
Bible, English, 25
Bismarck, 39, 77
Blind, education of, 100
Body of Christ, 79
Borton, Dr. Hugh, 34, 42, 106, 148
Boxer Rebellion, 122
Boys' schools, 100
Britain, 13, 46, 114, 115, 122, 124, 131, 137
Brown, Delmer, 35, 47, 107, 115
Brown, Samuel R., 28
Buddhism, 19, 25, 36, 45, 48, 71, 72, 73, 74, 75, 76, 85, 155, 176, 181
  in China, XII
  in South East Asia, XII
  in Japan, XII
Buddhist Priest, 28, 72, 73, 76, 77, 82
  Buddhist monasteries, 73
  Buddhists, 144, 148, 165, 169
  Buddhist sects, 158
  Buddhist Society, 182
Bungaku Kai, 167
bureaucrats, 54, 55, 56, 57, 105, 108, 139, 141, 142, 172
  Japanese, 129
bureaucracy, 57, 108, 161, 172
  military, 142
  civil, 142
Bushido, 26, 88, 130, 148, 157

Cabinets, 24, 109, 110, 111, 116, 118
Canton Event, 12, 14
Capital, 8, 63, 80
  foreign, 8, 63
Capitalists, 141
Capitalism, 181
Cary, Otis, 99, 149, 155, 156, 159
Charter oath, 35, 36, 37
Chiba, ken, 59, 80
Child labor, 140
China, 12, 13, 16, 21, 26, 27, 28, 29, 36, 40, 53, 63, 65, 73, 113, 114, 122, 123, 128, 137
Choshu, 4, 9, 13, 14, 15, 22, 26, 37, 38, 41, 63, 111, 112, 116
  daimyo of, 13, 33
  samurai, 13, 33
Christian, 7, 19, 20, 23, 24, 25, 26, 27, 44, 59, 71, 73, 74
  community, 77, 79
  country, 76
  historian, 77
  ideas, 61, 80
  leaders, 77
  powers, 71
  religion, 46
Christian Girls Schools, 100
Christian global strategy, 177
Christian Socialists, 151
Christianity, definition of, 69
Clan bureaucrats, 38, 53, 73, 116
  Clan bureaucracy, 110

Clark, Colonel W. S., 98
Church,
  Baptist, 93
  councils, 44
  membership, 147
  rural, 7
Class, 180, 182
  association, 98
  farm, 142
  intellectual, 144, 153, 158, 162, 163
  labor, 142, 162, 182
  lower, 85, 132, 133, 152, 172, 180, 181
  lower middle, 133
  managerial, 134, 135, 153, 162
  middle, 67, 77, 101, 128, 130, 139, 142, 151, 152, 163, 170, 172, 179, 180
  orientation, 101, 161, 179
  peasant, 162
  poorer, 98
  professional, 134–5, 142, 162
  salaried, 144, 158, 162
  structure, 53, 126, 130, 131, 132, 133, 134, 135, 139
  technicians, 162
  upper, 76, 79, 84, 86, 98, 99, 151, 162, 180, 181, 182
  upper middle, 130
  upper upper, 133
Codes
  Judicial, 124, 135
  Commercial, 124, 135
Comity agreements, 147
Commercial Code, 106
Communism, XI, 153
Confucian, 35, 44, 49, 51, 60
  authoritarianism, 67, 152
  concept of filial piety, 105
  ethic, 51
  scholar, 72
  teachings, 97
  state absolutism, 35
  values, 81, 146
Confucianism, XII, 29, 45, 49, 73, 75, 149, 155, 157, 176
  school of Wang Yang-Ming, or Yomeigaku, 95, 96, 171
Congregational Church, 78, 84, 90, 92, 93, 151, 154, 155, 157, 160, 161, 163
  Conference of, 156
Conscript army, 97
Council of State, 23, 36, 38, 41
Constitution, 46, 47, 48, 49, 68, 76, 77, 105, 106, 108, 110, 111, 118, 124, 125, 144, 145, 148, 151, 161, 180
  article 28, 151
  promulgation of, 74
  text of, 48
Creed
  apostle's, 93, 154, 155
Curtis, Donker, 18

Daido Danketsu, 108, 111
Democracy, 51, 180
Developing economy, 57
  industry, 62
Development, 64, 65, 67, 69, 77
  economic, 64, 66
De Vries, Egbert
  "Man in Rapid Social Change", IX
Diet, 111
  executive branch, 111
"Disinherited" the, 171, 176
Dort, Synod of, 91
Doshisha University, 83, 98, 149, 156
Drew University, IX, 157
Dual Alliance, 115
Dutch, 10, 13, 14, 18

Ebina Danjo, 86, 149, 158
Echizen, 25, 26
Ecumenical concern, 147
Edict boards, 71, 74, 79, 174
Edo, 3, 4, 14, 15
Education, 173
  moral, 105
Emperor, 3, 5, 9, 12, 13, 14, 15, 16, 17, 19, 24, 25, 31, 35, 36, 37, 40, 41, 44, 45, 46, 48, 49, 51, 68, 71, 72, 76, 77, 81, 86, 89, 96, 105, 148, 152, 180
  court, 13
  divinity, 46
  forces, 14
  institution, 16, 47, 65, 68, 84, 105, 106, 111, 154, 174, 176, 179, 180
  loyalty to, 73
Emperor of China, 10
Enclosure Acts, 7
Engineers' and Firemen's Union, 165
England, 10, 12, 22, 115, 121, 124, 138, 140
  alliance with Japan, 1902, 122
entrepeneurs, 132, 134, 138, 141, 142
Episcopal Church, 90, 92, 94, 161, 180
  American, 27, 81
  Mission Board, 27

equality, 61
of women, 100
eta, 165
ethics, 182
Eto, Shimpei, 38, 40, 42, 58, 71
Europe, 5, 8, 39, 47, 48, 65, 76, 77, 141
Evangelical Alliance, 71, 88, 94, 154, 155, 161
Expansion, military, 45, 130
Expansionism, 49, 113, 116, 123, 125, 151
expansionist program, 120
Extra territoriality, 39, 106, 124, 144

Factory laws, 164–165
Farmer, 6, 7, 9, 43, 58, 59, 60, 80, 82, 83, 85, 132, 134
Ferris, Dr., 24
Ferris Institute, 167
Feudal system, 6, 7, 38, 53, 57
feudalism, 151, 161, 180
lord, 26
Filial piety, 60
Finance minister, 45, 48
Financial magnates, 56
leaders, 58
Financiers, 51, 55, 66
First high school in Tokyo, 149
Foreign loans, 57
Formosa, 40, 114, 116
Formosan expedition, 60
governor-general of, 116
Forward movement, 161
France, 10, 15, 49, 75, 114, 115
Freedom Party, 45
French, 13, 14, 15, 80
revolution, 61
Freylinghausen, Senator, 24
Fukuoka, 146
Fukuzawa Yukichi, 74, 75, 76, 86
Futagawa, 71

Garst, Charles, 120
Genro, 110, 118
Germany, 39, 49, 114, 115, 124, 131, 136
Bismarckian, 47, 77
Goble, Jonathan, 28
Gold standard, 128
Goto Shojiro, 36, 37, 40, 41, 43, 60, 61, 66, 83, 108
Government,
constitutional, 46
executive branch, 110
representative, 40, 41, 43, 45, 59, 60, 106, 107, 108, 116, 118, 124
responsible, 113, 115
Governors of Prefectures, 24
Great Britain, 24, 53, 75, 140
Greene, D. C., 167–168
Griffis, 72
Growth
economic, 172
numerical, 147, 161
Gumma Ken, 44, 80, 100
Gunboat diplomacy, 12

Hakodate, 10, 147
Harris, Townsend, 11, 15, 20, 21
Hay, Secretary, 122
Heidelberg Confession, 91, 93, 150, 155
Heiminsha, 120
Hepburn, Dr. J. C., 27, 28
Hideyoshi, 19, 20, 21
Higo, 28
Hiyaguchi, 100
Hiroshima, 113
Hizen, 4, 9, 19, 33, 37, 38, 40, 58
Hokkaido, 45, 82, 98
Hokkaido scandal, 61, 66
Holiness Sects, 180
Holland, 10, 75
Holland, J. M., 164
Home Department, 44
Home for Blind, 165
for Lepers, 165
Home Ministry, 46, 108
Honda Yoichi, 44, 86, 89, 93, 95, 97, 100, 157
Honshu, 81
Hoshi, Toru, 117, 163
Hotta, 11, 12
House of Peers, 24, 33, 96, 109, 111
of Representatives, 162, 163
Hyogo, 15

Ichikawa Yeinosuke, 71
Iglehart, C. W., Professor Emeritus of Missions, Union Theological Seminary, New York, X
Ii Naosuke, 11, 12
Imperial
household, 33, 141, 142, 149
household staff, 47
Imperial Rescript, 46, 105, 106, 124–5, 148, 149
on education, 180

APPEND IX A

India, IX, introd. XI, 73, 141, 143
Industrial Revolution, 7
  expansion, 130
  leaders, 142
Industrialists, 4, 9, 54, 55, 66, 128, 139
Inouye Kaoru, 37, 66, 107, 111, 142
Inouye, Tetsujiro, 148
Inside clans, 5
Internationalism
  economic, 152
Ise, 24
Itagaki, Taisuke, 36, 37, 40, 41, 42, 43, 44, 45, 50, 60, 61, 82, 83, 84, 108, 111, 112, 117, 160
Ito Hirobumi, 13, 34, 37, 39, 41, 42, 43, 46, 47, 48, 49, 64, 65, 72, 76, 77, 84, 105, 106, 110, 111, 112, 113, 116, 117, 118, 123, 125, 139, 153, 160
Iwakura Mission, 36, 40, 41, 58, 72, 74, 75
Iwakura Tomoyoshi, 33, 36, 39, 55, 71, 105, 118
Iwasaki, (Zaibatsu), 132, 136, 141, 142

Janes, Captain, 98
Japan Rail Company, 165
Japanese, 11, 12, 17, 19, 20, 25, 26
  castaways, 27
  culture, introd. XIV
  feudal society, 5
  governments, 22
  history, introd. XIV
  leaders, introd. XIII, 23
    medicine, 100
  military, introd. XIII
  officials, 18, 22
  politics, introd. XIII, 29, 42
  society, introd. XII, XIII, XIV, XV, 26, 29, 33
  traders, 15
Japanese Christianity, 30, 80, 149
"Jiyu Minken Undo", See People's Rights Movement
Jiyu-to, 45, 111, 112
Jogaku Zasshi, 167

Kagoshima, 4, 13, 24, 26, 80, 147
Kaigan church, 78
Kaishin-to, 45, 82, 111, 112
Kanagawa, 10, 23, 28
Kanamori, Tsurin, 150
Kataoka Kenkichi, 44, 45, 61, 83, 118, 145, 163
  as speaker of lower house, 118
Katayama Sen, 119, 120, 121, 165
Kato, Hiroyuki, 75, 86, 145
Katsura government, 123, 139
Kawakami Kiyoshi, 119, 165
Keiki, regent, 14
Kelsey, George, Professor, Drew Univ. Graduate School, IX
Kensei-honto, 108, 118
Kenseito Party, 117, 119, 163
Kido, Koin, 34, 36, 37, 40, 41, 42, 43, 55
Kinoshita, Naoe, 165, 166
Kitamura, Tokoku, 159
Kochi ken, 4, 182
Kokugakusha, 72
Kokumin no Tomo, 167
Kokuminto, 119
Komei, Awasu, 29
Konoike, (Zaibatsu), 16
Korea, 40, 73, 108, 113, 114, 121, 122, 123, 128, 137
  Korean affair, 43, 45, 172
Kotoku, 120, 121
Kozaki, 149
Kudo, Eichi, 25, 95, 97
Kuge, 3, 5, 33
  ex-kuge, 39
Kumamoto, 41
  band, 86, 95, 98
Kuroda, 66
Kyobu sho, 72
Kyodan, IX, 180
Kyoto, 3, 14
Kyushu, 4, 80

Labor, 166
  conditions, 134
  movement, 181
  unions, 153, 164, 166, 181
Laborers' Friendly Society, 166
Lafayette College, X
Laissez-faire, 135
Landholders, 66, 128
Landlord, 7, 9, 43, 58, 59, 60, 67, 80, 82, 83, 98, 132, 134, 141, 142, 146, 151, 161
  as entrepreneur, 62
  rural, 118, 119
Li, Hung-Chang, 114
Li-Lobanov Treaty of 1896, 121
Liaotung Peninsula, 114, 115, 121, 123

Liberalism, 117
Christian, 181
in political structure, 141, 171
Liggens, John, 21, 27
Lockwood, W. W., 53, 56, 64, 127, 128, 129, 132, 134, 136, 137, 138, 142, 153
Lords, 3, 4, 5, 6, 7, 8, 9, 35, 37, 38, 57, 63
of Satsuma, 13
Lower House, 113

Mainichi newspaper, 163, 166
Managerial group, 132–3
Manchu dynasty, 114, 122
Manchuria, 114, 121, 122, 123
south, 128
Manchurian Railroad, 121, 123
south - m. railway, 138
Manufacturers, 119
Marxism, XI
Materialism, 181, 182
Matsudaira, 25, 26
Matsukata, Masayoshi, 48, 61, 65, 111, 112, 116, 117
McLaren, W. W., 109, 110, 113, 126
McWilliams, W. R., X
Meiji, Emperor, 35
Meiji era, XII, XIII, XV, 3, 14, 23, 34, 35, 38, 56, 74, 101, 111, 130, 178, 181
constitution, 84, 101, 109
government, 23, 25
leaders, 53
renovation, 53, 95
rescript on education (1890), 50, 77, 81, 149, See also Imperial Rescript on Education
Merchants, 4, 6, 7, 8, 9, 16, 42, 51, 53, 53, 54, 58, 61, 63, 119, 128, 139
class, 8, 23, 30, 33, 80, 98
foreign, 106
Methodist, 157, 161, 163
Canadian, 94, 157, 160
Episcopal, 93, 94
Methodist Church South, 157
Methodism, 160
Militarism, 116, 123, 125, 128
Militarists, 120
Military faction, 117
Mill, J. S., 44, 74, 75
Minamoto no Yoritomo, 3
Minister - presidents, 116, 118
Ministry of commerce, 138
Missions
council of, 90, 91, 97
Mito, 12
Mitsubishi, (Zaibatsu), 66, 132, 136, 141
Mitsui, (Zaibatsu), 16, 60, 66, 132, 136, 142, 152
Mobility
occupational, 134
social, 8, 134
Mori, Arenori, 72, 106
Mosse, Dr. Albert, 108
Motoda, 49
Movement
Labor, 119, 121, 140, 165
Socialist, 119
Social-Democratic, 119
Murota Wakasa and Ayabe, 28

Nagasaki, IX, 4, 10, 18, 20, 22, 23, 24, 27, 28, 43, 71, 80, 91, 167
Prefecture, 25, 36
Nagoya, 7, 81
Nakamura, Kichizo, 166
Nakashima, Noboyuki, 163
National Christian Council of Japan, 161
National consciousness, introd. XIII, 16, 17
National character, 182
National development, 55
National scholars, 72
Nationalism, 49, 57, 92, 97, 125, 141, 144, 148, 149, 150, 162, 166, 170, 172, 174, 176
modern, 51, 115
New Testament, 23, 182
New theology, 150, 151, 157, 166, 172
Nobility, 7, 9, 47, 53, 57, 63, 66, 105
Nicene creed, 93
Niijima Jo, 39, 98
Nimura, 78, 88
Non-church group, 98, 154
Norman, E. H., 6, 16, 59, 109, 117, 128, 141
Numagawa, 24
Numerical growth of the church, 145

Ogawa, Yoshiyasu 77, 86, 88, 89, 92
Oi Kentaro, 119
Okayama, 146
Oki, 38
Okubo, Toshimichi, 33, 34, 36, 37, 39, 41, 42, 43, 44, 55, 105

Okuma Shigenobu, 34, 36, 37, 39, 41, 42, 43, 45, 46, 48, 60, 61, 65, 66, 72, 82, 105, 107, 108, 111, 112, 116, 117, 118, 119, 142, 160, 163
Okuno, Masatsuna, 89, 92
Oligarchy, 46, 47, 48, 51, 53, 60, 63, 66, 68, 75, 77, 84, 87, 101, 111, 112, 117, 173, 174, 177
Oligarchs, 46, 47, 67, 105, 108, 118
  power of, 174
Ono (Zaibatsu), 16
Opium wars, 12
"Open Door Policy", 122
Orphanges, 165
Osaka, 4, 7, 14, 15, 63, 91
Osaka affair, 14, 18, 23, 26, 114, 174
Outside clans, 4, 5, 9, 10, 12, 14, 16, 17, 21, 29
Oyama, Iwao, 111
Ozaki, Yukio, 43

Parkes, Sir Harry, 14
Party
  Liberal, 44, 45, 47, 48, 59, 60, 61, 62, 82, 83, 84, 117
  Progressive, 46
Peace preservation
  Regulation law, 65, 107, 108, 110, 119
Peasant, 5, 6, 7, 9, 50, 51, 53, 58, 59, 60, 62, 66, 67, 68, 80, 128, 132
Peking, 114
People's Rights Movement, 7, 47, 48, 59, 81, 83, 85, 98, 107, 146, 151, 161, 166, 171, 172
Perry, Commodore, 10, 18, 19, 20, 21, 27, 28, 40
Pescadores, 114
Population, 55
  growth, 126, 128, 130, 133
  movement, 126, 134
Portugal, 19, 20
Portuguese, 19
Power, 139, 143
  charismatic, 175
  economic, Introd. XIII, 63, 118, 170, 173
  industrial, 143
  of central government, 37
  of Japan, 49
  of lords, 6
  of outside clans, 4, 13
  of Shogunate, 3
  outside power, 10
  personal, 42
  political, Introd. XIII, XIV, 15, 118, 170, 173
  primary, 163
  socio-economic-political, 139, 173
  structure, 33, 45, 126, 135, 139, 163, 173
Prefectures, 37
Prefectural assemblies, 45
Presbyterian, 159, 163
  Churches, 91
  Mission Board, 27, 28, 90
Press, 60, 97, 111, 162
  laws restricting, 44, 180
Prison reform, 100
Prisoners
  rehabilitation of, 165
Private enterprise, 135
Privy council, 23, 41, 108, 110, 116, 118
Property qualification, 60, 66, 119
Prostitution, 100
  Cessation Act, 164
  licensed abolition of, 180
Protestant, 18, 22, 27
  Christian Movement, 30, 87, 145
  Christians, 78
  churches, 78
  ethic, 130
Protestant Christianity, IX, XII, XIII, XIV, XV, 26, 29, 74, 79, 98, 100, 144, 163, 171, 172, 173, 180
Protestant Christian Community, 174–175
Protestant Christian Movement, 69, 70, 154, 163, 167
Prussian political theory, 48

Rapid economic change, 54
Rapid social change, IX, 42, 176, 177
Rationalism, 155
Reformed Church in America, 28
  churches, 91
  Mission Board, 27, 90
Registers of lands, 37, 38, 57
Religion
  sociology of, Introd. XIV
Religious
  freedom, 144
  toleration, 72
Representatives, House of, 109, 110
Representative institutions, 42, 44, 80
  forms, 42

government, 59, 80, 83, 94, 100, 101, 105, 112
Respect for personality, 61, 180
Restoration, 5, 14, 15, 17, 21, 25, 26, 28, 29, 30, 33, 34, 35, 37, 38, 39, 40, 42, 43, 53, 54, 57, 63, 66, 70, 71, 79, 80, 89, 95, 97, 126, 171, 174, 180
movement, 37
post-restoration, 6
pre-restoration, 14, 16
Revolts
peasant, 6, 7
Rikken Seiyukai Party, 117, 118, 119
Rikugo Zasshi, 70, 167
Roman Catholic, 19, 22, 25, 36, 71, 180
Ronin, 5, 26
Roosevelt, Theodore, President, 122
Rousseau, 44, 74, 97
Russia, 10, 40, 53, 75, 114, 115, 118, 121, 122, 123
Russian interests, 143
Russo-Japanese War, 118, 120, 123, 125, 127, 128, 136, 144, 150, 151, 152, 154, 158, 161, 174
Rutgers
college, 24
grammar school, 24
Ryder, 23

Saga, 4, 28, 40
Saigo Takamori, 26, 34, 37, 40, 41, 42, 58, 71, 74
Saionji, 118, 139
Sakai, 120
Sakhalin, 123
Salaried clan officials, 128, 172
Salvation Army, 180
Samurai, 5, 7, 8, 13, 16, 22, 23, 25, 26, 29, 30, 33, 34, 35, 36, 37, 38, 39, 40, 41, 42, 43, 50, 51, 54, 55, 57, 58, 59, 60, 61, 62, 63, 67, 71, 83, 86, 89, 95, 97, 98, 99, 105, 130, 132, 141, 146, 148, 152, 153, 161, 168, 171, 172, 175
San Felipe, 20
Sangi, 38
Sanjo, Sanetome, 33, 36, 39
Sansom, Sir George, 16, 35, 74
Sapporo, 182
Satsuma, 4, 9, 14, 15, 19, 22, 24, 26, 33, 34, 36, 38, 40, 41, 63, 111, 112, 116
Rebellion, 26, 41, 58, 59, 61, 62, 97, 174
Satsuma-Choshu clan government, 110, 125
Scalapino, R. K., 143
"Seikosha", 51
Sekigahara, 3
Serata, admiral, 145
Shanghai, 22
Shikoku, 4, 20, 44, 61, 83, 182
Shimabara uprising, 72
Shimada, Saburo, 163, 166
Shimadzu Saburo, 14
Shimazaki, Toson, 167
Shimizu, 28
Shimoda, 10, 11
Shimonoseki, 4, 13, 15, 26
straits of, 24
treaty of, 114
Shingi Sho, 72
Shinto, 25, 36, 45, 48, 49, 71, 72, 73, 75, 76, 82, 96, 148, 158, 176
nationalism, 40, 73, 161
traditional, XIII, 73
Shintoists, 169
Shiomura, 28
Shippey, Frederick, Professor at Drew Univ. Graduate School, IX
Shizuoka prefecture, 80
Shogun, 3, 4, 12, 14, 40
ex-Shogun, 15
Shogunate, 3, 4, 7, 9, 11, 12, 13, 14, 22, 26, 29, 53, 161
anti-Shogunate, 12
Shushigaku (Confucianism), 29, 73, 95
Simmons, Dr. D. B., 28
Sino-Japanese War, 113, 114, 115, 116, 120, 121, 124, 125, 127, 128, 136, 144, 146, 150, 152, 162, 174
Social
change, 56
justice, 170, 177
stratification, 79
structure, 54, 141
welfare, 173
work, 180
Socialism, 121, 135, 153, 181
Socialist,
point of view, 120
movement, 121, 165
Socialists, 120, 121
Society
Japanese, 3, 9, 171, 173, 175
open, 177
stratified, 3
western feudal, 6
Sociology, XIV, XV

Sonno Hobutsu Daido Dan, 148
Soyejima, 36, 38, 40
Spain, 19, 20
Spencer, Herbert, 74, 97
"spheres of influence", 115
Spirit of nationalism, 113, 116, 157, 158, 170, 172
State absolutism, 50, 77, 87, 92, 124, 148, 149, 176
Status, 8, 43, 58
Sumitomo, (Zaibatsu), 16, 136
Suzuki, Bunji, 166
Sumiya, Mikio, IX, 74, 75, 89, 92, 97, 99, 145, 146, 150, 151, 152, 155, 159, 169, 173
Supreme Court, 41
Syle, Rev., 27

Takayama, Chogyu, 159
Tariff convention, 15
Tazoe, 120
Technicians, 51, 54, 58, 63, 67, 99, 128, 135
Temperance Society, 165
  temperance, 180
Terauchi, 123
Thompson, David, 28
Tokudaiji, Prince, 33
Tokugawa
  clan, 3, 4, 9, 14, 15, 17, 37, 38, 54, 57
  government, 171
  order, 34
  period, 5, 6, 7, 82, 98, 133
  retainers, 51, 63
  samurai, 80, 95
  shogunate, 33, 36, 83, 89
Tokugawa Ieyasu, 20
Tokugawa, Nariaki, 12
Tokutomi Soho, 119, 116
Tokyo, 14, 59, 63, 65, 80, 81, 83, 90, 91, 93, 100, 107, 158, 163, 182
  mayor, 24
  missionary conference of 1900, 161
Tokyo Imperial University (Tokyo University), IX, 23, 75
Tosa, 4, 14, 19, 20, 33, 37, 38
Trade, 4, 8, 11, 12, 20, 33, 39, 40
  export, 63, 141
  foreign, 15, 19, 61, 62, 66
  international, 64, 143, 152
  relations, 20
  unions, 137, 139
  world, 142
Traditional
  handicrafts, 56
  values, 172
Traditionalism, 130, 152
Treaties, 10, 11, 13, 14, 19, 20, 66, 81
  amity and commerce of, 11, 40
  international, 39
  revision of, 39, 41, 65, 112, 144
  trade, 15, 39, 50, 77, 84, 106, 107
  unequal, 15, 47, 49, 57, 58, 64, 75, 76, 77, 99, 107, 108, 121, 124, 125, 141, 143, 146, 148, 152, 168, 171, 172, 177
Treaty,
  ports, 79
  Commerce and Navigation (1911), 124
  Portsmouth, 123
Triple Intervention, 114, 115
Tsungli Yamen, 114

Uchimura, Kanzo, 98, 120, 149, 151, 154, 159, 161, 166, 167, 169, 175
Ueda, 81
Uemura, Masahisa, 86, 89, 92, 95, 159, 162, 166, 167, 169, 175
Union Theological Seminary in Tokyo, 179
Unitarianism, 87, 92, 149
"United Church of Christ in Japan", 78, 90, 92, 93, 97, 145, 149, 150, 154, 155, 157
United States, 10, 11, 19, 23, 24, 27, 53, 75, 90, 121, 122, 131, 139, 140, 141, 157, 159, 166
United States
  Minister, 20
  Naval Academy, 24
  Navy, 10
Universal suffrage, 45
Upper House, 112
Uruga Bay, 10
Uryu, Admiral, 145

Verbeck, Guido, 21, 22, 23, 24, 28, 39, 43

Waseda University, 48
Weber, Max, XIV
"welfare of the nation", 17, 48, 64
  of Japan, XIII, 99, 172, 173, 174
Western
  capitalism, 130
  civilization, 29

imperialism, 98
nations, 10, 36
powers, XIV, 10
Westminster Confession, 91, 93, 150, 155
Williams, C. M., 23, 27, 28
Williams, S. R., 21
Williams, Dr. S. Wells, 26, 27
Wood, Henry, 27
Workers, 132
Workmen's Society, 120
World Council of Churches, 88
division of studies, IX
World War I, 129, 137
World War II, XII, XIII, 16, 130, 132, 135, 136, 169

Xavier, St. Francis, 19

Yalu River, 122
Yamagata Aritomo, 39, 43, 46, 48, 65, 111, 116, 117, 118, 121, 125, 139, 152
Yamaji Aizan, 77, 165
Yanaga, 115
Yano, Riyu, 28
Yasuda, (Zaibatsu), 16, 136
Yawata Steel Works, 136
Yedo, 20
Young Mens Christian Association, 150
Yokohama, 77, 87, 93, 95, 99, 154
Specie bank, 138
Yokoi, Rev. Tokio, 25, 149
Yorozu-Choho, 120
Yuasa, 44, 100

Zaibatsu, 61, 132, 136, 137, 138, 139, 142, 152, 161